TEACHINGS OF QUEEN KUNTĪ

Books by His Divine Grace A.C. Bhaktivedanta Swami Prabhupāda

Bhagavad-gītā As It Is
Śrīmad-Bhāgavatam (*completed by disciples*)
Śrī Caitanya-caritāmṛta
Kṛṣṇa, the Supreme Personality of Godhead
Teachings of Lord Caitanya
The Nectar of Devotion
The Nectar of Instruction
Śrī Īśopaniṣad
Light of the Bhāgavata
Easy Journey to Other Planets
Teachings of Lord Kapila, the Son of Devahūti
Teachings of Queen Kuntī
Message of Godhead
The Science of Self-Realization
The Perfection of Yoga
Beyond Birth and Death
On the Way to Kṛṣṇa
Rāja-vidyā: The King of Knowledge
Elevation to Kṛṣṇa Consciousness
Kṛṣṇa Consciousness: The Matchless Gift
Kṛṣṇa Consciousness: The Topmost Yoga System
Perfect Questions, Perfect Answers
Life Comes from Life
The Nārada-bhakti-sūtra (*completed by disciples*)
The Mukunda-mālā-stotra (*completed by disciples*)
Geetār-gān (*Bengali*)
Vairāgya-vidyā (*Bengali*)
Buddhi-yoga (*Bengali*)
Bhakti-ratna-boli (*Bengali*)
Back to Godhead magazine (*founder*)

Books compiled from the teachings of Śrīla Prabhupāda after his lifetime

The Journey of Self-Discovery
Civilization and Transcendence
The Laws of Nature
Renunciation Through Wisdom
Beyond Illusion and Doubt

TEACHINGS OF QUEEN KUNTĪ

His Divine Grace
A. C. Bhaktivedanta Swami Prabhupāda
Founder-*Ācārya* of the International Society for Krishna Consciousness

THE BHAKTIVEDANTA BOOK TRUST

Readers interested in the subject matter of this book are invited to contact the International Society for Krishna Consciousness (see address list in back of book) or any of the following information centers.

Karuna Bhavan
Bankhouse Rd, Lesmahagow
Lanarkshire, ML11 0ES, Scotland
Tel: +44 (0)1555 894790
Fax: +44 (0)1555 894526
karunabhavan@aol.com
www.iskcon.org.uk/scotland

ISKCON
83 Middle Abbey Street
Dublin 1, Republic of Ireland
Tel: +353 (0)1 8729775
mail@krishna.ie
www.krishna.ie

ISKCON Reader Services
P.O. Box 730, Watford
WD25 8ZE, United Kingdom
Tel: +44 (0)1923 857244
readerservices@pamho.net
www.iskcon.org.uk

Teachings of Queen Kuntī was prepared from Śrīla Prabhupāda's commentated translation of *Śrīmad-Bhāgavatam* 1.8.18–43, along with excerpts of lectures he gave on these verses in April of 1973 in New York and Los Angeles. The editor was Śrīla Prabhupāda's disciple Hayagrīva Dāsa (Howard Wheeler, M.A.).

www.krishna.com

ISBN 978-1-84599-061-9

Printed in 2007

Contents

Introduction

The tragic and heroic figure of Queen Kuntī emerges from an explosive era in the history of ancient India. As related in the *Mahābhārata,* India's grand epic poem of 110,000 couplets, Kuntī was the wife of King Pāṇḍu and the mother of five illustrious sons known as the Pāṇḍavas. As such, she was one of the central figures in a complex political drama that culminated fifty centuries ago in the Kurukṣetra War, a devastating war of ascendancy that changed the course of world events. The *Mahābhārata* describes the prelude to the holocaust as follows:

Pāṇḍu became king because his elder brother Dhṛtarāṣṭra had been born blind, a condition that excluded him from direct succession. Some time after Pāṇḍu ascended to the throne, Dhṛtarāṣṭra married Gāndhārī and fathered one hundred sons. This was the ruling family of the Kaurava dynasty, of whom the eldest was the ambitious and cruel Duryodhana.

Meanwhile, Pāṇḍu had taken two wives, Mādrī and Kuntī. Originally named Pṛthā, Kuntī was the daughter of Śūrasena, the chief of the glorious Yadu dynasty. The *Mahābhārata* relates that Kuntī "was gifted with beauty and character; she rejoiced in the law [*dharma*] and was great in her vows." She also possessed an unusual benediction. When she was a child, her father Śūrasena had given her in adoption to his childless cousin and close friend Kuntibhoja (hence the name "Kuntī"). In her stepfather's house, Kuntī's duty was to look after the welfare of guests. One day the powerful sage and mystic Durvāsā came there and was pleased by Kuntī's selfless service. Foreseeing that she would have difficulty conceiving sons, Durvāsā gave her the benediction that she could invoke any demigod and by him obtain progeny.

After Kuntī married Pāṇḍu, he was placed under a curse that prevented him from begetting children. So he renounced the throne and retired with his wives to the forest. There Kuntī's special benediction enabled her to conceive (at her husband's request) three glorious sons. First she invoked Dharma, the demigod of religion. After worshiping him and repeating an invocation Durvāsā had taught her, she united with Dharma and, in time, gave birth to a boy. As soon as the child was born, a voice with no visible source said, "This child will be called Yudhiṣṭhira, and he will be very virtuous. He will be splendid, determined, renounced, and famous throughout the three worlds."

Having been blessed with this virtuous son, Pāṇḍu then asked Kuntī for a son of great physical strength. Thus Kuntī invoked Vāyu, the demigod of the wind, who begot the mighty Bhīma. Upon Bhīma's birth the supernatural voice said, "This child will be the foremost of all strong men."

Thereafter Pāṇḍu consulted with great sages in the forest and then asked Kuntī to observe vows of austerity for one full year. At the end of this period Pāṇḍu said to Kuntī, "O beautiful one, Indra, the King of heaven, is pleased with you, so invoke him and conceive a son." Kuntī then invoked Indra, who came to her and begot Arjuna. As soon as the prince was born, the same celestial voice boomed through the sky: "O Kuntī, this child will be as strong as Kārtavīrya and Śibi [two powerful kings of Vedic times] and as invincible in battle as Indra himself. He will spread your fame everywhere and acquire many divine weapons." Subsequently, Pāṇḍu's junior wife Mādrī bore two sons named Nakula and Sahadeva. These five sons of Pāṇḍu (Yudhiṣṭhira, Bhīma, Arjuna, Nakula, and Sahadeva) then came to be known as the Pāṇḍavas.

Now, since Pāṇḍu had retired from the throne and gone to the forest, Dhṛtarāṣṭra had temporarily assumed the throne until Pāṇḍu's eldest son Yudhiṣṭhira came of age. However, long before that time Pāṇḍu died as a result of the curse, and Mādrī gave up her life as well by ascending his funeral pyre. That left the five Pāṇḍavas in the care of Queen Kuntī.

After Pāṇḍu's death, the sages living in the forest brought the five young princes and Kuntī to the Kaurava court at Hastināpura (near present-day Delhi). In Hastināpura, the capital city of the kingdom, the five boys were raised in royal style under the guidance of Dhṛtarāṣṭra and the noble Vidura, Pāṇḍu's half brother.

But a smooth transfer of power was not to be. Although Dhṛtarāṣṭra had at first recognized the primogeniture of Yudhiṣṭhira, he later allowed himself to be used by his eldest son, the power-hungry Duryodhana, who wished to ascend the throne in place of Yudhiṣṭhira. Driven by uncontrollable jealousy, Duryodhana plotted against the Pāṇḍavas, and with the hesitant approval of the weak Dhṛtarāṣṭra, he inflicted many sufferings upon them. He made several attempts on their lives in Hastināpura, and then he brought them to a provincial palace and tried to assassinate them by having it set on fire. All the while, the five youthful Pāṇḍavas were accompanied by their courageous mother Kuntī, who suffered Duryodhana's atrocities in the company of her beloved sons.

Miraculously, however, Kuntī and the Pāṇḍavas repeatedly escaped death, for they were under the loving protection of Lord Kṛṣṇa, who had incarnated to perform His earthly pastimes. Ultimately Duryodhana, a clever politician, cheated the Pāṇḍavas out of their kingdom (and their freedom) in a gambling match. As a result of the match, the Pāṇḍavas' wife Draupadī was abused by the Kauravas, and the Pāṇḍavas themselves were forced to spend thirteen years in exile in the forest – to the great sorrow of Kuntī.

When the thirteen-year exile had ended, the Pāṇḍavas returned to Hastināpura to reclaim their kingdom. But Duryodhana bluntly refused to relinquish it. Then, after some unsuccessful attempts to quell the hostilities, Yudhiṣṭhira sent Kṛṣṇa Himself to secure the return of the Pāṇḍava kingdom by peaceful means. But even this effort failed – because of Duryodhana's obstinacy – and both sides prepared for battle. To place Yudhiṣṭhira on the throne – or to oppose him – great warriors from all corners of the earth assembled, setting the scene for what would prove to be a devastating world war.

Fierce fighting raged for eighteen days on the historic plain of Kurukṣetra (near Hastināpura), and in the end all but a handful of the many millions of warriors were dead. Only Lord Kṛṣṇa, the Pāṇḍavas, and a few others survived the massacre. The Kauravas (Duryodhana and his brothers) were devastated. In a desperate gesture of revenge,

Aśvatthāmā, one of the surviving Kauravas, mercilessly murdered the five sons of Draupadī while they were sleeping. Queen Kuntī thus suffered a final blow – the loss of her grandchildren.

Arrested and dragged to the Pāṇḍavas' camp like a bound animal, Aśvatthāmā was let free only by the astounding compassion of Draupadī, the slaughtered boys' mother and Kuntī's daughter-in-law, who pleaded for his life. But the shameless Aśvatthāmā made one more attempt to kill the last heir of the Pāṇḍavas, their unborn grandson in the womb of Uttarā, by hurling the supreme *brahmāstra* weapon. When she saw the missile flying straight at her, Uttarā immediately ran to the shelter of Lord Kṛṣṇa, who was just about to depart for Dvārakā, His majestic capital city. Kṛṣṇa protected the Pāṇḍavas and their mother Kuntī from imminent death by stopping the weapon's uncontrollable heat and radiation with His own Sudarśana disc.

Having delivered the Pāṇḍavas from this last calamity, and seeing that all His plans were fulfilled, Lord Kṛṣṇa was again preparing to leave. For years Duryodhana had tormented Queen Kuntī's family, but Kṛṣṇa had protected them at every turn – and now He was going away. Kuntī was overwhelmed, and she prayed to Kṛṣṇa from the core of her heart.

Kuntī was Lord Kṛṣṇa's aunt (He had incarnated as the son of her brother Vasudeva), yet despite this conventional tie with the Lord, she fully understood His exalted and divine identity. She knew full well that He had descended from His abode in the spiritual world to rid the earth of demoniac military powers and reestablish righteousness. Just before the great war, Kṛṣṇa had revealed all this to her son Arjuna in words immortalized in the *Bhagavad-gītā* (4.7–8):

> Whenever and wherever there is a decline in religious practice, O descendant of Bharata, and a predominant rise of irreligion – at that time I incarnate Myself. In order to deliver the pious and annihilate the miscreants, as well as to reestablish the principles of religion, I advent Myself millennium after millennium.

Kṛṣṇa had accomplished His purpose of "annihilating the miscreants" by orchestrating the destruction of the unholy Kauravas. Then He installed Yudhiṣṭhira on the throne to establish the Pāṇḍava reign, and He consoled the slain warriors' relatives. The scene of the Lord's imminent departure provides the setting for Queen Kuntī's exalted prayers.

As Kuntī approached the Lord's chariot and began to address Him, her immediate purpose was to persuade Him to remain in Hastināpura and protect the Pāṇḍava government from reprisals:

> O my Lord ... are You leaving us today, though we are completely dependent on Your mercy and have no one else to protect us, now when all kings are at enmity with us? (*Bhāgavatam* 1.8.37)

From this supplication we should not mistakenly conclude that Kuntī's prayers were self-serving. Although her sufferings were far greater than those any ordinary person could endure, she does not beg relief. On the contrary, *she prays to suffer even more,* for she reasons that her suffering will increase her devotion to the Lord and bring her ultimate liberation:

> My dear Kṛṣṇa, Your Lordship has protected us from the poisoned cake, from a great fire, from cannibals, from the vicious assembly, from sufferings during our exile in the forest, and from the battle where great generals fought....I wish that all those calamities would happen again and again so that we could see You again and again, for seeing You means that we will no longer see repeated births and deaths. (*Bhāgavatam* 1.8.24–25)

Kuntī's words – the simple and illuminating outpourings of the soul of a great and saintly woman devotee – reveal both the deepest transcendental emotions of the heart and the most profound philosophical and theological penetrations of the intellect. Her words are words of glorification impelled by a divine love steeped in wisdom:

> O Lord of Madhu, as the Ganges forever flows to the sea without hindrance, let my attraction be constantly drawn unto You without being diverted to anyone else. (*Bhāgavatam* 1.8.42)

Kuntī's spontaneous glorification of Lord Kṛṣṇa and her description of the spiritual path are immortalized in the *Mahābhārata* and the

Bhāgavata Purāṇa (*Śrīmad-Bhāgavatam*), and they have been recited, chanted, and sung by sages and philosophers for thousands of years.

As they appear in the First Canto of the *Bhāgavatam,* Queen Kuntī's celebrated prayers consist of only twenty-six couplets (verses 18 through 43 of the eighth chapter), yet they are considered a philosophical, theological, and literary masterpiece. The present book (*Teachings of Queen Kuntī*) includes those inspired verses and an illuminating commentary by His Divine Grace A.C. Bhaktivedanta Swami Prabhupāda, founder-*ācārya* of the International Society for Krishna Consciousness (ISKCON) and renowned Vedic scholar and spiritual leader. In addition to this commentary (originally written in 1962), *Teachings of Queen Kuntī* contains further explanations that Śrīla Prabhupāda gave in a series of lectures delivered in the spring of 1973 at ISKCON's centers in New York and Los Angeles. At that time he analyzed the verses in significantly greater detail and shed even more light upon them. This book offers the reader a deeper look into what it means to live immersed in a spiritual life and opens a window into the thoughts and experiences of both Queen Kuntī and Śrīla Prabhupāda, two elevated practitioners of the yoga of devotional mysticism.

The Publishers

1

The Original Person

kunty uvāca
namasye puruṣaṁ tvādyam
īśvaraṁ prakṛteḥ param
alakṣyaṁ sarva-bhūtānām
antar bahir avasthitam

Śrīmatī Kuntī said: O Kṛṣṇa, I offer my obeisances unto You because You are the original personality and are unaffected by the qualities of the material world. You are existing both within and without everything, yet You are invisible to all.

Śrīmad-Bhāgavatam 1.8.18

Śrīmatī Kuntīdevī was quite aware that Kṛṣṇa is the original Personality of Godhead, although He was playing the part of her nephew. Such an enlightened lady could not commit a mistake by offering obeisances unto her nephew. Therefore, she addressed Him as the original *puruṣa* beyond the material cosmos. Although all living entities are also transcendental, they are neither original nor infallible. The living entities are apt to fall down under the clutches of material nature, but the Lord is never like that. In the *Vedas,* therefore, He is described as the chief among all living entities (*nityo nityānāṁ cetanaś cetanānām*). Then again He is addressed as *īśvara,* or the controller. The living entities or the demigods like Candra and Sūrya are also to some extent *īśvara,* but none of them is the supreme *īśvara,* or the ultimate controller. Kṛṣṇa is the *parameśvara,* or the Supersoul. He is both within and without. Although He was present before Śrīmatī Kuntī as her nephew, He was also within her and everyone else. In the *Bhagavad-gītā* (15.15) the Lord says, "I am situated in everyone's heart, and only due to Me one remembers, forgets, and is cognizant, etc. Through all the *Vedas* I am to be known because I am the compiler of the *Vedas,* and I am the teacher of the *Vedānta.*" Queen Kuntī affirms that the Lord, although both within and without all living beings, is still invisible. The Lord is, so to speak, a puzzle for the common man. Queen Kuntī experienced personally that Lord Kṛṣṇa was present before her, yet He entered within the womb of Uttarā to save her embryo from the attack of Aśvatthāmā's *brahmāstra.* Kuntī herself was puzzled about whether Śrī Kṛṣṇa is all-pervasive or localized. In fact, He is both, but He reserves the right of not being exposed to persons who are not surrendered souls. This checking curtain is called the *māyā* energy of the Supreme Lord, and it controls the limited vision of the rebellious soul. It is explained as follows.

2

Beyond the Senses

māyā-javanikācchannam
ajñādhokṣajam avyayam
na lakṣyase mūḍha-dṛśā
naṭo nāṭya-dharo yathā

Being beyond the range of limited sense perception, You are the eternally irreproachable factor covered by the curtain of deluding energy. You are invisible to the foolish observer, exactly as an actor dressed as a player is not recognized.

Śrīmad-Bhāgavatam 1.8.19

In the *Bhagavad-gītā* Lord Śrī Kṛṣṇa affirms that less intelligent persons mistake Him to be an ordinary man like us, and thus they deride Him. The same is confirmed herein by Queen Kuntī. The less intelligent persons are those who rebel against the authority of the Lord. Such persons are known as *asuras*. The *asuras* cannot recognize the Lord's authority. When the Lord Himself appears among us, as Rāma, Nṛsiṁha, Varāha, or in His original form as Kṛṣṇa, He performs many wonderful acts which are humanly impossible. As we shall find in the Tenth Canto of this great literature, Lord Śrī Kṛṣṇa exhibited His humanly impossible activities even from the days of His lying on the lap of His mother. He killed the Pūtanā witch, although she smeared her breast with poison just to kill the Lord. The Lord sucked her breast like a natural baby, and He sucked out her very life also. Similarly, He lifted the Govardhana Hill, just as a boy picks up a frog's umbrella, and stood several days continuously just to give protection to the residents of Vṛndāvana. These are some of the superhuman activities of the Lord described in the authoritative Vedic literatures like the *Purāṇas, Itihāsas* (histories), and *Upaniṣads.* He has delivered wonderful instructions in the shape of the *Bhagavad-gītā.* He has shown marvelous capacities as a hero, as a householder, as a teacher, and as a renouncer. He is accepted as the Supreme Personality of Godhead by such authoritative personalities as Vyāsa, Devala, Asita, Nārada, Madhva, Śaṅkara, Rāmānuja, Śrī Caitanya Mahāprabhu, Jīva Gosvāmī, Viśvanātha Cakravartī, Bhaktisiddhānta Sarasvatī, and all other authorities of the line. He Himself has declared as much in many places of the authentic literatures. And yet there is a class of men with demoniac mentality who are always reluctant to accept the Lord as the Supreme Absolute Truth. This is partially due to their poor fund of knowledge and partially due to their stubborn obstinacy, which results from various misdeeds in the past and present. Such persons could not recognize Lord Śrī Kṛṣṇa even when He was present before them. Another difficulty is that those who depend more on their imperfect senses cannot realize Him as the Supreme Lord. Such persons are like the modern scientist. They want to know everything by their experimental knowledge. But it is not possible to know the Supreme Person by imperfect experimental knowledge. He is described herein as *adhokṣaja,* or beyond the range of experimental knowledge. All our senses are imperfect. We claim to observe everything and anything, but we must admit that we can observe things under certain material conditions only, which are also beyond our control. The Lord is beyond the observation of sense perception. Queen Kuntī accepts this deficiency of the conditioned soul, especially of the woman class, who are less intelligent. For the less intelligent there must be such things as temples, mosques, or churches so that they may begin to recognize the authority of the Lord and hear about Him from authorities in such holy places. For the less intelligent, this beginning of spiritual life is essential, and only foolish men decry the establishment of such places of worship, which are required to raise the standard of spiritual attributes for the mass of people. For less intelligent persons, bowing down before the authority of the Lord, as generally done in the temples, mosques, or churches, is as beneficial as it is for the advanced devotees to meditate upon Him by active service.

3

The Most Intelligent Woman

tathā paramahaṁsānāṁ
munīnām amalātmanām
bhakti-yoga-vidhānārthaṁ
kathaṁ paśyema hi striyaḥ

You Yourself descend to propagate the transcendental science of devotional service unto the hearts of the advanced transcendentalists and mental speculators, who are purified by being able to discriminate between matter and spirit. How, then, can we women know You perfectly?

Śrīmad-Bhāgavatam 1.8.20

Even the greatest philosophical speculators cannot have access to the region of the Lord. It is said in the *Upaniṣads* that the Supreme Truth, the Absolute Personality of Godhead, is beyond the range of the thinking power of the greatest philosopher. He is unknowable by great learning or by the greatest brain. He is knowable only by one who has His mercy. Others may go on thinking about Him for years together, yet He is unknowable. This very fact is corroborated by the Queen, who is playing the part of an innocent woman. Women in general are unable to speculate like philosophers, but they are blessed by the Lord because they believe at once in the superiority and almightiness of the Lord, and thus they offer obeisances without reservation. The Lord is so kind that He does not show special favor only to one who is a great philosopher. He knows the sincerity of purpose. For this reason only, women generally assemble in great number in any sort of religious function. In every country and in every sect of religion it appears that the women are more interested than the men. This simplicity of acceptance of the Lord's authority is more effective than showy insincere religious fervor.

Kuntīdevī prayed to the Lord very submissively, and this is the symptom of a Vaiṣṇava. The Lord, Kṛṣṇa, had come to Kuntīdevī to offer respect to her by taking the dust of her feet. Because Kṛṣṇa considered Kuntīdevī His aunt, He used to touch her feet. But although Kuntīdevī, a great devotee, was in such an exalted position, practically on the level of Yaśodāmayī, Kṛṣṇa's mother, she was so submissive that she prayed, "Kṛṣṇa, You are meant to be understood by the *paramahaṁsas,* the most advanced transcendentalists, but I am a woman, so how can I see You?"

According to the Vedic system, there are four social divisions (*cātur-varṇyaṁ mayā sṛṣṭam*). The highest members of the social order are the *brāhmaṇas,* those who are intelligent, and then come the *kṣatriyas* (military men and administrators), the *vaiśyas* (farmers and businessmen), and finally the *śūdras* (ordinary laborers). One's place in this system is determined by one's qualities and work (*guṇa-karma*). The *Bhagavad-gītā* mentions *striyo vaiśyās tathā śūdrāḥ,* and the *Śrīmad-Bhāgavatam* speaks of *strī-śūdra-dvija-bandhūnām.* According to these references women, *śūdras,* and *dvija-bandhus* are considered to belong to the same category. The word *dvija-bandhu* refers to one who is born in an exalted *brāhmaṇa* or *kṣatriya* family but who has no qualifications of his own.

One's social standing, according to the Vedic system, is determined by one's qualifications. This is very practical. Suppose a man is born the son of a high-court judge. This does not mean that he himself is also a high-court judge. Yet because one happens to take birth in a *brāhmaṇa* family, even if he has no qualifications and is rascal number one, he claims to be a *brāhmaṇa,* and although his qualifications are less than those of a *śūdra,* people accept him as a *brāhmaṇa.* This has caused the downfall of the Vedic civilization. The *brāhmaṇas* in India are sometimes very much against my movement because I train and accept *brāhmaṇas* from Europe and America. But we do not care about their arguments, nor will any other reasonable man. Śrī Caitanya Mahāprabhu said:

pṛthivīte āche yata nagarādi grāma
sarvatra pracāra haibe mora nāma

"In every town, city, and village of the world, the Kṛṣṇa consciousness movement will be preached."

How is it, then, that Europeans and Americans will not become *brāhmaṇas*? In fact, one who comes to Kṛṣṇa consciousness has already surpassed brāhmaṇism. As stated in *Bhagavad-gītā* (14.26):

māṁ ca yo 'vyabhicāreṇa
bhakti-yogena sevate
sa guṇān samatītyaitān
brahma-bhūyāya kalpate

"One who takes to *bhakti-yoga* surpasses the modes of material nature and comes immediately to the transcendental platform [*brahma-bhūta*]." Not to speak of becoming a *brāhmaṇa,* the person who fully engages in *bhakti-yoga* attains the highest transcendental platform.

The stereotyped, crippled idea that only a person born in a *brāhmaṇa* family can become a *brāhmaṇa* has killed Vedic civilization, but now we are reviving the correct understanding that the attainment of perfection is meant for everyone. In *Bhagavad-gītā* (9.32) Lord Kṛṣṇa says:

māṁ hi pārtha vyapāśritya
ye 'pi syuḥ pāpa-yonayaḥ

striyo vaiśyās tathā śūdrās
te 'pi yānti paraṁ gatim

"O son of Pṛthā, those who take shelter in Me – though they be lowborn, women, *vaiśyas,* or *śūdras* – can approach the supreme destination." Thus although women, *śūdras,* and *vaiśyas* are ordinarily considered to belong to a lower class, when one becomes a devotee he or she goes beyond such designations. Women, *śūdras,* and *vaiśyas* are ordinarily regarded as less intelligent, but if one takes to Kṛṣṇa consciousness one is the most intelligent, as stated in the *Caitanya-caritāmṛta* (*kṛṣṇa yei bhaje sei baḍa catura*). And Caitanya Mahāprabhu says:

ei rūpe brahmāṇḍa bhramite kona bhāgyavān jīva
guru-kṛṣṇa-prasāde pāya bhakti-latā-bīja

"Among all the living entities wandering throughout the universe, one who is very fortunate receives, by the mercy of the spiritual master and the mercy of Kṛṣṇa, the seed of devotional service." (*Caitanya-caritāmṛta, Madhya* 19.151) The Kṛṣṇa consciousness movement does not consist of wretched, unfortunate men. No. It consists of the most fortunate. One who has taken to Kṛṣṇa consciousness is to be considered the most fortunate because he has found the way to act so that his life will be perfect. One who is Kṛṣṇa conscious and discharging his duties nicely is the most fortunate and the most perfect. This is humbly stated here by Kuntīdevī.

Although Kuntī had the body of a woman, she was a devotee. Therefore she was not like an ordinary unintelligent woman. Rather, she was the most intelligent, for she recognized Kṛṣṇa to be the Supreme Godhead: "He has come to me to offer me respect, materially appearing to be my nephew, but He is the Supreme Personality of Godhead." Therefore in a previous verse she said, *alakṣyaṁ sarva-bhūtānām antar bahir avasthitam:* "You are not seen by ordinary men, although You are everywhere, inside and outside." In another verse also she said, *na lakṣyase mūḍha-dṛśā:* "Fools and rascals cannot see You." This indicates that Kuntī saw Him. Unless she were able to see Kṛṣṇa as He is, how could she say, *na lakṣyase mūḍha-dṛśā*? She also said, *prakṛteḥ param:* "You are transcendental to this material creation."

Now here also, in this verse, Kuntī continues to express herself with humility. This humility is very good in devotional service. Therefore Śrī Kṛṣṇa Caitanya Mahāprabhu teaches us, *tṛṇād api sunīcena taror api sahiṣṇunā:* "One should be more tolerant than the tree and humbler than the grass to make progress in spiritual life." This is necessary because for one who is living in this material world there will be so many disturbances, just as if one were traveling on the ocean. One cannot expect a very peaceful situation on the ocean; even a big ship may also be unsteady, and at any moment there may be tumultuous waves. Similarly, in this material world we should always expect danger; one cannot expect a very peaceful life within this material world. The *śāstra,* the Vedic literature, says, *padaṁ padaṁ yad vipadām* (*Bhāgavatam* 10.14.58): at every step there is danger. But if one becomes a devotee, then one can escape (*māyām etāṁ taranti te*).

If one takes to Kṛṣṇa consciousness, in the beginning there will be many disturbances caused by Māyā, the material energy of illusion. Māyā will test us to see how firmly we are fixed in Kṛṣṇa consciousness. Because she is also an agent of Kṛṣṇa, she does not allow anyone the freedom to disturb Kṛṣṇa. Therefore she tests very rigidly to see whether we have taken to Kṛṣṇa consciousness to disturb Kṛṣṇa or are actually serious. That is Māyā's business. So in the beginning there will be tests by Māyā, and we shall feel so many disturbances while making progress in Kṛṣṇa consciousness. But if we follow the rules and regulations and chant regularly as prescribed, then we shall remain steady. If we neglect these principles, Māyā will capture us immediately. Māyā is always ready. We are in the ocean, and at any moment we may be disturbed. Therefore one who is not disturbed at all is called *paramahaṁsa.*

Kuntīdevī therefore says, *tathā paramahaṁsānām:* "You are meant to be understood by the *paramahaṁsas.*" The word *parama* means "ultimate," and *haṁsa* means "swan." So *paramahaṁsa* means "the perfect swan." If we give a swan milk mixed with water, the swan will take the milk and leave aside the water. Similarly, this material world is made of two natures – the inferior nature and the superior nature. The superior nature means spiritual life, and the inferior nature is material life. Thus a person who gives up the material part of this world and takes only the spiritual part is called *paramahaṁsa.*

One should know that the activities of the body are due to the soul within the body. That is the real fact. The body is only the outward covering. Similarly, one should know that Kṛṣṇa is the real center of all activities, and one who knows this is a *paramahaṁsa*. Thus *bhakti-yoga* is for the *paramahaṁsa,* one who knows that Kṛṣṇa is the central fact. Kṛṣṇa says in *Bhagavad-gītā, ahaṁ sarvasya prabhavo mattaḥ sarvaṁ pravartate:* "I am the source of everything; everything emanates from Me." So one who knows, not only theoretically but practically, that Kṛṣṇa is the cause of all causes – one who is convinced of this – is a *paramahaṁsa.*

Kuntīdevī says, "You are meant for the *paramahaṁsas,* not for the rascals and fools. You are meant for the *paramahaṁsas* and *munis.*" The word *munīnām* refers to those who are thoughtful or to mental speculators, and the word *amalātmanām* refers to one who has no dirty things in his heart. The heart of a materialistic person is full of dirty things. What are those dirty things? Lust and greed. All materialistic persons are lusty and greedy, and therefore their hearts are understood to be full of dirty things, but *amalātmanām* refers to those who are freed from these two contaminations.

Bhakti-yoga is meant for those whose hearts are cleansed, not for the lusty and greedy. Of course, those who are lusty and greedy may try to advance, and gradually they may do so, but once one is situated in *bhakti-yoga* there is no more lust or greed. *Viraktir anyatra ca* (*Bhāgavatam* 11.2.42). This is the test – when one is free from lusty desires and greed, then he is situated in *bhakti-yoga* and is actually a *paramahaṁsa.* Kuntīdevī humbly submits, "You are meant for the *paramahaṁsas* and *munis,* those who are cleansed in heart and are engaged in *bhakti-yoga.* But what are we? We are simply women. We are in a lower class. How can we understand You?" Although she understands everything, she still takes the position of an ordinary woman and says, "How can I understand You?" This is humility.

4

Approaching Kṛṣṇa, the All-pervading Truth

kṛṣṇāya vāsudevāya
devakī-nandanāya ca
nanda-gopa-kumārāya
govindāya namo namaḥ

Let me therefore offer my respectful obeisances unto the Lord, who has become the son of Vasudeva, the pleasure of Devakī, the boy of Nanda and the other cowherd men of Vṛndāvana, and the enlivener of the cows and the senses.

Śrīmad-Bhāgavatam 1.8.21

The Lord, being thus unapproachable by any material assets, out of unbounded and causeless mercy descends on the earth as He is in order to show His special mercy upon His unalloyed devotees and to diminish the upsurges of the demoniac persons. Queen Kuntī specifically adores the incarnation, or descent, of Lord Kṛṣṇa above all other incarnations because in this particular incarnation He is more approachable. In the Rāma incarnation He remained a king's son from His very childhood, but in the incarnation of Kṛṣṇa, although He was the son of a king, He at once left the shelter of His real father and mother (King Vasudeva and Queen Devakī) just after His appearance and went to the lap of Yaśodāmayī to play the part of an ordinary cowherd boy in the blessed Vrajabhūmi, which is very sanctified because of His childhood pastimes. Therefore Lord Kṛṣṇa is more merciful than Lord Rāma. He was undoubtedly very kind to Kuntī's brother Vasudeva and the family. Had He not become the son of Vasudeva and Devakī, Queen Kuntī could not claim Him to be her nephew and thus address Kṛṣṇa in parental affection. But Nanda and Yaśodā are more fortunate because they could relish the Lord's childhood pastimes, which are more attractive than all other pastimes. There is no parallel to His childhood pastimes as exhibited at Vrajabhūmi, which are the prototypes of His eternal affairs in the original Kṛṣṇaloka, described as the *cintāmaṇi-dhāma* in the *Brahma-saṁhitā*. Lord Śrī Kṛṣṇa descended Himself at Vrajabhūmi with all His transcendental entourage and paraphernalia. Śrī Caitanya Mahāprabhu therefore confirmed that no one is as fortunate as the residents of Vrajabhūmi, and specifically the cowherd girls, who dedicated their everything for the satisfaction of the Lord. His pastimes with Nanda and Yaśodā and His pastimes with the cowherd men and especially with the cowherd boys and the cows have caused Him to be known as Govinda. Lord Kṛṣṇa as Govinda is more inclined to the *brāhmaṇas* and the cows, indicating thereby that human prosperity depends more on these two items, namely brahminical culture and cow protection. Lord Kṛṣṇa is never satisfied where these are lacking.

In the beginning of her prayers, Kuntīdevī said, *namasye puruṣaṁ tvādyam īśvaraṁ prakṛteḥ param:* "I offer my obeisances unto the person, *puruṣa,* who is *prakṛteḥ param,* beyond this material manifestation." Thus in the beginning Kuntīdevī gave us the understanding that

God is the supreme *puruṣa,* the Supreme Person. He is not impersonal. He is a person, but He is not a person of this material world or this material creation, and He does not have a material body. This is to be understood. The poor fund of knowledge held by the impersonalists cannot accommodate how the Supreme Absolute Truth can be a person, because whenever they think of a person they think of a person of this material world. That is their defect. Why should God be a person of this material world? Therefore in the beginning Kuntīdevī cleared away this misunderstanding by saying that the Lord is *prakṛteḥ param,* beyond this material creation. Yet He is a person, and now by the grace of Kuntī we can understand that this Supreme Person, although *alakṣyam,* invisible, has now visibly appeared as Kṛṣṇa.

Kuntīdevī says, *kṛṣṇāya vāsudevāya.* The word *vāsudeva* is sometimes understood to mean "the all-pervading." The impersonalists have this conception of Vāsudeva, and therefore Kuntīdevī points out, "That Vasudeva, the all-pervading, is Kṛṣṇa." *Īśvaraḥ sarva-bhūtānāṁ hṛd-deśe 'rjuna tiṣṭhati:* Kṛṣṇa, the Supreme Lord, is present in everyone's heart. Thus He is all-pervading.

Kṛṣṇa, the original person, exists in three features: as the Supreme Personality of Godhead, as the all-pervading Paramātmā (the Supersoul), and as the impersonal Brahman effulgence. Those who are interested in *bhakti-yoga* have no interest in the impersonal Brahman effulgence, which is for common men. If one were an inhabitant of the sun, what interest would he have in the sunshine? That would be most insignificant for him. Similarly, those who are advanced in spiritual life are not interested in the impersonal Brahman effulgence. Rather, they are interested in *puruṣa,* the Supreme Person, Vāsudeva. As stated in *Bhagavad-gītā,* this realization of the Supreme Person takes place after many, many births (*bahūnāṁ janmanām ante*). The *jñānīs,* the impersonalists, who are attached to the Brahman effulgence, try to understand the Absolute Truth by dint of their knowledge, but they do not know that their knowledge is imperfect and limited whereas Kṛṣṇa, the Absolute Truth, is unlimited. We cannot approach the unlimited by our limited knowledge. That is not possible.

By the grace of devotees like Kuntīdevī, we can understand that the all-pervading Absolute Truth, Vāsudeva, Paramātmā, is present as Kṛṣṇa (*kṛṣṇāya vāsudevāya*). This realization of Vāsudeva is not possible for impersonalists very easily. Kṛṣṇa says in *Bhagavad-gītā* (7.19):

bahūnāṁ janmanām ante
jñānavān māṁ prapadyate
vāsudevaḥ sarvam iti
sa mahātmā sudurlabhaḥ

"After many births and deaths, he who is actually in knowledge surrenders unto Me, knowing Me to be the cause of all causes and all that is. Such a great soul is very rare." The word *mahātmā* means "broad-minded." One who cannot understand Kṛṣṇa is not broad-minded but cripple-minded. If one becomes broad-minded, then by the grace of Kṛṣṇa one can understand Kṛṣṇa.

The process of understanding Kṛṣṇa is *sevonmukha* – by rendering service. *Sevonmukhe hi jihvādau.* Realization of Vāsudeva is possible by rendering service, beginning with the tongue. The tongue has two functions – to vibrate and to taste. So if one repeatedly hears and vibrates the Hare Kṛṣṇa *mantra* and tastes *prasāda,* food offered to Kṛṣṇa, by this very simple method one will realize Vāsudeva, Kṛṣṇa. Kṛṣṇa will reveal Himself. It is not that by our endeavor alone we can understand Kṛṣṇa, but our endeavor in loving service will make us qualified, and then Kṛṣṇa will reveal Himself (*svayam eva sphuraty adaḥ*).

Kṛṣṇa is very much anxious to take us back home, back to Godhead, but we are stubborn and do not wish to go. Therefore He is always looking for the opportunity to take us back home. He is just like an affectionate father. When a son who is a rascal leaves his father and goes loitering in the street, with no food and no shelter, and suffers very much, the father is always anxious to bring the boy back home. Similarly, Kṛṣṇa is the supreme father, and all the living entities within this material world are exactly like misled children of a wealthy man who have left home to loiter in the street. Therefore the greatest benefit one can bestow upon one's fellow human being is to give him Kṛṣṇa consciousness. No kind of material profit will satisfy the living entity, but if he is given Kṛṣṇa consciousness he will actually be satisfied. A bewildered boy loitering in the street may be reminded, "My dear boy, why are you suffering so much? You are the son of a very rich man who has so much property. Why are you loitering in the street?" And if he comes to understand, "Yes, I am the son of this important man. Why shall I loiter in the street?" he may then return home. Therefore the best service is to inform those who have forgotten Kṛṣṇa, "You are part and parcel of Kṛṣṇa. You are the son of Kṛṣṇa, who is full in all opulence. Why are you rotting in this material world?" This is the greatest service. *Māyā*, illusion, is very strong, but it is the duty of every devotee of Kṛṣṇa to try to enlighten everyone to Kṛṣṇa consciousness. Kuntīdevī, for example, first said that although Kṛṣṇa, the Supreme Person, is within and without, to rascals and fools He is invisible. Therefore she points out, "Here is the Lord – Kṛṣṇa."

Kṛṣṇa is the all-pervading Supreme Personality of Godhead (*kṛṣṇāya vāsudevāya*), but He is very much pleased to become the son of Devakī (*devakī-nandanāya*). Devakī-nandana is also mentioned in the *Atharva Veda*. Kṛṣṇa comes as Devakī-nandana, and His father is Nanda-gopa, Nanda Mahārāja. Kṛṣṇa likes to be related with His devotees who act as father and mother. Although here in this material world we try to make our relationship with the Supreme by accepting Him as father, Kṛṣṇa wants to become the son. He takes pleasure in becoming the son of a devotee. Ordinary men want God as their father, but that is not very pleasing to Kṛṣṇa because the son always bothers the father: "Give me this, give me this, give me this."

Of course, Kṛṣṇa has immense potencies by which He can supply as much as everyone wants. *Eko bahūnāṁ yo vidadhāti kāmān.* He supplies food to the elephant, and He supplies food to the ant, so why not to the human being? But rascals do not know this. They work like asses day and night to find bread, and if they go to church, there also they pray, "Give me bread." They are concerned only with the bread problem.

Although the living entity is the son of the richest, most opulent person, he has created a bread problem. This is called ignorance. He thinks, "If I do not solve my bread problem, if I do not drive my trucks day and night, how can I live?" This is the nonsense of our modern civilization. Where is there a bread problem? Kṛṣṇa can supply unlimited amounts of bread. There are thousands of elephants in Africa, and Kṛṣṇa supplies food to them. So if He can supply food to the elephants, why not to the human beings? The *Bhāgavatam* therefore says, "Don't waste your time with this bread problem."

tasyaiva hetoḥ prayateta kovido
na labhyate yad bhramatām upary adhaḥ

We should not waste our time with solving economic problems. Economic development is nonsense. Of course, this proposal is very revolutionary, and people may even hate me for it. "What is Swamiji saying?" they may ask. But actually it is a fact. This economic development is madness. Suppose one has a rich father and enough food. Suppose one knows, "My father is the richest man in the city." Then where is one's economic problem? Actually, that is our position. We have no economic problem. Everything is completely provided. We want water. Just see – there are oceans of water. Of course, we want pure water, and although the ocean has so much water, when water is scarce we shall have to take help from Kṛṣṇa, who will evaporate the water and turn it into clouds, and then when the rain falls down the water will be sweet. Otherwise we cannot drink it.

Everything is under control, and everything – water, light, heat, and so on – is complete.

oṁ pūrṇam adaḥ pūrṇam idaṁ
pūrṇāt pūrṇam udacyate
pūrṇasya pūrṇam ādāya
pūrṇam evāvaśiṣyate

"The Personality of Godhead is perfect and complete, and because He is completely perfect, all emanations from Him, such as this phenomenal world, are perfectly equipped as complete wholes. Whatever is produced of the complete whole is also complete in itself. Because He is the complete whole, even though so many complete units emanate from Him, He remains the complete balance." (*Īśopaniṣad,* Invocation)

Kṛṣṇa's stock is never exhausted. We must simply become obedient to Him, and the supply will be there. Therefore a Kṛṣṇa conscious person has no economic problem; everything is sufficiently supplied by Kṛṣṇa.

In Los Angeles the neighbors of our temple are sometimes very envious. "You do not work," they say to our Kṛṣṇa conscious devotees. "You have no anxiety. You have four cars. You are eating so nicely. How is that?" Actually, they are right. Somehow or other we are getting everything we need, and we have no problems, for if one simply becomes a sincere servant of Kṛṣṇa, everything is provided. They are envious of us because we do not work but still we have so much. But why don't they come join us? That they will not do. "Come with us," we say. "Chant Hare Kṛṣṇa." "No, no, no. That I cannot do." "All right. Then work with your trucks." By zooming around in their cars and trucks, they have made their own lives dangerous, and they have created danger for others also. At any moment there may be an accident. But they say that this is civilization. Nonsense. This is not civilization. Civilization means calmness, prosperity, and *śānti,* peace. In peace and prosperity one should be Kṛṣṇa conscious always.

People work so hard, day and night, simply for a little food, not knowing that their food has already been provided. *Avidyā-karma-saṁjñānyā tṛtīyā śaktir iṣyate* (*Viṣṇu Purāṇa* 6.7.61). This material world is full of ignorance (*avidyā*). Therefore our endeavor should be to become free from this ignorance. It is only for this reason that we should work – to come out of ignorance. We are thinking, "I am this material body. I have to work day and night, and then I shall get my food, and I shall live." This is ignorance. We have lived this life of ignorance in forms other than that of a human being. We have lived in bird life, in beast life, and so on, but now, in this life, we should be peaceful, calm, and quiet, and should simply inquire about the Absolute Truth (*jīvasya tattva-jijñāsā, athāto brahma-jijñāsā*). That should be one's occupation.

We are simply sitting down and inquiring about Kṛṣṇa, and this is what one should do. This is life. Why should one work day and night like an ass? What kind of life is this? No. This is not life. Therefore the *Bhāgavatam* says to one who is intelligent (*kovida*), "Your life should be engaged for this purpose – for understanding the Absolute Truth." Then how will my economic problem be solved? The answer is that happiness one desires from economic development will come automatically in due course of time. *Tal labhyate duḥkha-vad anyataḥ* (*Bhāgavatam* 1.5.18). We are looking for happiness. Are you looking for distress? "No, sir."

Then why does distress come upon you? If you are not eager for calamities and distress, why do they come upon you? According to our *karma,* our life holds some portion of happiness and some portion of distress. Therefore, if distress comes without invitation, happiness will also come without invitation.

We are already destined to have a certain amount of happiness and a certain amount of distress, and we cannot change that. The change we should make, therefore, is to get free from this material condition of life. That should be our only business. According to our *karma,* we are sometimes taking birth in a higher planetary system as demigods and sometimes taking birth as cats and dogs or as germs in stool. Therefore Caitanya Mahāprabhu said:

> *ei rūpe brahmāṇḍa bhramite kona bhāgyavān jīva*
> *guru-kṛṣṇa-prasāde pāya bhakti-latā-bīja*

"According to their *karma,* all living entities are wandering throughout the entire universe. Some of them are being elevated to the upper planetary systems, and some are going down into the lower planetary systems. Out of many millions of wandering living entities, one who is very fortunate gets an opportunity to associate with a bona fide spiritual master by the grace of Kṛṣṇa. By the mercy of both Kṛṣṇa and the spiritual master, such a person receives the seed of the creeper of devotional service." (*Caitanya-caritāmṛta, Madhya* 19.151) Only a fortunate living entity gets the opportunity to associate with Kṛṣṇa and Kṛṣṇa's devotee, and in this way he gets the seed of devotional service, the chanting of the Hare Kṛṣṇa *mantra,* and then his life becomes sublime.

Kuntīdevī, therefore, is pointing our attention toward Kṛṣṇa, the Supreme Person, who is *alakṣya,* invisible to all. Who is that invisible person? Here – Kṛṣṇa. "Oh, Kṛṣṇa," one may say. "There are so many Kṛṣṇas." Therefore Kuntīdevī says, "I am offering my prayers to Vāsudeva, the son of Vasudeva." "There are many Vāsudevas." "No. *Nanda-gopa-kumārāya:* I am praying to the foster son of Mahārāja Nanda." In this way, three times she points out, "Here is Kṛṣṇa."

Kṛṣṇa officially takes birth as the son of Devakī and Vasudeva, but in His childhood He enjoys the company of mother Yaśodā and Nanda Mahārāja. This is Kṛṣṇa's pastime. *Ānanda-līlāmaya-vigrahāya:* Kṛṣṇa's pastimes are all jubilant. *Ānanda-mayo 'bhyāsāt* (*Vedānta-sūtra* 1.1.12): He is by nature full of bliss. We shall never find Kṛṣṇa unhappy. Kṛṣṇa is always happy, and whoever associates with Him is also happy. Therefore He is known as Govinda. The word *go* means "senses." We are looking for sense gratification, and if we associate with Kṛṣṇa we shall enjoy our senses abundantly, just like the *gopīs* who are dancing with Kṛṣṇa. Thus there is no scarcity of sense gratification, but this sense gratification in association with Kṛṣṇa is not gross sense gratification; rather, it is the spiritual sense gratification enjoyed in the spiritual world. *Ānanda-cin-maya-sad-ujjvala-vigrahasya.* That *ānanda,* or pleasure, is not the third-class *ānanda* we enjoy with our bodily senses. Such bodily enjoyment is not *ānanda* but illusion. We are thinking, "I am enjoying," but that *ānanda* is not factual, because we cannot enjoy this material pleasure of the senses for long. Everyone has experience that this material pleasure comes to an end. Spiritual enjoyment, however, does not end; rather, it increases. That is the difference. *Ānanda-cinmaya-sad-ujjvala-vigrahasya govindam ādi-puruṣaṁ tam ahaṁ bhajāmi* (*Brahma-saṁhitā* 5.32). Therefore we have to associate with Govinda.

Here also it is said, *govindāya namo namaḥ:* "I offer my respectful obeisances to Govinda." The Kṛṣṇa consciousness movement is so sublime that it puts one directly in contact with Govinda. The worship of the Deity of Kṛṣṇa in the temple is also direct contact with Govinda. *Śrī-vigrahārādhana-nitya-nānā-śṛṅgāra-tan-mandira-mārjanādau* (*Śrī Gurv-aṣṭaka* 3). The *vigraha,* the Deity of Kṛṣṇa, appears by Kṛṣṇa's mercy. Because Kṛṣṇa is *alakṣya,* invisible, He becomes visible to give us the facility to see Him. It is not that Kṛṣṇa is stone, wood, or metal. Kṛṣṇa is always Kṛṣṇa, but because we cannot see anything beyond material elements like wood, stone, and metal, He appears in a form made of these elements. But He is neither wood, metal, nor stone. When we associate with the Deity, we associate with Kṛṣṇa personally. Because Kṛṣṇa is invisible, He very kindly takes a form that is visible to us. This is Kṛṣṇa's mercy. Do not think, "Oh, here is a stone Kṛṣṇa." Kṛṣṇa is everything, and therefore Kṛṣṇa is stone also, but He is not the kind of stone that cannot act. Even in the form of stone or metal, Kṛṣṇa can act as Kṛṣṇa, and one who worships the Deity will perceive that. *Svayam eva sphuraty adaḥ.* The Deity, although apparently stone, may speak with a devotee. There are many instances in which this has happened.

I am very pleased, therefore, when my disciples nicely dress the Deity, offer the Deity nice foodstuffs, and keep the temple very clean. *Śrī-mandira-mārjanādau. Mārjana* means "cleansing." Whether one dresses Kṛṣṇa or cleanses the temple, the spiritual benefit one receives is the same. Don't think, "I am only a cleanser, and he is a dresser." No, the person who is dressing the Deity and the person who is cleansing the temple are the same because Kṛṣṇa is absolute. Therefore, one should engage in Kṛṣṇa's service in any way, and one's life will be successful. This is the Kṛṣṇa consciousness movement.

By the grace of Kuntīdevī we can understand that Kṛṣṇa, Vāsudeva, is the Supreme Personality of Godhead. The word *vāsudeva* also indicates that the Lord is understood when one comes to the platform of pure goodness, which is also called *vasudeva,* or *viśuddha-sattva. Sattvaṁ viśuddhaṁ vasudeva-śabditam* (*Bhāgavatam* 4.3.23). To understand the Supreme Lord, we must first come to the platform of *sattva,* goodness, but goodness here in the material world is sometimes contaminated by the lower qualities ignorance and passion. By hearing about Kṛṣṇa, however, one comes to the platform of pure goodness. *Śṛṇvatāṁ sva-kathāḥ kṛṣṇaḥ puṇya-śravaṇa-kīrtanaḥ.* We should try to hear and chant about Kṛṣṇa always, twenty-four hours a day, and in this way the dirty things will be cleansed from our hearts. It is not that one should only attend a *bhāgavata-saptāha,* an official reading of *Śrīmad-Bhāgavatam* for seven days. That is another form of exploitation. In the *Bhāgavatam* it is said, *naṣṭa-prāyesv abhadreṣu nityaṁ bhāgavata-sevayā.* The word *nityam* means "daily" or "twenty-four hours a day." One should always read *Śrīmad-Bhāgavatam* and carry out the order of one's spiritual master. The word *bhāgavata* may refer either to the spiritual master or to the book *Śrīmad-Bhāgavatam.* So one should always serve the person *bhāgavata* or the book *Bhāgavata. Bhagavaty uttama-śloke bhaktir bhavati naiṣṭhikī.* Then one will be fixed immovably (*naiṣṭhikī*) in devotional service to the Supreme Personality of Godhead.

In this way, one should realize the benefits of the Kṛṣṇa consciousness movement by the prescribed spiritual process and try to distribute these benefits to other people. To awaken the dormant Kṛṣṇa consciousness of others is the greatest welfare activity in the world. We can actually see that devotees who were not Kṛṣṇa conscious four or five years ago have been awakened and are now Kṛṣṇa conscious. Similarly, others can be awakened also. There is no difficulty. The process is the same.

By following in the footsteps of devotees like Kuntī, we shall be able to understand Kṛṣṇa's identity. For example, we may ask a person's identity by asking, "What is your father's name?" So *Śrīmad-Bhāgavatam* presents God with His father's name, His mother's name, and even His address. We are not impersonalists with a vague idea of God. If one takes advantage of the Kṛṣṇa consciousness movement, one can understand God perfectly and completely.

5

The Vision of Lotuses

namaḥ paṅkaja-nābhāya
namaḥ paṅkaja-māline
namaḥ paṅkaja-netrāya
namas te paṅkajāṅghraye

My respectful obeisances are unto You, O Lord, whose abdomen is marked with a depression like a lotus flower, who are always decorated with garlands of lotus flowers, whose glance is as cool as the lotus, and whose feet are engraved with lotuses.

Śrīmad-Bhāgavatam 1.8.22

Here are some of the specific symbolical marks on the spiritual body of the Personality of Godhead which distinguishes His body from the bodies of all others. They are all special features of the body of the Lord. The Lord may appear as one of us, but He is always distinct by His specific bodily features. Śrīmatī Kuntī claims herself unfit to see the Lord because of her being a woman. This is claimed because women, *śūdras* (the laborer class), and the *dvija-bandhus,* or the wretched descendants of the higher three classes, are unfit by intelligence to understand transcendental subject matter concerning the spiritual name, fame, attributes, forms, etc., of the Supreme Absolute Truth. Such persons, although they are unfit to enter into the spiritual affairs of the Lord, can see Him as the *arcā-vigraha,* who descends on the material world just to distribute favors to the fallen souls, including the above-mentioned women, *śūdras,* and *dvija-bandhus.* Because such fallen souls cannot see anything beyond matter, the Lord condescends to enter into each and every one of the innumerable universes as the Garbhodaka-śāyī Viṣṇu, who grows a lotus stem from the lotuslike depression in the center of His transcendental abdomen, and thus Brahmā, the first living being in the universe, is born. Therefore, the Lord is known as the Paṅkajanābhi. The Paṅkajanābhi Lord accepts the *arcā-vigraha* (His transcendental form) in different elements, namely a form within the mind, a form made of wood, a form made of earth, a form made of metal, a form made of jewels, a form made of paint, a form drawn on sand, etc. All such forms of the Lord are always decorated with garlands of lotus flowers, and there should be a soothing atmosphere in the temple of worship to attract the burning attention of the nondevotees always engaged in material wranglings. The meditators worship a form within the mind. Therefore, the Lord is merciful even to the women, *śūdras,* and *dvija-bandhus,* provided they agree to visit the temple and worship the different forms made for them. Such temple visitors are not idolaters, as alleged by some men with a poor fund of knowledge. All the great *ācāryas* established such temples of worship in all places just to favor the less intelligent, and one should not pose himself as transcending the stage of temple worship while one is actually in the category of the *śūdras* and the women or less. One should begin to see the Lord from His lotus feet, gradually rising to the thighs, waist, chest, and face. One should not try to look at the face of the Lord without being accustomed to seeing the lotus feet of the Lord. Śrīmatī Kuntī, because of her being the aunt of the Lord, did not begin to see the Lord from the lotus feet because the Lord might feel ashamed, and thus Kuntīdevī, just to save a painful situation for the Lord, began to see the Lord just above His lotus feet, i.e., from the waist of the Lord, gradually rising to the face, and then down to the lotus feet. In the round, everything there is in order.

If one sees a lotus flower, one can immediately remember Kṛṣṇa. For example, if one loves one's child and one sees any of the child's garments, or his shoes or a small ship or any of his playthings, one will immediately remember the child: "Oh, these are my child's shoes. These are my child's playthings. This is his garment." This is the nature of love. So if one actually loves God, Kṛṣṇa, one can remember Him always.

It is not difficult to remember Kṛṣṇa. Here Kuntīdevī describes Kṛṣṇa with reference to lotus flowers. Similarly, when Kṛṣṇa describes Himself in *Bhagavad-gītā,* He says, *raso 'ham apsu kaunteya:* "I am the taste of liquids." So one can remember Kṛṣṇa by tasting water. Even if one is drinking liquor, if he thinks, "The taste of this drink is Kṛṣṇa," he will one day turn out to be a great saintly person. So I can request even drunkards to become Kṛṣṇa conscious, what to speak of others, because Kṛṣṇa says, *raso 'ham apsu kaunteya:* "I am the taste of liquids." Generally in this context "liquid" is taken to mean water. But liquor is also liquid; it is only sugar and molasses or some other combination fermented and distilled. Of course, it is bad because it creates intoxication. Although in one sense nothing is bad, liquor is bad because it creates bad effects. In America there are many drunkards. There is no scarcity of them. But I may request even the drunkards, "When drinking wine, kindly remember that the taste of this drink is Kṛṣṇa. Just begin in this way, and one day you will become a saintly, Kṛṣṇa conscious person."

So Kṛṣṇa is available under any circumstances, if we want to catch Him. Kṛṣṇa says in *Bhagavad-gītā* (10.10):

teṣāṁ satata-yuktānāṁ
bhajatāṁ prīti-pūrvakam
dadāmi buddhi-yogaṁ taṁ
yena mām upayānti te

"To those who are constantly devoted and who worship Me with love, I give the understanding by which they can come to Me." If one is actually very serious in searching for Kṛṣṇa, Kṛṣṇa is everywhere. *Aṇḍāntara-stha-paramāṇu-cayāntara-sthaṁ govindam ādi-puruṣaṁ tam ahaṁ bhajāmi* (*Brahma-saṁhitā* 5.35). Kṛṣṇa is present within the universe, within our hearts, and even within the atom. So it is not difficult to find Him, but one must know the process by which to do so. This process is very simple, and by the order of Śrī Caitanya Mahāprabhu we are distributing this process to everyone, without charge. The process is to chant Hare Kṛṣṇa. As soon as one chants Hare Kṛṣṇa, one will immediately understand Kṛṣṇa.

Similarly, simply by hearing or chanting the verses of *Śrīmad-Bhāgavatam,* one can be purified. Whatever knowledge exists in the world is present in *Śrīmad-Bhāgavatam.* It includes literature, poetry, astronomy, philosophy, religion, and love of Godhead. *Śrīmad-bhāgavataṁ pramāṇam amalam.* If one simply reads *Śrīmad-Bhāgavatam,* he gains the topmost education, for if one studies *Śrīmad-Bhāgavatam* he will be well versed in every subject matter. Even if one does not understand a single word of the *mantras* of *Śrīmad-Bhāgavatam,* the vibrations themselves have such power that simply by chanting one will be purified. *Śṛṇvatāṁ sva-kathāḥ kṛṣṇaḥ puṇya-śravaṇa-kīrtanaḥ.* The word *puṇya* means "pious," *śravaṇa* means "hearing," and *kīrtana* means "chanting." One who chants or hears the verses of *Śrīmad-Bhāgavatam* becomes pious automatically. To become pious one generally has to endeavor a great deal, but if one simply hears the verses of *Śrīmad-Bhāgavatam* or *Bhagavad-gītā* one becomes pious automatically. Therefore it is a rigid principle in every temple of our Kṛṣṇa consciousness movement that there must be a daily class for hearing and chanting. Our movement is meant for training spiritual leaders, but without hearing and chanting it is impossible to become a leader. Of course, in the material world it is possible, but not in the spiritual world.

mālī hañā sei bīja kare āropaṇa
śravaṇa-kīrtana-jale karaye secana
(*Caitanya-caritāmṛta, Madhya* 19.152)

Hearing and chanting waters the seed of devotional service, which develops one's original consciousness.

So here, in these prayers, Kuntīdevī, a great devotee, is giving us an opportunity to become Kṛṣṇa conscious simply by concentrating our mind on *paṅkaja,* the lotus flower. *Paṅka* means "mud," and *ja* means "generate." Although the lotus flower is generated from mud, it is a most important flower, and Kṛṣṇa likes it very much. Kuntīdevī therefore describes all the parts of Kṛṣṇa's body with reference to lotus flowers, so that as soon as one sees a lotus flower one will immediately think of Kṛṣṇa: "Oh, Kṛṣṇa's navel is just like a lotus, and from Kṛṣṇa's navel grew the stem of the lotus upon which Brahmā, the creator of this universe, was born. This universe includes so many planets, seas, mountains, and cities with motorcars and other paraphernalia, but the entire universe began from that lotus."

Namaḥ paṅkaja-māline. From Kṛṣṇa comes the wonderful lotus flower that contains the seed of the entire universe. But He is not the source of only one such flower. Kṛṣṇa is not so poor that He simply produces one lotus flower and then is finished. No. Just as there may be a garland with many flowers, Kṛṣṇa is the source of innumerable universes, which may be compared to a big garland of lotuses. This is God. *Yasyaika-niśvasita-kālam athāvalambya/ jīvanti loma-vilajā jagad-aṇḍa-nāthāḥ* (*Brahma-saṁhitā* 5.48). Kṛṣṇa is unlimited. We are very much concerned with this one planet, but Kṛṣṇa's creation contains an unlimited number of planets. We cannot count how many planets there are, any more than one can count how many hairs there are on one's head. This is the nature of Kṛṣṇa's creation. To give another example, on one tree there is an unlimited number of leaves. Similarly, there is an unlimited number of planets, and there are unlimited universes. Therefore, Kṛṣṇa is unlimited.

Kṛṣṇa's navel resembles a lotus, He is garlanded with lotuses, and His eyes are also compared to the petals of a lotus (*ālola-candraka-lasad-vanamālya-vaṁśī, Brahma-saṁhitā* 5.31). So if we simply think of only this one verse, which describes Kṛṣṇa's body with reference to the lotus, we can meditate our whole life on how beautiful Kṛṣṇa is, how wise Kṛṣṇa is, and how Kṛṣṇa manifests His creation. This is meditation – thinking of Kṛṣṇa. *Dhyānāvasthita-tad-gatena manasā paśyanti yam-yoginaḥ.* A *yogī* is one who always thinks of Kṛṣṇa.

Those who think of something impersonal are not *yogīs*. Their meditation simply involves undergoing more and more labor (*kleśo 'dhikataras teṣām avyaktāsakta-cetasām*), and they cannot reach anything substantial. Therefore after meditation they say, "Come on, give me a cigarette. Come on, my throat is now dry. Give me a cigarette." That is not meditation. Meditation means thinking of Kṛṣṇa always (*satataṁ cintayanto mām*) and endeavoring to advance in Kṛṣṇa consciousness with a firm vow (*yatantaś ca dṛḍha-vratāḥ*).

We have to be purified. *Paraṁ brahma paraṁ dhāma pavitraṁ paramaṁ bhavān.* Because Kṛṣṇa is pure, we cannot approach Kṛṣṇa impurely. But if we think of Kṛṣṇa always and meditate upon Kṛṣṇa, then we shall be purified. *Puṇya-śravaṇa-kīrtanaḥ.* That meditation can be possible by hearing and chanting, and then thinking of Kṛṣṇa will automatically come. That is the process of Kṛṣṇa consciousness. *Śravaṇaṁ kīrtanaṁ viṣṇoḥ smaraṇam.* The word *smaraṇam* means "remembering." If we chant and hear, then remembrance will automatically come, and then we shall engage in worshiping Kṛṣṇa's lotus feet (*sevanam*). Then we shall engage in the temple worship (*arcanam*) and offering prayers (*vandanam*). We shall engage ourselves as Kṛṣṇa's servants (*dāsyam*), we shall become Kṛṣṇa's friends (*sakhyam*), and we shall surrender everything to Kṛṣṇa (*ātma-nivedanam*). This is the process of Kṛṣṇa consciousness.

6

The Master of the Senses

yathā hṛṣīkeśa khalena devakī
kaṁsena ruddhāti-ciraṁ śucārpitā
vimocitāhaṁ ca sahātmajā vibho
tvayaiva nāthena muhur vipad-gaṇāt

O Hṛṣīkeśa, master of the senses and Lord of lords, You have released Your mother, Devakī, who was long imprisoned and distressed by the envious King Kaṁsa, and me and my children from a series of constant dangers.

Śrīmad-Bhāgavatam 1.8.23

Devakī, the mother of Kṛṣṇa and sister of King Kaṁsa, was put into prison along with her husband, Vasudeva, because the envious King was afraid of being killed by Devakī's eighth son (Kṛṣṇa). The King killed all the sons of Devakī who were born before Kṛṣṇa, but Kṛṣṇa escaped the danger of child-slaughter because He was transferred to the house of Nanda Mahārāja, Lord Kṛṣṇa's foster father. Kuntīdevī, along with her children, was also saved from a series of dangers. But Kuntīdevī was shown far more favor because Lord Kṛṣṇa did not save the other children of Devakī, whereas He saved the children of Kuntīdevī. This was done because Devakī's husband, Vasudeva, was living, whereas Kuntīdevī was a widow and there was none to help her except Kṛṣṇa. The conclusion is that Kṛṣṇa bestows more favor upon a devotee who is in greater dangers. Sometimes He puts His pure devotees in such dangers because in that condition of helplessness the devotee becomes more attached to the Lord. The more the attachment is there for the Lord, the more success is there for the devotee.

Devakī, the devotee who became the mother of Kṛṣṇa, was not an ordinary woman. After all, who can become the mother of the Supreme Personality of Godhead? Kṛṣṇa agrees to become the son only of the most advanced devotee. In their previous lives, Devakī and her husband underwent severe austerities, and when Kṛṣṇa therefore appeared before them, wanting to give them a benediction, they told Him that they wanted a son like God. But where can there be another person equal to God? That is not possible. God is *asamaurdhva;* that is, no one can be equal to or greater than Him. There cannot be any competition. One cannot say, "I am God, you are God, he is God, we are all God." No. One who says this is a dog, not God, for God is great, and He has no competitor. No one is equal to Him; everyone is lower. *Ekale īśvara kṛṣṇa āra saba bhṛtya:* the only master is Kṛṣṇa, God, and everyone else is His servant, including even great demigods like Brahmā, Viṣṇu, and Śiva, not to speak of others. *Śiva-viriñci-nutam.* In the *śāstra,* the Vedic scriptures, it is said that Lord Kṛṣṇa is offered respect even by Lord Śiva and Lord Brahmā, the topmost demigods.

Above the human beings there are demigods. As we human beings are above the lower animals, above us there are demigods, the most important of whom are Lord Brahmā and Lord Śiva. Lord Brahmā is the creator of this universe, Lord Śiva is its destroyer, and Lord Viṣṇu, who is Kṛṣṇa Himself, is its maintainer. For the maintenance of this material world there are three *guṇas,* or modes of material nature – *sattva-guṇa* (the mode of goodness), *rajo-guṇa* (the mode of passion), and *tamo-guṇa* (the mode of ignorance). Lord Viṣṇu, Lord Brahmā, and Lord Śiva have each taken charge of one of these modes – Lord Viṣṇu of *sattva-guṇa,* Lord Brahmā of *rajo-guṇa,* and Lord Siva of *tamo-guṇa.* Yet these three controllers are not under the influence of the *guṇas.* Just as the superintendent of a jail is not a prisoner but the controlling officer, so Lord Śiva, Lord Viṣṇu, and Lord Brahmā control these three *guṇas* and are not under the control of the *guṇas.*

But above all others, the supreme controller is Kṛṣṇa, who is known as Hṛṣīkeśa. The word *hṛṣīka* means "senses." We are enjoying our senses, but ultimately the controller of the senses is Kṛṣṇa. Consider my hand, for example. I claim, "This is my hand. I can fight you with a good fist." I am very much proud. But I am not the controller; the controller is Kṛṣṇa, because if He withdraws my hand's power to act, the hand will be paralyzed. Although I claim, "It is my hand, and I shall use it," when it is paralyzed I cannot do anything. Therefore, I should understand that although I possess this hand by the grace of Kṛṣṇa, I am not its controller. This is Kṛṣṇa consciousness.

A sane man will think, "If this hand is ultimately controlled by Kṛṣṇa, then it is meant for Kṛṣṇa." This is a commonsense understanding. I claim, "This is my hand, this is my leg, this is my ear." Even a child will speak this way. If we ask a child, "What is this?" he will say, "It is my hand." But regardless of what we claim, actually it is not our hand; it is given to us. Because I wanted to use my hand in so many ways, Kṛṣṇa has given it to me: "All right, take this hand and use it." So it is a gift from Kṛṣṇa, and therefore a sane man always consciously thinks, "Whatever I have in my possession, beginning with this body and my senses, is actually not mine. I have been given all these possessions to use, and if everything ultimately belongs to Kṛṣṇa, why not use everything for Kṛṣṇa?" This is intelligence, and this is Kṛṣṇa consciousness.

Everyone is part and parcel of Kṛṣṇa (*mamaivāṁśo jīva-loke jīva-bhūtaḥ,* and therefore everyone's senses are also Kṛṣṇa's. When we use the senses for Kṛṣṇa's service, we attain the perfection of life. Therefore, *hṛṣīkeṇa hṛṣīkeśa-sevanaṁ bhaktir ucyate:* when by our senses (*hṛṣīkeṇa*) we serve Hṛṣīkeśa, the real master of the senses, that service is called *bhakti.* This is a very simple definition of *bhakti. Hṛṣīkeśa-sevanam,* not *hṛṣīka-sevanam* – service to the supreme master of the senses, not to the senses themselves. When we use our senses for sense gratification, we are in *māyā,* illusion, but when we use our senses for the gratification of the master of the senses, that service is called *bhakti.*

In this material world, everyone is generally using his senses for sense gratification. That is *māyā,* illusion, and that is the cause of one's bondage. But when one comes to Kṛṣṇa consciousness, when one becomes purified and understands that these senses are actually meant for satisfying Kṛṣṇa, then he is a liberated person (*mukta-puruṣa*).

īhā yasya harer dāsye
karmaṇā manasā girā
nikhilāsv apy avasthāsu
jīvan-muktaḥ sa ucyate

"A person who acts in the service of Kṛṣṇa with his body, mind, intelligence, and words is a liberated person, even within the material world." One should come to understand, "My senses are meant to serve the master of the senses, Hṛṣīkeśa." The master of the senses is sitting within everyone's heart. In the *Bhagavad-gītā* (15.15) the Lord says, *sarvasya cāhaṁ hṛdi sanniviṣṭo:* "I am seated in everyone's heart." *Mattaḥ smṛtir jñānam apohanaṁ ca:* "And from Me come remembrance, knowledge, and forgetfulness."

Kṛṣṇa is so merciful that if we want to use our senses in a certain way, He will give us the chance to do so. The senses are not ours; they are Kṛṣṇa's, but Kṛṣṇa gives us the opportunity to use them according to our desires. For example, each of us has a tongue, and suppose we want to eat stool. We may say, "Kṛṣṇa, I want to taste stool," and Kṛṣṇa will say, "Yes, take this body of a hog and eat stool." The master is present – Kṛṣṇa. He will give us an appropriate body and remind us, "My dear living entity, you wanted to eat stool. Now you have the proper body in which to do so." Similarly, if one wants to become a demigod, Kṛṣṇa will give one a chance to do that also. There are 8,400,000 forms of life, and if one wants to engage one's senses in a particular type of body, Kṛṣṇa will give one the chance: "Come on. Here is the body you want. Take it." But eventually one will become exasperated by using one's senses. Ultimately one will become senseless. Therefore Kṛṣṇa says, *sarva-dharmān parityajya mām ekaṁ śaraṇaṁ vraja:* "Don't act like this. Your senses are meant for serving Me. You are misusing your senses and are therefore being entrapped in different types of bodies. Therefore, to get relief from this tedious business of accepting one body and then giving it up to accept another and again another in continued material existence, just give up this process of sense gratification and surrender unto Me. Then you will be saved." This is Kṛṣṇa consciousness.

At the present moment, our senses are contaminated. I am thinking, "I am American, so my senses should be used for the service of my country, my society, my nation." Or else I am thinking, "I am Indian, and my senses are Indian senses, and therefore they should be used for India." In ignorance, one does not know that the senses belong to Kṛṣṇa. Instead, one thinks that one has American senses, Indian senses, or African senses. This is called *māyā,* illusion. In material life, the senses are covered by designations such as "American," "Indian," and "African," but when our senses are no longer contaminated by all these designations (*sarvopādhi-vinirmuktam*), *bhakti* begins.

To think "I am an American. Why shall I take to Kṛṣṇa consciousness and worship a Hindu god?" is foolishness. If one thinks, "I am Muhammadan," "I am Christian," or "I am Hindu," one is in illusion. One must purify the senses so that one can understand, "I am a spirit soul, and the supreme spirit soul is Kṛṣṇa. I am part and parcel of Kṛṣṇa, and therefore it is my duty to serve Kṛṣṇa." When one thinks in this way, one immediately becomes free. At that time, one is no longer American, Indian, African, this, or that. At that time, one is Kṛṣṇa-ized, or Kṛṣṇa conscious. That is what is wanted. Therefore Kuntīdevī says, "My dear Kṛṣṇa, Hṛṣīkeśa, You are the master of the senses."

For sense gratification we have fallen into this material condition and are suffering in different varieties of life. Because this is the material world, even Kṛṣṇa's mother was put into suffering. Devakī was so advanced that she became the mother of Kṛṣṇa, but still she was put into difficulties by her own brother, Kaṁsa. That is the nature of this material world. The living entities in this world are so jealous that if one's personal interest is hampered, one will immediately be ready to give trouble to others, even to one's nearest relatives.

The word *khala* means "jealous." This material world is a world of jealousy and envy. I am envious of you, and you are envious of me. The Kṛṣṇa consciousness movement, however, is meant for one who is no longer jealous or envious. By becoming free from jealousy and envy, one becomes a perfect person. *Dharmaḥ projjhita-kaitavo 'tra paramo nirmatsarāṇāṁ satām* (*Bhāgavatam* 1.1.2). Those who are jealous and envious are within this material world, and those who are not are in the spiritual world. Therefore, we can test ourselves. If we are jealous or envious of our friends or other associates, we are in the material world, and if we are not jealous we are in the spiritual world. There need be no doubt of whether we are spiritually advanced or not. We can test ourselves. *Bhaktiḥ pareśānubhavo viraktir anyatra ca* (*Bhāgavatam* 11.2.42). When we eat, we can understand for ourselves whether our hunger is satisfied; we don't have to take a certificate from others. Similarly, we can test for ourselves whether we are in the material world or the spiritual world. If we are jealous or envious, we are in the material world, and if we are not we are in the spiritual world.

If one is not jealous, one can serve Kṛṣṇa very well, because jealousy and envy begin with being jealous of Kṛṣṇa. For example, some philosophers think, "Why should Kṛṣṇa be God? I am also God." This is the beginning of material life – to be envious of Kṛṣṇa. "Why should Kṛṣṇa be the enjoyer?" they think. "I shall also be the enjoyer. Why should Kṛṣṇa enjoy the *gopīs*? I shall become Kṛṣṇa and make a society of *gopīs* and enjoy." This is *māyā*. No one but Kṛṣṇa can be the enjoyer. Kṛṣṇa therefore says in *Bhagavad-gītā, bhoktāraṁ yajña:* "I am the only enjoyer." If we supply ingredients for Kṛṣṇa's enjoyment, we attain the perfection of life. But if we want to imitate Kṛṣṇa, thinking, "I shall become God and enjoy like Him," then we are in *māyā*. Our natural position is to provide enjoyment for Kṛṣṇa. In the spiritual world, for example, Kṛṣṇa enjoys, and the *gopīs,* the transcendental cowherd girls, supply the ingredients for Kṛṣṇa's enjoyment. This is *bhakti.*

Bhakti is a relationship between master and servant. The servant's duty is to serve the master, and the master supplies whatever the servant needs.

nityo nityānāṁ cetanaś cetanānām
eko bahūnāṁ yo vidadhāti kāmān
(*Kaṭha Upaniṣad* 2.2.13)

The Vedic literature informs us that Kṛṣṇa can supply all the necessities for one's life. There is no scarcity and no economic problem. We simply have to try to serve Kṛṣṇa, and then everything will be complete.

If Kṛṣṇa desires, there may be ample supplies. In America, for example, there is an ample supply of everything needed, although in other countries this is not so. For instance, when I went to Switzerland I saw that everything there is imported. The only thing supplied locally is snow. This is all under Kṛṣṇa's control. If one becomes a devotee, one will be amply supplied with food, and if one does not become a devotee one will be covered with snow. Everything is under Kṛṣṇa's control, so actually there is no scarcity. The only scarcity is a scarcity of Kṛṣṇa consciousness.

Of course, the world is full of dangers. But Kuntīdevī says, "Because Devakī is Your devotee, You saved her from the distresses imposed upon her by her envious brother." As soon as Devakī's brother heard that his sister's eighth son would kill him, he was immediately ready to kill Devakī. But Devakī's husband pacified him. It is the duty of a husband to protect his wife, and therefore Devakī's husband said, "My dear brother-in-law, why are you envious of your sister? After all, your sister will not kill you; it is her son who will kill you. That is the problem. So I shall deliver all the sons to you, and then you may do whatever you like with them. Why should you kill this innocent, newly married girl? She is your younger sister, and you should protect her, just as you would protect your daughter. Why should you kill her?" In this way he placated Kaṁsa, who believed Vasudeva's word that he would bring all the sons so that if Kaṁsa wanted he could kill them. Vasudeva thought, "Let me save the present situation. After all, if Kaṁsa later gets a nephew, he may forget this envy." But Kaṁsa never forgot. Instead, he kept Devakī and Vasudeva in prison for a long time (*ati-ciram*) and killed all their sons. Finally, Kṛṣṇa appeared and saved Vasudeva and Devakī.

Therefore, we must depend on Kṛṣṇa, like Devakī and Kuntī. After Kuntī became a widow, the envious Dhṛtarāṣṭra was always planning ways to kill her sons, the five Pāṇḍavas. "Because by chance I was born blind," he thought, "I could not inherit the throne of the kingdom, and instead it went to my younger brother. Now he is dead, so at least my sons should get the throne." This is the materialistic propensity. One thinks, "I shall be happy. My sons will be happy. My community will be happy. My nation will be happy." This is extended selfishness. No one is thinking of Kṛṣṇa and how Kṛṣṇa will be happy. Rather, everyone is thinking in terms of his own happiness: "How shall I be happy? How will my children, my community, my society, and my nation be happy?" Everywhere we shall find this. Everyone is struggling for existence, not thinking of how Kṛṣṇa will be happy. Kṛṣṇa consciousness is very sublime. We should try to understand it from *Śrīmad-Bhāgavatam* and *Bhagavad-gītā* and try to engage our senses for the service of the master of the senses (*hṛṣīkeṇa hṛṣīkeśa-sevanam*). Then we shall actually be happy.

7

Dangerous Encounters

viṣān mahāgneḥ puruṣāda-darśanād
asat-sabhāyā vana-vāsa-kṛcchrataḥ
mṛdhe mṛdhe 'neka-mahārathāstrato
drauṇy-astrataś cāsma hare 'bhirakṣitāḥ

My dear Kṛṣṇa, Your Lordship has protected us from a poisoned cake, from a great fire, from cannibals, from the vicious assembly, from sufferings during our exile in the forest, and from the battle where great generals fought. And now You have saved us from the weapon of Aśvatthāmā.

Śrīmad-Bhāgavatam 1.8.24

The list of dangerous encounters is submitted herein. Devakī was once put into difficulty by her envious brother, otherwise she was well. But Kuntīdevī and her sons were put into one difficulty after another for years and years together. They were put into trouble by Duryodhana and his party due to the kingdom, and each and every time the sons of Kuntī were saved by the Lord. Once Bhīma was administered poison in a cake, once they were put into the house made of shellac and set afire, and once Draupadī was dragged out, and attempts were made to insult her by stripping her naked in the vicious assembly of the Kurus. The Lord saved Draupadī by supplying an immeasurable length of cloth, and Duryodhana's party failed to see her naked. Similarly, when they were exiled in the forest, Bhīma had to fight with the man-eater demon Hiḍimba Rākṣasa, but the Lord saved him. So it was not finished there. After all these tribulations, there was the great Battle of Kurukṣetra, and Arjuna had to meet such great generals as Droṇa, Bhīṣma, and Karṇa, all powerful fighters. And at last, even when everything was done away with, there was the *brahmāstra* released by the son of Droṇācārya to kill the child within the womb of Uttarā, and so the Lord saved the only surviving descendant of the Kurus, Mahārāja Parīkṣit.

Here Kuntī remembers all the dangers through which she passed before the Pāṇḍavas regained their kingdom. In *Bhagavad-gītā* Lord Kṛṣṇa says, *kaunteya pratijānīhi na me bhaktaḥ praṇaśyati:* "My dear Arjuna, you may declare to the world that My devotee is never vanquished." The Pāṇḍavas, the sons of Pāṇḍu, were great devotees of Lord Kṛṣṇa, but because people in the material world are interested in material things, the Pāṇḍavas were put into many dangers. Their materialistic uncle Dhṛtarāṣṭra was always planning to kill them and usurp the kingdom for his own sons. That was his policy from the very beginning.

Once Dhṛtarāṣṭra constructed a house of lac, which was so inflammable that when touched with a match it would immediately burst into fire. Then he told his nephews and his sister-in-law, Kuntī, "I've constructed a very nice house, and you should go live there for some time." But Dhṛtarāṣṭra's brother Vidura informed them of Dhṛtarāṣṭra's policy: "He wants you to go to that house so that you may burn to ashes." When Dhṛtarāṣṭra's son Duryodhana understood that Vidura had thus informed the Pāṇḍavas, he was very angry. Such is the nature of politics. Then, although the Pāṇḍavas knew, "Our uncle's plan is to send us into that house and set it afire," they agreed to go there. After all, Dhṛtarāṣṭra was their guardian, and they did not want to be disobedient to the order of a superior. But they dug a tunnel under that house, and when the house was set on fire they escaped.

Another time, when the Pāṇḍavas were at home, Dhṛtarāṣṭra gave them poison cakes, but they escaped from being poisoned. Then *puruṣāda-darśanāt:* they met a man-eating demon named Hiḍimba Rākṣasa, but Bhīma fought with him and killed him.

On another occasion, the Pāṇḍavas were cheated in a game of chess in the royal assembly of the Kurus. Dhṛtarāṣṭra, Bhīṣmadeva, Droṇācārya, and other elderly persons were present, and somehow or other Draupadī, the wife of the Pāṇḍavas, was placed as a bet. "Now if you lose," the Kurus told the Pāṇḍavas, "Draupadī will no longer be your wife." So when the Pāṇḍavas lost the game, Karṇa and Duḥśāsana immediately captured her. "Now you no longer belong to your husbands," they told her. "You are our property. We can deal with you as we like."

Previously, Karṇa had been insulted during Draupadī's *svayaṁvara.* In those days a very qualified princess would select her own husband in a ceremony called a *svayaṁvara.* In modern America, of course, any girl may select a husband as she likes, although for a common girl this is actually not very good. But even in those times an uncommon, highly qualified girl who knew how to select a good husband was given the chance to do so. Even this, however, was limited by very strict conditions. Draupadī's father, for example, placed a fish on the ceiling, and he stipulated that in order to qualify to marry his daughter, a prince had to shoot an arrow and pierce the eye of the fish, without directly seeing the fish but seeing only its reflection in a pot of water on the floor. When these conditions were declared, many princes came to compete, for responding to a challenge is a principle for a *kṣatriya,* a heroic leader.

In the assembly for Draupadī's *svayaṁvara,* Karṇa was present. Draupadī's real purpose was to accept Arjuna as her husband, but Karṇa was there, and she knew that if he competed, Arjuna would not be able to succeed. At that time it was not known that Karṇa was a *kṣatriya.* He was born the son of Kuntī before her marriage, but that was a secret. Karṇa had been maintained by a carpenter, and therefore he was known as a *śūdra,* a member of the lowest occupational division of society. Draupadī took advantage of this by saying, "In this assembly, only *kṣatriyas* may compete. I do not want any carpenter to come here and take part in the competition." In this way, Karṇa was excluded.

Karṇa regarded this as a great insult, and therefore when Draupadī was lost in the game, he was the first to come forward. He was Duryodhana's great friend, and he said, "Now we want to see the naked beauty of Draupadī." Present at that meeting were elderly persons like Dhṛtarāṣṭra, Bhīṣma, and Droṇācārya, but they did not protest. They did not say, "What is this? You are going to strip a lady naked in this assembly?" Because they did not protest, they are described as *asat-sabhāyāḥ,* an assembly of uncultured men. Only an uncultured man wants to see a woman naked, although nowadays that has become fashionable. According to the Vedic culture, a woman is not supposed to be naked before anyone except her husband. Therefore, because these men wanted to see Draupadī naked in that great assembly, they were all rascals. The word *sat* means "gentle," and *asat* means "rude." Therefore Kuntīdevī prays to Lord Kṛṣṇa, "You saved Draupadī in that assembly of rude men." When the Kurus were taking away Draupadī's *sārī* to see her naked, Kṛṣṇa supplied more and more cloth for the *sārī,* and therefore they could not come to the end of it. Finally, with heaps of cloth stacked in the room, they became tired and realized she would never be naked. They could understand, "It is impossible."

At first, Draupadī had tried to hold on to her *sārī.* But what could she do? After all, she was a woman, and the Kurus were trying to strip her naked. So she cried and prayed to Kṛṣṇa, "Save my honor," but she also tried to save herself by holding on to her *sārī.* Then she thought, "It is impossible to save my honor in this way," and she let go and simply raised her arms and prayed, "Kṛṣṇa, if You like You can save me." Thus the Lord responded to her prayers.

Therefore, it is not very good to try to save oneself. Rather, one should simply depend on Kṛṣṇa: "Kṛṣṇa, if You save me, that is all right. Otherwise, kill me. You may do as You like." As Bhaktivinoda Ṭhākura says:

mānasa, deha, geha—yo kichu mora
arpiluṅ tuya pade, nanda-kiśora

"My dear Lord, whatever I have in my possession I surrender unto You. And what do I have? I have this body and mind, I have a little home and my wife and children, but whatever I have, I surrender everything unto You." This is full surrender.

A devotee of Kṛṣṇa surrenders unto Kṛṣṇa without reservation, and therefore he is called *akiñcana*. The word *kiñcana* refers to something one reserves for oneself, and *akiñcana* means that one does not keep anything for oneself. Of course, although actually one should surrender in this way, in the material world one should not artificially imitate those who are fully surrendered. According to the example set by Rūpa Gosvāmī, whatever possessions one has, one should give fifty percent for Kṛṣṇa and twenty-five percent for one's relatives, who will also expect something, and one should keep twenty-five percent for personal emergencies. Before his retirement, Rūpa Gosvāmī divided his money in this way, although later, when his brother Sanātana Gosvāmī, another great devotee, was arrested, Rūpa Gosvāmī spent everything. This is full surrender. Similarly, Draupadī fully surrendered to Kṛṣṇa without trying to save herself, and then unlimited yards of cloth were supplied, and the Kurus could not see her naked.

But then, in the next game of chess, the bet was that if the Pāṇḍavas lost the game they would go to the forest for twelve years. Thereafter they were to remain incognito for one year, and if detected they would have to live in the forest again for another twelve years. This game also the Pāṇḍavas lost, so for twelve years they lived in the forest and for one year incognito. It was while they were living incognito that Arjuna won Uttarā.

These incidents are all recorded in the book known as the *Mahābhārata*. The word *mahā* means "great" or "greater," and *bhārata* refers to India. Thus the *Mahābhārata* is the history of greater India. Sometimes people regard these accounts as stories or mythology, but that is nonsense. The *Mahābhārata* and the *Purāṇas* are histories, although they are not chronological. If the history of such a vast period of time was recorded chronologically, how many pages would it have to be? Therefore, only the most important incidents are selected and described in the *Mahābhārata*.

Kuntī prays to Kṛṣṇa by describing how He saved the Pāṇḍavas on the Battlefield of Kurukṣetra. *Mṛdhe mṛdhe 'neka-mahārathāstrataḥ.* On the Battlefield of Kurukṣetra there were great, great fighters called *mahā-rathas.* Just as military men in modern days are given titles like lieutenant, captain, commander, and commander-in-chief, formerly there were titles like *eka-ratha, ati-ratha,* and *mahā-ratha.* The word *ratha* means "chariot." So if a warrior could fight against one chariot, he was called *eka-ratha,* and if he could fight against thousands of chariots he was called *mahā-ratha.* All the commanders on the Battlefield of Kurukṣetra were *mahā-rathas.* Many of them are mentioned in *Bhagavad-gītā.* Bhīṣma, Karṇa, and Droṇācārya were especially great commanders. They were such powerful fighters that although Arjuna was also a *mahā-ratha,* before them he was nothing. But by the grace of Kṛṣṇa he was able to kill Karṇa, Bhīṣma, Droṇācārya, and the others and come out victorious. While speaking with Śukadeva Gosvāmī, Mahārāja Parīkṣit also referred to this. "The Battlefield of Kurukṣetra," he said, "was just like an ocean, and the warriors were like many ferocious aquatic animals. But by the grace of Kṛṣṇa, my grandfather Arjuna crossed over this ocean very easily."

This is very significant. We may have many enemies who may be very powerful fighters, but if we remain under the protection of Kṛṣṇa, no one can do us any harm. *Rakhe kṛṣṇa māre ke māre kṛṣṇa rakhe ke.* "He whom Kṛṣṇa protects, no one can kill, but if Kṛṣṇa wants to kill someone, no one can give him protection." For example, suppose a very rich man is suffering from disease. He may have a first-class physician, medicine, and hospital available for him, but still he may die. This means that Kṛṣṇa desired, "This man must die." Therefore, the so-called protective methods we have devised will be useless if Kṛṣṇa does not desire us to live. The demon Rāvaṇa was very powerful, but when Kṛṣṇa in the form of Lord Rāmacandra desired to kill him, no one could protect him. Rāvaṇa was a great devotee of Lord Śiva and was praying to Lord Śiva, "Please come save me from this danger." But Lord Śiva did not come. Then Pārvatī, Lord Siva's wife, asked Lord Śiva, "What is this? He is such a great devotee and has served you so much, and now he is in danger and is asking your help. Why are you not going to help him?" Then Lord Śiva replied, "My dear Pārvatī, what shall I do? I cannot give him protection. It is not possible. Why shall I go?" Therefore, if God wants to kill someone, no one can give him protection, and if God wants to protect someone, no one can kill him. *Rakhe kṛṣṇa māre ke māre kṛṣṇa rakhe ke.*

Thus Kuntī is remembering how Kṛṣṇa saved her and her sons one time after another. This is *smaraṇam,* thinking of Kṛṣṇa. "Kṛṣṇa, You are so kind to us that You saved us from many great dangers. Without You there was no hope."

Then the last danger was *drauṇy-astra,* the weapon of Aśvatthāmā, the son of Droṇa. Aśvatthāmā performed a most abominable act by killing the five sons of the Pāṇḍavas. Of course, in the Battle of Kurukṣetra both sides belonged to the same family, and practically everyone was killed, but the five sons of the Pāṇḍavas survived. So Aśvatthāmā thought, "If I kill these five sons of the Pāṇḍavas and present their heads to Duryodhana, he will be very much pleased." Therefore, when the five sons were sleeping, he severed their heads, which he then presented to Duryodhana. At that time, Duryodhana was incapacitated. His spine was broken, and he could not move. Aśvatthāmā said, "I have brought the five heads of the Pāṇḍavas, my dear Duryodhana." At first, Duryodhana was very glad, but he knew how to test the heads to see whether they were in fact the heads of the Pāṇḍavas. When he pressed the heads, the heads collapsed, and Duryodhana said, "Oh, these are not the heads of the Pāṇḍavas. They must be the heads of their sons." When Aśvatthāmā admitted that this was so, Duryodhana fainted, and when he revived he said, "You have killed all our hopes. I had hoped that in our family at least these five sons would survive, but now you have killed them." Thus in lamentation he died.

Subsequently, Arjuna arrested Aśvatthāmā and was going to kill him. In fact, Kṛṣṇa ordered, "Kill him. He is not a *brāhmaṇa;* he is less than a *śūdra.*" But then Draupadī said, "I am suffering because of the death of my sons, and this rascal is the son of our Guru Mahārāja, Droṇācārya, who has done so much for us. If Aśvatthāmā dies, then Droṇācārya's wife, our mother *guru,* will be very much unhappy. So release him and let him go away." Thus Arjuna freed Aśvatthāmā. But then Aśvatthāmā, having been insulted, retaliated by unleashing a *brahmāstra.* The *brahmāstra* is something like a nuclear weapon. It can go to the enemy, wherever he is, and kill him. Aśvatthāmā knew, "The last descendant of the Kuru family is Parīkṣit, the son of Abhimanyu. He is in the womb of Uttarā, so let me kill him also, and then the entire dynasty will be finished."

When that weapon was unleashed, Parīkṣit Mahārāja's mother, Uttarā, felt that she was going to have a miscarriage, and therefore she approached Kṛṣṇa, saying, "Please save me." Kṛṣṇa, by His mystic power, therefore entered the womb of Uttarā and saved the child. After the Battle of Kurukṣetra, Parīkṣit Mahārāja, who was still in the womb of his mother, was the last remaining descendant of the Pāṇḍavas, and in mature time, when he was born, only his grandfathers were still alive. Parīkṣit Mahārāja was the son of Abhimanyu, who was the son of Arjuna and Subhadrā, Kṛṣṇa's sister. When Abhimanyu was sixteen years old, he went to fight, and seven great commanders joined forces to kill him. Subhadrā had only one grandchild, Parīkṣit Mahārāja. As soon as he grew up, the entire estate of the Pāṇḍavas was entrusted to him, and all the Pāṇḍavas left home and went to the Himalayas. This history is described in the *Mahābhārata*. Many great misfortunes befell the Pāṇḍavas, but in all circumstances they simply depended on Kṛṣṇa, who always saved them. Queen Kuntī's response to these misfortunes is recorded in the next verse.

8

Let There Be Calamities

vipadaḥ santu tāḥ śaśvat
tatra tatra jagad-guro
bhavato darśanaṁ yat syād
apunar bhava-darśanam

I wish that all those calamities would happen again and again so that we could see You again and again, for seeing You means that we will no longer see repeated births and deaths.

Śrīmad-Bhāgavatam 1.8.25

Generally, the distressed, the needy, the intelligent, and the inquisitive who have performed some pious activities worship or begin to worship the Lord. Others, who are thriving on misdeeds only, regardless of status, cannot approach the Supreme due to being misled by the illusory energy. Therefore, for a pious person, if there is some calamity there is no other alternative than to take shelter of the lotus feet of the Lord. Constantly remembering the lotus feet of the Lord means preparing for liberation from birth and death. Therefore, even though there are so-called calamities, they are welcome because they give us an opportunity to remember the Lord, which means liberation.

One who has taken shelter of the lotus feet of the Lord, which are accepted as the most suitable boat for crossing the ocean of nescience, can achieve liberation as easily as one leaps over the holes made by the hooves of a calf. Such persons are meant to reside in the abode of the Lord, and they have nothing to do with a place where there is danger in every step.

This material world is certified by the Lord in the *Bhagavad-gītā* as a dangerous place full of calamities. Less intelligent persons prepare plans to adjust to those calamities, without knowing that the nature of this place is to be full of calamities. They have no information of the abode of the Lord, which is full of bliss and without trace of calamity. The duty of the sane person, therefore, is to be undisturbed by worldly calamities, which are sure to happen in all circumstances. Suffering all sorts of unavoidable misfortunes, one should make progress in spiritual realization, because that is the mission of human life. The spirit soul is transcendental to all material calamities; therefore, the so-called calamities are called false. A man may see a tiger swallowing him in a dream, and he may cry for this calamity. Actually there is no tiger and there is no suffering; it is simply a case of dreams. In the same way, all calamities of life are said to be dreams. If someone is lucky enough to get in contact with the Lord by devotional service, it is all gain. Contact with the Lord by any one of the nine devotional services is always a forward step on the path going back to Godhead.

In this very interesting verse, it is described that *vipadaḥ* – calamities or dangers – are very good if such dangers and calamities remind us of Kṛṣṇa.

tat te 'nukampāṁ susamīkṣamāṇo
bhuñjāna evātma-kṛtaṁ vipākam
(*Bhāgavatam* 10.14.8)

How does a devotee receive dangers? There must be dangers because this material world is full of dangers. But foolish people who do not know this try to avoid the dangers. Thus they struggle for existence. Everyone is trying to become happy and avoid danger. This is our material business. Everyone is trying for *ātyantikaṁ sukham,* ultimate happiness. A working man thinks, "Let me work very hard now and put money in the bank, so that when I get old I shall enjoy life without working." This is the inner intention of everyone. No one wants to work; as soon as one gets some money, he wants to retire from work and become happy. But that is not possible. One cannot become happy in that way.

Here Kuntīdevī speaks of *apunar bhava-darśanam.* The prefix *a* means "not," and *punar bhava* means "repetition of birth and death." The real danger is the repetition of birth and death. That must be stopped.

The material world is full of dangers (*padaṁ padaṁ yad vipadām*). For example, if one is on the ocean one may have a very strong ship, but that ship can never be safe; because one is at sea, at any time there may be dangers. The Titanic was safe, but on its first voyage it sank, and many important men lost their lives. So danger there must be, because we are in a dangerous position. This material world itself is dangerous. Therefore, our business now should be to cross over this sea of danger as soon as possible. As long as we are at sea, we are in a dangerous position, however strong our ship may be. That's a fact. But we should not be disturbed by the sea waves; instead, we should just try to cross over the sea and get to the other side. That should be our business.

As long as we are in this material world, there must be calamities because this is the place of calamity. But even with calamities our business should be to develop our Kṛṣṇa consciousness, so that after giving up this body we may go back home, back to Kṛṣṇa.

On the Battlefield of Kurukṣetra, Arjuna said to Kṛṣṇa, "Whatever You are saying is all right. I am not this body. I am a soul, and this is also true of everyone else. So when the body is annihilated, the soul will continue to exist. But when I see that my son is dying or my grandfather is dying and that I am killing, how can I be solaced simply by knowing that they are not dying, but that only their bodies are changing? I am accustomed to thinking of them with affection in terms of the body, and so there must be grief and suffering."

Kṛṣṇa did not deny what Arjuna said. "Yes," He replied. "That's a fact. Because you are in the bodily concept of life, there must be suffering. So you must tolerate it, that's all. There is no other remedy." As mentioned in *Bhagavad-gītā* (2.14), Lord Kṛṣṇa told Arjuna:

mātrā-sparśās tu kaunteya
śītoṣṇa-sukha-duḥkha-dāḥ
āgamāpāyino 'nityās
tāṁs titikṣasva bhārata

"O son of Kuntī, the nonpermanent appearance of heat and cold, happiness and distress, and their disappearance in due course, are like the appearance and disappearance of winter and summer seasons. They arise from sense perception, O scion of Bharata, and one must learn to tolerate them without being disturbed."

In America it may sometimes be very chilly in the morning, and that may make taking one's morning bath a little difficult. But does that mean that those who are devotees will stop taking their prescribed morning bath? No. Even if it is chilly, they must take this regular bath. The duty must be done, even if there is a little suffering involved. That is called *tapasya,* or austerity. *Tapasya* means that we must proceed with our business of Kṛṣṇa consciousness despite all the dangers and calamities of this world. This is called *tapasya,* or voluntary acceptance of the difficulties of life.

Sometimes those who have undertaken strict vows of *tapasya* will ignite a ring of fire all around themselves, and in the scorching heat of the sun in the hot summer they will sit down in the midst of that fire and meditate. Similarly, in the chilly cold of winter they will immerse themselves in water up to the neck and meditate. Such vows are prescribed in strict systems of *tapasya.* But Lord Caitanya Mahāprabhu does not give us such a prescription. Instead, He gives us a very nice program: chant, dance, and take *prasāda,* food offered first to Lord Kṛṣṇa. But still we are unwilling. We are so fallen that we cannot accept even this *tapasya*. Although this kind of *tapasya* is very easy to perform and very pleasant (*su-sukhaṁ kartum avyayam*), still we are not agreeable. We may even prefer to rot in the street. Some people prefer to drink and have sex and live in the street. So what can be done?

The Kṛṣṇa consciousness movement is giving all facilities so that people may come here, chant, dance, live very peacefully, take *kṛṣṇa-prasāda,* and be happy, but people will not accept it. That is called misfortune. Caitanya Mahāprabhu, portraying the people of this age, therefore said, "I am so unfortunate that I have no attachment for chanting Hare Kṛṣṇa." Lord Caitanya prayed:

nāmnām akāri bahudhā nija-sarva-śaktis
tatrārpitā niyamitaḥ smaraṇe na kālaḥ
etādṛśī tava kṛpā bhagavan mamāpi
durdaivam īdṛśam ihājani nānurāgaḥ
(*Śikṣāṣṭaka* 2)

Kṛṣṇa, the transcendental holy name of God, has all potencies, Lord Caitanya said. Kṛṣṇa has unlimited potencies, and similarly in the holy name of Kṛṣṇa there are unlimited potencies. Kṛṣṇa has thousands and thousands of names, of which the name *kṛṣṇa* is the chief, and there are no hard and fast rules for chanting. It is not that one must chant at a certain time. No. At any time one may chant. Furthermore, Kṛṣṇa's name is identical with Kṛṣṇa Himself. Therefore the holy name of Kṛṣṇa *is* Kṛṣṇa.

We should not think that Kṛṣṇa is living in His abode, Goloka Vṛndāvana, and that His name is different from Him. In the material world, of course, in the material conception, a name is different from the fact it represents. But in the absolute world there are no such differences. The name is as potent as Kṛṣṇa is. We have a tongue, and if we use this tongue to chant Hare Kṛṣṇa, we shall immediately come directly in touch with Kṛṣṇa, because the name *kṛṣṇa* and the person Kṛṣṇa are not different. We may think that Kṛṣṇa is far, far away, but in fact Kṛṣṇa is within us. He is far away, but at the same time He is the nearest. But even if we think that Kṛṣṇa is far, far away, His name is present. We can chant Hare Kṛṣṇa, and Kṛṣṇa will immediately become available. Kṛṣṇa is available in this easy way, for which there are no hard and fast rules. We can chant at any time and immediately get Kṛṣṇa. Just see the mercy of Kṛṣṇa!

Therefore Caitanya Mahāprabhu says, *etādṛśī tava kṛpā bhagavan mamāpi durdaivam īdṛśam ihājani nānurāgaḥ:* "My dear Lord, You have given me such generous facilities by which to contact You, but I am so unfortunate that I have no attachment for these things. I have attachment for so many other things, but I have no attachment for chanting Hare Kṛṣṇa. This is my misfortune." Kṛṣṇa is so magnanimous that He is present before us by the transcendental vibration of His name, which has all the potencies of Kṛṣṇa Himself, and if we remain in contact with that name we shall get all the benefits of Kṛṣṇa's benedictions. But still we are not inclined to chant the Hare Kṛṣṇa *mantra.* This is our misfortune.

A devotee, however, is never disturbed by dangers, reverses, or calamities. Rather, he welcomes them. Because he is a surrendered soul, he knows that both dangers and festivals are but different demonstrations of Kṛṣṇa, who is absolute. In the *śāstra,* the Vedic literature, it is said that religion and irreligion, which are complete opposites, are merely the front portion and the back portion of God. But is there any difference between God's front and God's back? God is absolute, and therefore a devotee, either in opulence or in danger, is undisturbed, knowing that both of these are Kṛṣṇa.

When a devotee is in danger, he thinks, "Now Kṛṣṇa has appeared before me as danger." In His form of Nṛsiṁhadeva, the Lord was dangerous to the demon Hiraṇyakaśipu, but the same Nṛsiṁhadeva was the supreme friend to the devoted Prahlāda Mahārāja. God is never dangerous to the devotee, and the devotee is never afraid of dangers, because he is confident that the danger is but another feature of God. "Why should I be afraid?" the devotee thinks. "I am surrendered to Him."

Therefore Kuntīdevī says, *vipadaḥ santu:* "Let there be calamities." *Vipadaḥ santu tāḥ śaśvat:* "Let all those calamities happen again and again." Because she knows how to remember Kṛṣṇa at times of danger, she is welcoming danger. "My dear Lord," she says, "I welcome dangers, because when dangers come I can remember You." When Prahlāda

Mahārāja's father was putting him into dangerous predicaments, Prahlāda was always thinking of Kṛṣṇa. So if we are put into a dangerous position and that danger gives us an impetus to remember Kṛṣṇa, that is welcome: "Oh, I am getting this opportunity to remember Kṛṣṇa." Why is this welcome? It is welcome because seeing Kṛṣṇa or remembering Kṛṣṇa means advancing in spiritual life so that we will not have to suffer any more of these dangers. *Tyaktvā dehaṁ punar janma naiti mām eti so 'rjuna* (*Bhagavad-gītā* 4.9). If one becomes advanced in Kṛṣṇa consciousness, the result will be that after giving up the body (*tyaktvā deham*) one will not have to take birth again in this material world (*punar janma naiti*). This is to be desired.

Suppose I am very comfortable at the present moment. My body may be comfortable, but there will be death, and then another birth. After giving up my present body, if I get the body of a cat or a dog, what is the meaning of my comfortable position? Death is sure, and after death one must surely accept another body. We may not know what kind of body we shall get, but we can know from the *śāstra*, the Vedic literature. The *śāstra* says that according to our particular mentality, we will get a particular kind of body. Although I may be in a comfortable position, if I keep myself in the mentality of a dog, I shall get my next life as a dog. Therefore, what is the value of this comfortable position? I may be in a comfortable position for twenty years, thirty years, fifty years, or at the utmost one hundred years. Yet if, when I give up this body, my mentality causes me to become a cat, a dog, or a mouse, what is the benefit of this comfortable position? But people do not consider this. They think, especially in the present age, "I am now in a comfortable position. I have enough money and a good estate. I have ample comforts and enough food. When this body is finished, I am not going to take birth again, so as long as I am living, let me enjoy life." This is the modern philosophy of hedonism, but it does not correspond to the facts.

Kuntī, however, is aware of birth and death, and she is anxious not to repeat this process. This is indicated by the words *apunar bhava-darśanam*. If one always sees Kṛṣṇa, one is in Kṛṣṇa consciousness, for Kṛṣṇa consciousness means always thinking of Kṛṣṇa. One's consciousness should be absorbed in Kṛṣṇa thought. Therefore the spiritual master gives different varieties of engagements to devotees in Kṛṣṇa consciousness. For example, under the direction of the spiritual master the devotees may sell books in Kṛṣṇa consciousness. But if the devotees think that the energy invested in selling books should be diverted into selling jewelry, that is not a very good idea. Then they would become nothing more than jewelers. We should be very much careful not to be diverted from Kṛṣṇa consciousness. Even if there is danger or suffering in Kṛṣṇa consciousness, we should tolerate it. We should even welcome such danger, and we should pray in appreciation to Kṛṣṇa.

How should we pray? *Tat te 'nukampāṁ susamīkṣamāṇaḥ:* "My dear Lord, it is Your great mercy that I have been put into this dangerous position." That is the viewpoint of a devotee. He doesn't regard danger as danger. Rather, he thinks, "It is Kṛṣṇa's mercy." What kind of mercy? *Bhuñjāna evātma-kṛtaṁ vipākam:* "Because of my past activities, I was meant to suffer very much. But You are mitigating that suffering and giving me only a little." In other words, by the grace of Kṛṣṇa a devotee may receive only token punishment.

In court an important man is sometimes found to be a culprit, and the judge may be able to fine him a hundred thousand dollars and know that the man can pay it. But he may tell the man, "You just give one cent." That is also punishment, but it is greatly minimized. Similarly, we have to suffer for our past deeds. That is a fact, and we cannot avoid it. But *karmāṇi nirdahati kintu ca bhakti-bhājām* (*Brahma-saṁhitā* 5.54): the sufferings of those who engage in devotional service in Kṛṣṇa consciousness are minimized. For example, one may have been destined to be killed, but instead of being killed with a knife, he may instead get some little cut on his finger. In this way, for those who engage in devotional service, the reactions of past activities are minimized. Lord Kṛṣṇa assures His devotees, *ahaṁ tvāṁ sarva-pāpebhyo mokṣayiṣyāmi:* "I shall give you protection from the reactions of sinful life." So even if a devotee has a history of very grievous criminal activities behind him, instead of being killed he may only get a little cut on his finger. Why then should a devotee fear danger?

We should simply depend on Kṛṣṇa consciousness, because if we live Kṛṣṇa consciously under all circumstances, we shall not return to this material world (*apunar bhava-darśanam*). If we repeatedly think of Kṛṣṇa, see Kṛṣṇa, read of Kṛṣṇa, work for Kṛṣṇa, and somehow or other remain in Kṛṣṇa consciousness, we benefit in such a way that we shall be saved from taking birth again in the material world. That is true benefit. But if we become a little comfortable because of other, materialistic engagements and we forget Kṛṣṇa and have to take birth again, then what is our benefit? We should be very careful about this. We should act in such a way that our Kṛṣṇa consciousness can under no circumstances be disturbed, even if there is heavy suffering. That is the instruction of Kuntīdevī.

Before winning the Battle of Kurukṣetra, all the Pāṇḍavas were put into many dangers, as already described in the previous verses. They were given poison, they were put into a house of lac that was later set afire, and sometimes they were even confronted with great man-eating demons. They lost their kingdom, they lost their wife, they lost their prestige, and they were exiled to the forest. But throughout all those dangers, Kṛṣṇa was there. When the Kauravas were trying to strip Draupadī naked, Kṛṣṇa was there supplying cloth to protect her honor. Kṛṣṇa was always there.

Therefore, when the Pāṇḍavas went to see their grandfather, Bhīṣmadeva, on his deathbed, Bhīṣmadeva began to cry. "These boys, my grandsons, are all very pious," he said. "Mahārāja Yudhiṣṭhira, the oldest of the brothers, is the most pious person. He is even called Dharmarāja, the king of religion. Bhīma and Arjuna are both devotees, and they are such powerful heroes that they can kill thousands of men. Their wife, Draupadī, is directly the goddess of fortune, and it has been enjoined that wherever she is, there will be no scarcity of food. Thus they all form a wonderful combination, and moreover, Lord Kṛṣṇa is always with them. But still they are suffering." Thus he began to cry, saying, "I do not know what is Kṛṣṇa's arrangement, because such pious devotees are also suffering."

Therefore, we should not think, "Because I have become a devotee, there will be no danger or suffering." Prahlāda Mahārāja suffered greatly, and so did other devotees like the Pāṇḍavas and Haridāsa Ṭhākura. But we should not be disturbed by such sufferings. We must have firm faith, firm conviction, knowing, "Kṛṣṇa is present, and He will give me protection." Don't try to take the benefit of any shelter other than Kṛṣṇa. Always take to Kṛṣṇa.

In *Bhagavad-gītā* Lord Kṛṣṇa says, *kaunteya pratijānīhi na me bhaktaḥ praṇaśyati:* "My dear Arjuna, you may declare to the world that My devotee is never vanquished." Now, one may ask, why did Kṛṣṇa advise Arjuna to declare this? Why did He not declare it Himself? The answer is that if Kṛṣṇa Himself made this declaration, it might be suspect, because Kṛṣṇa sometimes violates His own promise. But the promise of a devotee will never be violated. This is Kṛṣṇa's concern. "Oh, My devotee has declared this. I must see that his word is kept." This is Kṛṣṇa's position because of His affection for His devotee. Therefore Lord Kṛṣṇa said, "You declare it. If I declare it, people may not believe it, but if you declare it they will believe you because you are a devotee." Even though Kṛṣṇa may break His own promise, He wants to see that the promises of His devotees are fulfilled.

Therefore, we must take to Kṛṣṇa consciousness and adhere to this consciousness under all circumstances, even in the most dangerous position. We must keep our faith in Kṛṣṇa's lotus feet, and then there will be no danger.

9

Decreasing the Fever of Illusion

janmaiśvarya-śruta-śrībhir
edhamāna-madaḥ pumān
naivārhaty abhidhātuṁ vai
tvām akiñcana-gocaram

My Lord, Your Lordship can easily be approached, but only by those who are materially exhausted. One who is on the path of [material] progress, trying to improve himself with respectable parentage, great opulence, high education, and bodily beauty, cannot approach You with sincere feeling.

Śrīmad-Bhāgavatam 1.8.26

Being materially advanced means taking birth in an aristocratic family and possessing great wealth, an education, and attractive personal beauty. All materialistic men are mad after possessing all these material opulences, and this is known as the advancement of material civilization. But the result is that by possessing all these material assets one becomes artificially puffed up, intoxicated by such temporary possessions. Consequently, such materially puffed up persons are incapable of uttering the holy name of the Lord by addressing Him feelingly, "O Govinda, O Kṛṣṇa." It is said in the *śāstras* that by once uttering the holy name of the Lord, the sinner gets rid of a quantity of sins that he is unable to commit. Such is the power of uttering the holy name of the Lord. There is not the least exaggeration in this statement. Actually the Lord's holy name has such powerful potency. But there is a quality to such utterances also. It depends on the quality of feeling. A helpless man can feelingly utter the holy name of the Lord, whereas a man who utters the same holy name in great material satisfaction cannot be so sincere. A materially puffed up person may utter the holy name of the Lord occasionally, but he is incapable of uttering the name in quality. Therefore, the four principles of material advancement, namely (1) high parentage, (2) good wealth, (3) high education, and (4) attractive beauty, are, so to speak, disqualifications for progress on the path of spiritual advancement. The material covering of the pure spirit soul is an external feature, as much as fever is an external feature of the unhealthy body. The general process is to decrease the degree of the fever and not to aggravate it by maltreatment. Sometimes it is seen that spiritually advanced persons become materially impoverished. This is no discouragement. On the other hand, such impoverishment is a good sign as much as the falling of temperature is a good sign. The principle of life should be to decrease the degree of material intoxication which leads one to be more and more illusioned about the aim of life. Grossly illusioned persons are quite unfit for entrance into the kingdom of God.

In one sense, of course, material opulences are God's grace. To take birth in a very aristocratic family or nation like America, to be very rich, to be advanced in knowledge and education, and to be endowed with beauty are gifts of pious activities. A rich man attracts the attention of others, whereas a poor man does not. An educated man attracts attention, but a fool attracts no attention at all. Materially, therefore, such opulences are very beneficial. But when a person is materially opulent in this way, he becomes intoxicated: "Oh, I am a rich man. I am an educated man. I have money."

One who drinks wine will become intoxicated and may think that he is flying in the sky or that he has gone to heaven. These are effects of intoxication. But an intoxicated person does not know that all these dreams are within the limits of time and will therefore come to an end. Because he is unaware that these dreams will not continue, he is said to be in illusion. Similarly, one is intoxicated by thinking, "I am very rich, I am very educated and beautiful, and I have taken birth in an aristocratic family in a great nation." That's all right, but how long will these advantages exist? Suppose one is an American and is also rich, beautiful, and advanced in knowledge. One may be proud of all this, but how long will this intoxication exist? As soon as the body is finished, it will all be finished, just like the intoxicated dreams of a person who has been drinking.

These dreams are on the mental platform, the egoistic platform, and the bodily platform. But I am not the body. The gross body and subtle body are different from my actual self. The gross body is made of earth, water, fire, air, and ether, and the subtle body is made of mind, intelligence, and false ego. But the living being is transcendental to these eight elements, which are described in the *Bhagavad-gītā* as the inferior energy of God.

Even if one is mentally very advanced, he does not know that he is under the influence of the inferior energy, just as an intoxicated person does not know what condition he is in. Opulence, therefore, places one in a position of intoxication. We are already intoxicated, and modern civilization aims at increasing our intoxication. In truth we should become free from this intoxication, but modern civilization aims at increasing it so that we may become more and more intoxicated and go to hell.

Kuntīdevī says that those who are intoxicated in this way cannot feelingly address the Lord. They cannot feelingly say, *jaya rādhā-mādhava:* "All glories to Rādhā and Kṛṣṇa!" They have lost their spiritual feeling. They cannot feelingly address the Lord, because they do not have knowledge. "Oh, God is for the poor man," they think. "The poor do not have sufficient food. Let them go to the church and pray, 'O God, give us our daily bread.' But I have enough bread. Why should I go to church?" This is their opinion.

Nowadays, therefore, because we are in a time of economic prosperity, no one is interested in going to the churches or temples. "What is this nonsense?" people think. "Why should I go to the church to ask for bread? We shall develop our economic condition, and then there will be a sufficient supply of bread." In Communist countries this mentality is especially prevalent. The Communists make propaganda in the villages by asking people to go to church and pray for bread. So the innocent people pray as usual, "O God, give us our daily bread." When the people come out of the church, the Communists ask, "Have you gotten bread?"

"No, sir," they reply.

"All right," the Communists say. "Ask us."

Then the people say, "O Communist friends, give us bread."

The Communist friends, of course, have brought a whole truckload of bread, and they say, "Take as much as you like. Now, who is better – the Communists or your God?"

Because the people are not very intelligent, they reply, "Oh, you are better." They don't have the intelligence to inquire, "You rascals, wherefrom have you brought this bread? Have you manufactured it in your factory? Can your factory manufacture grains?" Because they are *śūdras* (people who have very little intelligence), they don't ask these questions. A *brāhmaṇa*, however, one who is advanced in intelligence, will immediately inquire, "You rascals, wherefrom have you brought this bread? You cannot manufacture bread. You have simply taken the wheat given by God and transformed it, but this does not mean that it has become your property."

Simply transforming one thing into something else does not make the final product one's own property. For example, if I give a carpenter some wood, some tools, and a salary and he makes a very beautiful closet, to whom will the closet belong – to the carpenter or to me, the person who has supplied the ingredients? The carpenter cannot say, "Because I have transformed this wood into such a nice closet, it is mine." Similarly, we should say to atheistic men like the Communists, "Who is supplying the ingredients for your bread, you rascal? It is all coming from Kṛṣṇa. In *Bhagavad-gītā* Kṛṣṇa says, 'The elements of this material creation are all My property.' You have not created the sea, the land, the sky, the fire, or the air. These are not your creations. You may mix and transform these material things. You may take earth from the land and water from the sea, mix them and put them in a fire to make bricks, and then you may pile up all these bricks to make a skyscraper and claim that the skyscraper is yours. But where did you get the ingredients for the skyscraper, you rascal? You have stolen the property of God, and now you are claiming that it is your property." This is knowledge.

Unfortunately, those who are intoxicated cannot understand this. They think, "We have taken this land of America from the Red Indians, and now it is our property." They do not know that they are thieves. The *Bhagavad-gītā* clearly says that one who takes the property of God and claims it as his own is a thief (*stena eva saḥ*).

The devotees of Kṛṣṇa, therefore, have their own form of communism. According to Kṛṣṇa conscious communism, everything belongs to God. Just as the Russian and Chinese Communists think that everything belongs to the state, we think that everything belongs to God. This is merely an extension of the same philosophy, and to understand it one simply needs a little intelligence. Why should one think that his state belongs to only a small number of people? In fact this is all the property of God, and every living entity has a right to use this property because every living being is a child of God, who is the supreme father. In *Bhagavad-gītā* (14.4), Lord Kṛṣṇa says, *sarva-yoniṣu kaunteya ... ahaṁ bīja-pradaḥ pitā:* "I am the seed-giving father of all living entities. In whatever forms they may live, all living entities are My sons."

We living entities are all sons of God, but we have forgotten this, and therefore we are fighting. In a happy family, all the sons know, "Father is supplying food to us all. We are brothers, so why should we fight?" Similarly, if we become God conscious, Kṛṣṇa conscious, the fighting in the world will come to an end. "I am American," "I am Indian," "I am Russian," "I am Chinese" – all these nonsensical designations will be finished. The Kṛṣṇa consciousness movement is so purifying that as soon as people become Kṛṣṇa conscious their political and national fighting will immediately be over, because they will come to their real consciousness and understand that everything belongs to God. The children in a family all have the right to accept privileges from the father. Similarly, if everyone is part and parcel of God, if everyone is a child of God, then everyone has the right to use the property of the father. That right does not belong only to the human beings; rather, according to *Bhagavad-gītā,* that right belongs to all living entities, regardless of whether they are in the bodies of human beings, animals, trees, birds, beasts, insects, or whatever. That is Kṛṣṇa consciousness.

In Kṛṣṇa consciousness we do not think, "My brother is good, and I am good, but all others are bad." This is the kind of narrow, crippled consciousness we reject. Rather, in Kṛṣṇa consciousness we look equally toward all living entities. As stated in *Bhagavad-gītā* (5.18):

vidyā-vinaya-sampanne
brāhmaṇe gavi hastini
śuni caiva śvapāke ca
paṇḍitāḥ sama-darśinaḥ

"The humble sage, by virtue of true knowledge, sees with equal vision a learned and gentle *brāhmaṇa,* a cow, an elephant, a dog, and a dog-eater [outcaste]."

One who is *paṇḍita,* one who is learned, sees all living entities to be on an equal level. Therefore, because a Vaiṣṇava, or devotee, is learned, he is compassionate (*lokānāṁ hita-kāriṇau*), and he can work in such a way as to actually benefit humanity. A Vaiṣṇava feels and actually sees that all living entities are part and parcel of God and that somehow or other they have fallen into contact with this material world and have assumed different types of bodies according to different *karma.*

Those who are learned (*paṇḍitāḥ*) do not discriminate. They do not say, "This is an animal, so it should be sent to the slaughterhouse so that a man may eat it." No. Why should the animals be slaughtered? A person who is actually Kṛṣṇa conscious is kind to everyone. Therefore one tenet of our philosophy is "No meat-eating." Of course, people may not accept this. They will say, "Oh, what is this nonsense? Meat is our food. Why should we not eat it?" Because they are intoxicated rascals (*edhamāna-madaḥ*), they will not hear the real facts. But just consider: if a poor man is lying helpless in the street, can I kill him? Will the state excuse me? I may say, "I have only killed a poor man. There was no need for him in society. Why should such a person live?" But will the state excuse me? Will the authorities say, "You have done very nice work"? No. The poor man is also a citizen of the state, and the state cannot allow him to be killed. Now, why not expand this philosophy? The trees, the birds, and the beasts are also sons of God. If one kills them, one is as guilty as one who kills a poor man on the street. In God's eyes, or even in the vision of a learned man, there is no discrimination between poor and rich, black and white. No. Every living entity is part and parcel of God. And because a Vaiṣṇava sees this, he is the only true benefactor of all living entities.

A Vaiṣṇava tries to elevate all living beings to a platform of Kṛṣṇa consciousness. A Vaiṣṇava does not see, "Here is an Indian, and there is an American." Someone once asked me, "Why have you come to America?" But why should I not come? I am a servant of God, and this is the kingdom of God, so why should I not come? To hinder the movements of a devotee is artificial, and one who does so commits a sinful act. Just as a policeman may enter a house without trespassing, a servant has the right to go anywhere, because everything belongs to God. We have to see things in this way, as they are. That is Kṛṣṇa consciousness.

Now, Kuntīdevī says that those who are increasing their own intoxication cannot become Kṛṣṇa conscious. A fully intoxicated person may talk nonsense, and he may be told, "My dear brother, you are talking nonsense. Just see. Here is your father, and here is your mother." But because he is intoxicated, he will not understand, nor will he even care to understand. Similarly, if a devotee tries to show a materially intoxicated rascal, "Here is God," the rascal will not be able to understand it. Therefore Kuntīdevī says, *tvām akiñcana-gocaram,* indicating that to be free from the intoxication caused by high birth, opulence, education, and beauty is a good qualification.

Nonetheless, when one becomes Kṛṣṇa conscious, these same material assets can be used for the service of Kṛṣṇa. For example, the Americans who have joined the Kṛṣṇa consciousness movement were materially intoxicated before they became devotees, but now that their intoxication is over, their material assets have become spiritual assets that may be helpful in furthering the service of Kṛṣṇa. For example, when these

American devotees go to India, the Indian people are surprised to see that Americans have become so mad after God. Many Indians strive to imitate the materialistic life of the West, but when they see Americans dancing in Kṛṣṇa consciousness, then they realize that this is what is actually worthy of being followed.

Everything can be used in the service of Kṛṣṇa. If one remains intoxicated and does not use one's material assets for the service of Kṛṣṇa, they are not very valuable. But if one can use them for the service of Kṛṣṇa, they become extremely valuable. To give an example, zero has no value, but as soon as the digit one is placed before the zero, the zero immediately becomes ten. If there are two zeros, they become one hundred, and three zeros become one thousand. Similarly, we are intoxicated by material assets that are actually no better than zero, but as soon as we add Kṛṣṇa, these tens and hundreds and thousands and millions of zeros become extremely valuable. The Kṛṣṇa consciousness movement therefore offers a great opportunity to the people of the West. They have an overabundance of the zeros of materialistic life, and if they simply add Kṛṣṇa their life will become sublimely valuable.

10

The Property of the Impoverished

namo 'kiñcana-vittāya
nivṛtta-guṇa-vṛttaye
ātmārāmāya śāntāya
kaivalya-pataye namaḥ

My obeisances are unto You, who are the property of the materially impoverished. You have nothing to do with the actions and reactions of the material modes of nature. You are self-satisfied, and therefore You are the most gentle and are master of the monists.

Śrīmad-Bhāgavatam 1.8.27

A living being is finished as soon as there is nothing to possess. Therefore a living being cannot be, in the real sense of the term, a renouncer. A living being renounces something for gaining something more valuable. A student sacrifices his childish proclivities to gain better education. A servant gives up his job for a better job. Similarly, a devotee renounces the material world not for nothing but for something tangible in spiritual value. Śrīla Rūpa Gosvāmī, Sanātana Gosvāmī, and Śrīla Raghunātha dāsa Gosvāmī and others gave up their worldly pomp and prosperity for the sake of the service of the Lord. They were big men in the worldly sense. The Gosvāmīs were ministers in the government service of Bengal, and Śrīla Raghunātha dāsa Gosvāmī was the son of a big *zamīndār* of his time. But they left everything to gain something superior to what they previously possessed. The devotees are generally without material prosperity, but they have a very secret treasure-house in the lotus feet of the Lord. There is a nice story about Śrīla Sanātana Gosvāmī. He had a touchstone with him, and this stone was left in a pile of refuse. A needy man took it, but later on wondered why the valuable stone was kept in such a neglected place. He therefore asked Sanātana Gosvāmī for the most valuable thing, and then he was given the holy name of the Lord. *Akiñcana* means "one who has nothing to give materially." A factual devotee, or *mahātmā,* does not give anything material to anyone, because he has already left all material assets. He can, however, deliver the supreme asset, namely the Personality of Godhead, because He is the only property of a factual devotee. The touchstone of Sanātana Gosvāmī, which was thrown in the rubbish, was not the property of the Gosvāmī, otherwise it would not have been kept in such a place. This specific example is given for the neophyte devotees just to convince them that material hankerings and spiritual advancement go ill together. Unless one is able to see everything as spiritual in relation with the Supreme Lord, one must always distinguish between spirit and matter. A spiritual master like Śrīla Sanātana Gosvāmī, although personally able to see everything as spiritual, set this example for us only because we have no such spiritual vision.

Advancement of material vision or material civilization is a great stumbling block for spiritual advancement. Such material advancement entangles the living being in the bondage of a material body followed by all sorts of material miseries. Such material advancement is called *anartha,* or things not wanted. Actually this is so. In the present context of material advancement one uses lipstick at a cost of fifty cents, and there are so many unwanted things which are all products of the material conception of life. By diverting attention to so many unwanted things, human energy is spoiled without achievement of spiritual realization, the prime necessity of human life. The attempt to reach the moon is another example of spoiling energy because even if the moon is reached, the problems of life will not be solved. The devotees of the Lord are called *akiñcanas* because they have practically no material assets. Such material assets are all products of the three modes of material nature. They foil spiritual energy, and thus the less we possess such products of material nature, the more we have a good chance for spiritual progress.

The Supreme Personality of Godhead has no direct connection with material activities. All His acts and deeds, which are exhibited even in this material world, are spiritual and without affection for the modes of material nature. In the *Bhagavad-gītā* the Lord says that all His acts, even His appearance and disappearance in and out of the material world, are transcendental, and one who knows this perfectly shall not take his birth again in this material world, but will go back to Godhead.

The material disease is due to hankering after and lording it over material nature. This hankering is due to an interaction of the three modes of nature, and neither the Lord nor the devotees have attachment for such false enjoyment. Therefore, the Lord and the devotees are called *nivṛtta-guṇa-vṛtti.* The perfect *nivṛtta-guṇa-vṛtti* is the Supreme Lord because He never becomes attracted by the modes of material nature, whereas the living beings have such a tendency. Some of them are entrapped by the illusory attraction of material nature.

Because the Lord is the property of the devotees, and the devotees are the property of the Lord reciprocally, the devotees are certainly transcendental to the modes of material nature. That is a natural conclusion. Such unalloyed devotees are distinct from the mixed devotees who approach the Lord for mitigation of miseries and poverty or because of inquisitiveness and speculation. The unalloyed devotees and the Lord are transcendentally attached to one another. For others, the Lord has nothing to reciprocate, and therefore He is called *ātmārāma,* self-satisfied.

Self-satisfied as He is, He is the master of all monists who seek to merge into the existence of the Lord. Such monists merge within the personal effulgence of the Lord called the *brahma-jyotir,* but the devotees enter into the transcendental pastimes of the Lord, which are never to be misunderstood as material.

To be materially impoverished is the first qualification of a devotee. One who does not possess anything in this material world but simply possesses Kṛṣṇa is called *akiñcana.* The word *akiñcana* means "one who has lost all material possessions." As long as we have even the slightest tinge of an idea of becoming happy materially in some way or other, we shall have to accept a material body. Nature is so kind that according to the way we want to enjoy this material world, she will give us a suitable body, under the direction of the Lord. Because the Lord is situated in everyone's heart, He knows everything. Therefore, knowing that we still want something material, He will give us another material body: "Yes, take it." Kṛṣṇa wants us to have full experience through which to understand that by material gain we shall never be happy. This is Kṛṣṇa's desire.

Because we are part and parcel of Kṛṣṇa, who has full freedom, we too have full freedom, although the quantity of that freedom is quite minute. Although the quantity of salt in a drop of seawater is not comparable to the quantity of salt in the ocean, the chemical composition of both the drop and the ocean is the same. Similarly, whatever we have in a minute quantity is present in its fullness in Kṛṣṇa (*janmādy asya yataḥ*). For example, we have a propensity to steal, to take things that belong to others. Why? Because Kṛṣṇa has the same propensity. Unless the propensity to steal is present in the Absolute Truth, how can it be present in us? Kṛṣṇa is known as "the butter thief." But Kṛṣṇa's stealing and our stealing are different. Because we are materially contaminated, our stealing is abominable, whereas on the spiritual, absolute platform the same stealing is so nice that it is enjoyable. Mother Yaśodā therefore enjoys Kṛṣṇa's activities of stealing. This is the difference between material and spiritual.

Any activities that are spiritual are all-good, and any activities that are material are all-bad. This is the difference between spiritual and material. The so-called morality and goodness of this material world is all bad, but in the spiritual world even so-called immorality is good. This we must understand. For example, to dance with the wives of others at the dead of night is immoral, at least according to the Vedic civilization. Even today in India, a young woman will never be allowed to go to a young man at the dead of night to dance with him. But we shall find in *Śrīmad-Bhāgavatam* that as soon as all the *gopīs,* the young cowherd girls of Vṛndāvana, heard Kṛṣṇa's flute, they immediately came to dance with Him. Now, according to material conceptions this is immoral, but from the spiritual point of view this is in accord with the greatest morality. Caitanya Mahāprabhu therefore said, *ramyā kācid upāsanā vraja-vadhū-vargeṇa yā kalpitā:* "Oh, there is no better mode of worship than that which was conceived by the *vraja-vadhūs,* the damsels of Vṛndāvana." After Caitanya Mahāprabhu accepted the renounced order of life, He very strictly avoided association with women. Even in His family life, He never played any jokes with women. He was very humorous, but only with men, not with women. Once He spoke some joking words with His wife, Viṣṇupriyā. When Śacīmātā, Lord Caitanya's mother, was searching for something, He jokingly said, "Maybe your daughter-in-law has taken it." But in His whole life these are the only joking words we find in relation to women. He was very strict. After He accepted *sannyāsa,* the renounced order, no woman could even come near Him to offer obeisances; rather, they would offer obeisances from a distant place. Nonetheless, Caitanya Mahāprabhu said, *ramyā kācid upāsanā vraja-vadhū-vargeṇa yā kalpitā:* "There is no conception of worship better than that which was conceived by the damsels of Vṛndāvana." What was their conception? They wanted to love Kṛṣṇa, at any risk. And this is never immoral.

That which is in relationship to Kṛṣṇa can never be immoral. To give another example, Lord Kṛṣṇa in His incarnation as Nṛsiṁhadeva killed Hiraṇyakaśipu, the father of Prahlāda Mahārāja, while Prahlāda Mahārāja stood nearby without protesting. Now, is this moral? Who would like to see his own father being killed? Who would just stand there and not protest? No one would approve of such behavior and say that it is moral. Nonetheless, this actually happened. Not only that, but Prahlāda Mahārāja even made a garland to place upon the neck of the killer. "My dear Lord Killer," he said, "please take this garland. You have killed my father, and You are very good." This must be understood spiritually. If one's father is being attacked and one cannot protect him, one must protest and cry for help. But because Prahlāda Mahārāja's father was killed by Kṛṣṇa in the form of Lord Nṛsiṁhadeva, Prahlāda Mahārāja prepared a garland for the killer. After his father was killed, Prahlāda said to Nṛsiṁhadeva, "My dear Lord, now that my father has been killed, everyone is happy. Now please withdraw Your angry mood."

A *sādhu,* a saintly person, never approves of killing, not even the killing of an animal, but Prahlāda Mahārāja said, *modeta sādhur api vṛścika-sarpa-hatyā:* "Even a saintly person is pleased when a scorpion or a snake is killed." A scorpion or a snake is also a living entity, and a *sādhu* is never satisfied when he sees another living entity killed, but Prahlāda Mahārāja said, "Even a *sādhu* is pleased when a snake or a scorpion is killed. My father was just like a snake or a scorpion, and therefore now that he has been killed, everyone is happy." Hiraṇyakaśipu was a very dangerous demon who gave trouble to devotees, and when such a demon is killed even saintly persons are satisfied, although ordinarily they never want anyone killed. Therefore, although it may appear that Lord Kṛṣṇa or Prahlāda Mahārāja acted immorally, in fact they acted in accord with the highest morality.

Kṛṣṇa is *akiñcana-vitta,* the only solace for one who has lost everything material. In the *Caitanya-caritāmṛta,* Lord Kṛṣṇa says, "If someone wants Me but at the same time wants material prosperity, he is a fool." Kṛṣṇa is so kind that if one wants material prosperity but at the same time wants to become a devotee, Kṛṣṇa makes him a failure in material life. Therefore people are very much afraid of coming to Kṛṣṇa consciousness. "Oh," they think, "my material prosperity will be finished."

Generally, people go to a church or temple to pray to God for material prosperity: "O God, give us our daily bread." But although they are approaching God for material prosperity – "Give me this, give me that" – they are also considered pious because they approach God, unlike the atheists, who never approach Him. "Why shall I approach God?" the atheist says. "I shall create my own wealth, and by advancement of science I shall be happy." One who thinks "For my own prosperity I shall depend on my own strength and my own knowledge" is a *duṣkṛtī*, a most sinful person, but one who thinks "My prosperity depends on the mercy of God" is pious.

It is a fact that without the sanction of God, nothing can be achieved. *Tāvat tanur idaṁ tanūpekṣitānām.* We have discovered many methods by which to counteract distress, but when freedom from such distress is not sanctioned by God, these methods will fail. For example, a sick man may have very good medicine and a qualified physician, but if we ask the physician, "Can you guarantee the life of this patient?" the doctor will always say, "No, I cannot do so. I try my best. That's all." An intelligent doctor knows, "The ultimate sanction is in the hand of God. I am simply an instrument. If God does not want the patient to live, then all my medicines and all my scientific medical knowledge will fail."

The ultimate sanction, therefore, is Kṛṣṇa. Those who are foolish do not know this, and therefore they are called *mūḍha*, rascals. They do not know that although whatever they are doing may be very good, if it is not ultimately sanctioned by God, by Kṛṣṇa, it will all be a failure. On the other hand, a devotee knows, "With whatever intelligence I have I may try to become happy, but without Kṛṣṇa's sanction I shall never be happy." This is the distinction between a devotee and a nondevotee.

As mentioned before, Kṛṣṇa says, "One who tries to approach Me to become Kṛṣṇa conscious but at the same time wants to become materially happy is not very intelligent. He is wasting his time." Our main business is to become Kṛṣṇa conscious. That is the main business of human life. If we waste our time striving for material improvement and forget to chant Hare Kṛṣṇa, that will be a great loss. Therefore Kṛṣṇa says, *āmi-vijña, ei mūrkhe 'viṣaya' kena diba* (*Caitanya-caritāmṛta, Madhya* 22.39): "A rascal may ask some material prosperity from Me in exchange for discharging devotional service. But why shall I give him material prosperity? Rather, whatever he has I shall take away."

When our material assets are taken away, we become very morose. But that is the test. That was stated by Kṛṣṇa Himself to Yudhiṣṭhira Mahārāja. Yudhiṣṭhira Mahārāja inquired from Kṛṣṇa, "We are completely dependent on You, but still we are suffering materially so much. Our kingdom has been taken away, our wife has been insulted, and our enemies attempted to burn us in our house. How can this be so?" Kṛṣṇa replied, *yasyāham anugṛhṇāmi hariṣye tad-dhanaṁ śanaiḥ:* "Yes, that is

My first business. If I especially favor someone, then I take away all his sources of income and place him into great difficulty." In this way, Kṛṣṇa is very dangerous.

I have actual experience in this connection. I do not wish to narrate this whole story, but it is a fact that I received Kṛṣṇa's special favor in this way. When I was twenty-five years old, my Guru Mahārāja, my spiritual master, ordered me to go preach. But I thought, "First of all I shall become a rich man, and then I shall use my money to finance the preaching work." I had good opportunities to become a very rich businessman. An astrologer even told me that I should have become as rich as the wealthiest man in India. There were very good chances. I was the manager of a big chemical factory. I started my own factory, and the business was very successful. But eventually everything collapsed, and in this way I was forced into the position of carrying out the orders of my Guru Mahārāja. When all my material assets were taken away, then I approached Kṛṣṇa, saying, "You are the only shelter." Therefore Kṛṣṇa is *akiñcana-vitta,* the property of the materially impoverished. When one is bereft of all material opulences, then one turns to Kṛṣṇa. And now I am realizing that I have not lost but gained.

So to lose material opulences for Kṛṣṇa's sake is not a loss. Rather, it is the greatest gain. When one becomes *akiñcana,* having nothing to possess, Kṛṣṇa becomes one's only riches. Expressing this understanding, Narottama dāsa Ṭhākura says:

hā hā prabhu nanda-suta vṛṣabhānu-sutā-yuta
karuṇā karaha ei-bāra
narottama dāsa kahe na ṭheliyā raṅga-pāya
tumi vinā ke āche āmāra

"Kṛṣṇa, but for You I have nothing to claim. I have no possessions. You are my only possession, so please don't neglect me."

This position is very nice. When one does not depend on anything material but simply depends on Kṛṣṇa, one has attained the first-class position of Kṛṣṇa consciousness. Therefore Kṛṣṇa is addressed as *akiñcana-vitta.* "When one becomes materially impoverished, You are the only wealth." *Namo 'kiñcana-vittāya nivṛtta-guṇa-vṛttaye.* "When one takes You as one's only possession, one immediately becomes free from the activities of the material nature." In other words, by accepting Kṛṣṇa in this way, one attains the transcendental position of the Absolute. *Ātmārāmāya:* "At that time, one becomes happy with You. Kṛṣṇa, You are happy with Yourself, and one who surrenders to You becomes happy, as You are." There is no difference between Kṛṣṇa's body and Kṛṣṇa Himself. He is entirely self, entirely spirit. We, on the other hand, have a body that is different from ourselves. I am self, but I possess a material body. But when we actually become dependent on Kṛṣṇa, who is completely self-satisfied, we can also be self-satisfied with Kṛṣṇa.

Kaivalya-pataye namaḥ. The Māyāvādī philosophers, the monists, want to become one with the Supreme. The Supreme is self-satisfied, and they also want to be self-satisfied by becoming one with the Supreme. Our philosophy of Kṛṣṇa consciousness is the same, but instead of becoming one with Kṛṣṇa, we depend on Kṛṣṇa. That is actual oneness. If we simply agree to abide by the orders of Kṛṣṇa and have no disagreement with Him, we are situated in actual oneness.

The Māyāvādī philosophers think, "Why shall I keep my individual, separate existence? I shall merge into the Supreme." But that is not possible. From the very beginning, we are separated parts of Kṛṣṇa. Kṛṣṇa therefore says in *Bhagavad-gītā,* "My dear Arjuna, you should know that you, I, and all the persons assembled on this battlefield were individuals in the past, we are individuals at present, and in the future we shall continue to remain individuals."

Nityo nityānāṁ cetanaś cetanānām. Kṛṣṇa is the supreme *nitya,* the supreme living force, among the innumerable living forces. We living entities (*jīva*) are innumerable (*ananta*); there is no counting how many we are. Similarly, Kṛṣṇa is also a living entity, but He is the chief, the supreme living entity. That is the difference. One leader may have many followers. Similarly, Kṛṣṇa, the supreme living entity, is the supreme leader, and we are subordinate, dependent living entities.

That we are dependent is not very difficult to understand. If Kṛṣṇa does not supply us food, we shall starve, because independently we cannot produce anything. *Eko bahūnāṁ yo vidadhāti kāmān:* Kṛṣṇa is maintaining everything, and we are being maintained. Therefore Kṛṣṇa is the real predominator, and we should be willing to be predominated.

That is our natural constitutional position. If we falsely want to become predominators in this material world, we are in illusion. We must give up this illusion and always try to be predominated by Kṛṣṇa. Then our life will be successful.

11
The Touch of Superior Energy

manye tvāṁ kālam īśānam
anādi-nidhanaṁ vibhum
samaṁ carantaṁ sarvatra
bhūtānāṁ yan mithaḥ kaliḥ

My Lord, I consider Your Lordship to be eternal time, the supreme controller, without beginning and end, the all-pervasive one. In distributing Your mercy, You are equal to everyone. The dissensions between living beings are due to social intercourse.

Śrīmad-Bhāgavatam 1.8.28

Kuntīdevī knew that Kṛṣṇa was neither her nephew nor an ordinary family member of her paternal house. She knew perfectly well that Kṛṣṇa is the primeval Lord who lives in everyone's heart as the Supersoul, Paramātmā. Another name of the Paramātmā feature of the Lord is *kāla,* or eternal time. Eternal time is the witness of all our actions, good and bad, and thus resultant reactions are destined by Him. It is no use saying that we do not know why we are suffering. We may forget the misdeed for which we may suffer at this present moment, but we must remember that Paramātmā is our constant companion and therefore He knows everything – past, present, and future. And because the Paramātmā feature of Lord Kṛṣṇa destines all actions and reactions, He is the supreme controller also. Without His sanction not a blade of grass can move. The living beings are given as much freedom as they deserve, and misuse of that freedom is the cause of suffering. The devotees of the Lord do not misuse their freedom, and therefore they are the good sons of the Lord. Others, who misuse freedom, are put into miseries destined by the eternal *kāla.* The *kāla* offers the conditioned souls both happiness and miseries. It is all predestined by eternal time. As we have miseries uncalled for, so we may have happiness also without being asked, for they are all predestined by *kāla.* No one is therefore either an enemy or friend of the Lord. Everyone is suffering and enjoying the result of his own destiny. This destiny is made by the living beings in course of social intercourse. Everyone here wants to lord it over the material nature, and thus everyone creates his own destiny under the supervision of the Supreme Lord. He is all-pervading and therefore He can see everyone's activities. And because the Lord has no beginning or end, He is known also as the eternal time, *kāla.*

What is explained herein by the devoted Kuntī is exactly confirmed by the Lord Himself in *Bhagavad-gītā* (9.29). There the Lord says:

samo 'haṁ sarva-bhūteṣu
na me dveṣyo 'sti na priyaḥ
ye bhajanti tu māṁ bhaktyā
mayi te teṣu cāpy aham

"I envy no one, nor am I partial to anyone. I am equal to all. But one who renders service unto Me in devotion is a friend, is in Me, and I am also a friend to him." God cannot be partial. Everyone is God's son, so how can God favor one son above another? That is not possible. But human beings discriminate. We write, "In God we trust," but one who trusts in God must be equally kind and merciful toward all living entities. That is God consciousness.

Kṛṣṇa says, "I have no enemies, nor have I friends." *Na me dveṣyo 'sti na priyaḥ.* The word *dveṣya* means "enemy." We are envious of our enemies and friendly toward our friends, but because Kṛṣṇa is absolute, even when He appears to be inimical toward some demon He is actually a friend. When Kṛṣṇa kills a demon, the demon's demoniac activities are killed, and he immediately becomes a saint and merges into the supreme impersonal effulgence, the *brahma-jyotir.*

The *brahma-jyotir* is one of three features of the Absolute Truth.

vadanti tat tattva-vidas
tattvaṁ yaj jñānam advayam
brahmeti paramātmeti
bhagavān iti śabdyate
(*Bhāgavatam* 1.2.11)

The Absolute Truth is one, but is perceived in three features, known as Brahman, Paramātmā, and Bhagavān. The original, complete feature of the Absolute Truth is Bhagavān, the Supreme Personality of Godhead, and His plenary representation is Paramātmā, Kṣīrodaka-śāyī Viṣṇu, who is situated in everyone's heart (*īśvaraḥ sarva-bhūtānāṁ hṛd-deśe 'rjuna tiṣṭhati*). The third feature of the Absolute Truth is Brahman, the all-pervading impersonal effulgence of the Absolute.

The Absolute Truth is equal to everyone, but one will realize the Absolute according to the way one approaches Him (*ye yathā māṁ prapadyante*). According to one's capacity for understanding, the Absolute Truth is revealed either as the impersonal Brahman, as the localized Paramātmā, or ultimately as Bhagavān.

To explain this by an example, we may sometimes see hills from our room, although we may not see them distinctly. In Los Angeles there are many hills, but when we see the hills from a distant place they look like something cloudy. However, if we go further toward a hill, we shall find that there is something distinct – a hill. And if we go all the way to the hill itself, we shall find many people working there, many houses, streets, cars, and so many varied things. Similarly, when one wants to know the Absolute Truth by one's tiny brain and thinks, "I shall conduct research to find the Absolute Truth," one will have a vague, impersonal idea. Then if one goes further and becomes a meditator, one will find that God is situated within one's heart. *Dhyānāvasthita-tad-gatena manasā paśyanti yaṁ yoginaḥ. Yogīs* – real *yogīs* – see the form of Viṣṇu within the heart by meditation. The devotees, however, meet the Supreme Person face to face, just as we meet face to face and speak face to face. The Supreme Personality of Godhead orders, "Supply Me this," and the devotee directly serves the Lord by supplying what He wants. Thus there are different realizations of the Absolute Truth, and although He is equal to everyone it is up to us to understand Him according to our advancement. Therefore Kuntī says, *samaṁ carantaṁ sarvatra:* "In distributing Your mercy, You are equal to everyone."

The word *carantam* means "moving." The Lord moves everywhere – within and without – and we simply have to make our vision clear so that we may see Him. By devotional service, we can purify our senses so that we may perceive the presence of God. Those who are less intelligent simply try to find God within, but those who are advanced in intelligence can see the Lord both within and without.

The yogic system of meditation is actually meant for those who are less intelligent. One who practices meditation in *yoga* must control the senses (*yoga indriya-saṁyamaḥ*). Our senses are very restless, and by practicing the different *āsanas,* or sitting postures, one must control the mind and senses so that one can concentrate upon the form of Viṣṇu within the heart. This is the *yoga* system recommended for those who are too much absorbed in the bodily concept of life. However, because *bhaktas,* devotees, are more advanced, they do not need to undergo a separate process to control their senses; rather, by engaging in devotional service they are already controlling their senses.

For example, if one is engaged in worshiping the Deity, cleansing the temple, decorating the Deity, cooking for the Deity, and so on, one's senses are already engaged in the service of the Absolute Truth, so where is the chance of their being diverted? *Hṛṣīkeṇa hṛṣīkeśa-sevanaṁ bhaktir ucyate: bhakti,* devotional service, simply means engaging our senses (*hṛṣīka*) in the service of the master of the senses (*hṛṣīkeśa*). Now our senses are engaged in sense gratification. I am thinking that because I am this body, I must satisfy my senses. In fact, however, this is a contaminated stage of life. When one comes to the understanding that he is not this body but a spiritual soul, part and parcel of God, he knows that his spiritual senses should be engaged in the service of the supreme spiritual being. Thus one attains liberation (*mukti*).

One attains liberation when one gives up the false idea that the body is the self and when one resumes his actual position of service to the Lord (*muktir hitvānyathā-rūpaṁ svarūpeṇa vyavasthitiḥ, Bhāgavatam* 2.10.6). When we are conditioned, we give up our original constitutional position, which is described by Caitanya Mahāprabhu as being that of eternal service to Kṛṣṇa (*jīvera svarūpa haya—kṛṣṇera 'nitya-dāsa'*). But as soon as we employ ourselves in the service of the Lord, we are liberated immediately. There is no need to pass through some preliminary process. This very act of engaging one's senses in the service of the Lord is evidence that one is liberated.

This liberation is open for everyone (*samaṁ carantam*). In *Bhagavad-gītā* Kṛṣṇa does not say to Arjuna, "Only you may come to Me and become liberated." No, the Lord is available for everyone. When He says, *sarva-dharmān parityajya mām ekaṁ śaraṇaṁ vraja* – "Give up all other duties and surrender unto Me" – He is speaking not only to Arjuna but to everyone. Arjuna was the original target, but in fact *Bhagavad-gītā* was spoken for everyone, for all human beings, and therefore one must take advantage of it.

Kṛṣṇa's impartiality is compared to that of the sun. The sun does not consider, "Here is a poor man, here is a low-class man, and here is a hog. I shall not distribute my sunshine to them." No, the sun is equal toward all, and one simply has to take advantage of it. The sunshine is available, but if we close our doors and want to keep ourselves in darkness, that is our decision. Similarly, Kṛṣṇa is everywhere, Kṛṣṇa is for everyone, and Kṛṣṇa is ready to accept us as soon as we surrender. *Samaṁ carantam.* There is no restriction. People may make a distinction between lower class and higher class, but Kṛṣṇa says, *māṁ hi pārtha vyapāśritya ye 'pi syuḥ pāpa-yonayaḥ* (*Bhagavad-gītā* 9.32):

"Even though one may supposedly be of a lower class, that doesn't matter. If he surrenders to Me he is also eligible to come back home, back to Godhead."

That same Kṛṣṇa is described by Kuntīdevī as eternal time. Everything takes place within time, but our time calculations of past, present, and future are relative. A small insect's measurement of past, present, and future is different from our past, present, and future, and similarly the past, present, and future of Brahmā, the chief creative living being within this universe, are different from ours. But Kṛṣṇa has no past, present, or future. Therefore He is eternal. We have a past, present, and future because we change from one body to another. The body we have now is dated. At a certain date I was born of my father and mother, and now this body will stay for some time. It will grow, it will produce some by-products, then it will become old and dwindle and then vanish, and then I shall have to accept another body. When the past, present, and future of my present body are finished, I shall accept another body, and again my past, present, and future will begin. But Kṛṣṇa has no past, present, or future, because He does not change His body. That is the difference between ourselves and Kṛṣṇa.

The eternal position of Kṛṣṇa is revealed in *Bhagavad-gītā.* There Kṛṣṇa said to Arjuna, "In the past, millions of years ago, I spoke this philosophy of *Bhagavad-gītā* to the sun-god." Arjuna appeared not to believe this. Of course, Arjuna knew everything, but for our education he said to Kṛṣṇa, "Kṛṣṇa, we are contemporaries, and since we were born at practically the same time, how can I believe that You spoke this philosophy so long ago to the sun-god?" Then Kṛṣṇa replied, "My dear Arjuna, you were also present then, but you have forgotten, whereas I have not. That is the difference." Past, present, and future pertain to persons who forget, but for one who does not forget, who lives eternally, there is no past, present, or future.

Kuntī therefore addresses Kṛṣṇa as eternal (*manye tvāṁ kālam*). And because He is eternal, He is the full controller (*īśānam*). By Kṛṣṇa's extraordinary behavior, Kuntī could understand that Kṛṣṇa is eternal and that Kṛṣṇa is the supreme controller. He has no beginning and no end (*anādi-nidhanam*), and therefore He is *vibhu,* the Supreme, the greatest.

We are *aṇu,* the smallest, and Kṛṣṇa is *vibhu,* the greatest. We are part and parcel of Kṛṣṇa, and therefore Kṛṣṇa is both the smallest and the greatest, whereas we are only the smallest. *Vibhu,* the greatest, must be all-inclusive. If one has a large bag one can hold many things, whereas in a small bag one cannot. Because Kṛṣṇa is *vibhu,* the greatest, He includes everything, even past, present, and future time, and He is all-pervading, present everywhere.

Without Kṛṣṇa, matter cannot develop. Atheistic scientists say that life comes from matter, but that is nonsense. Matter is one energy of Kṛṣṇa, and spirit is another. The spirit is superior energy, and matter is inferior energy. The matter develops when the superior energy is present. For example, two or three hundred years ago the land of America was not developed, but because some superior living entities from Europe came here, America is now very much developed. Therefore the cause of development is the superior energy. In Africa, Australia, and many other places there is still vacant land that is undeveloped. Why is it undeveloped? Because the superior energy of advanced living entities has not touched it. As soon as the superior energy touches it, the same land will develop so many factories, houses, cities, roads, cars, and so on.

The point of this example is that matter cannot develop by itself. That is not possible. Superior energy must touch it, and then it will be active. To give another example, a machine is matter – it is inferior energy – and therefore unless an operator comes to touch the machine, it will not act. One may have a very costly car, but unless a driver comes, in millions of years it will never go anywhere.

Thus it is common sense to understand that matter cannot work independently; it cannot work unless the superior energy, the living entity, touches it. So how can we conclude that life develops from matter? Rascal scientists may say this, but they do not have sufficient knowledge.

All the universes have developed because of Kṛṣṇa's presence, as mentioned in the *Brahma-saṁhitā* (*aṇḍāntara-stha-paramāṇu-cayāntara-stham*). The scientists are now studying atoms, and they are finding that electrons, protons, and other particles act in so many ways. Why are these particles active? Because Kṛṣṇa is present there. This is real scientific understanding.

One should scientifically understand Kṛṣṇa. Kṛṣṇa has no past, present, and future. He is eternal time, with no beginning and no end, and He is equal to everyone. We simply have to prepare ourselves to see Kṛṣṇa and understand Kṛṣṇa. That is the purpose of Kṛṣṇa consciousness.

12
Bewildering Pastimes

na veda kaścid bhagavaṁś cikīrṣitaṁ
tavehamānasya nṛṇāṁ viḍambanam
na yasya kaścid dayito 'sti karhicid
dveṣyaś ca yasmin viṣamā matir nṛṇām

O Lord, no one can understand Your transcendental pastimes, which appear to be human and so are misleading. You have no specific object of favor, nor do You have any object of envy. People only imagine that You are partial.

Śrīmad-Bhāgavatam 1.8.29

The Lord's mercy upon the fallen souls is equally distributed. He has no one as the specific object of hostility. The very conception of the Personality of Godhead as a human being is misleading. His pastimes *appear* to be exactly like a human being's, but actually they are transcendental and without any tinge of material contamination. He is undoubtedly known as partial to His pure devotees, but in fact He is never partial, as much as the sun is never partial to anyone. By utilizing the sun rays, sometimes even the stones become valuable, whereas a blind man cannot see the sun, although there are enough sun rays before him. Darkness and light are two opposite conceptions, but this does not mean that the sun is partial in distributing its rays. The sun rays are open to everyone, but the capacities of the receptacles differ. Foolish people think that devotional service is flattering the Lord to get special mercy. Factually the pure devotees who are engaged in the transcendental loving service of the Lord are not a mercantile community. A mercantile house renders service to someone in exchange for values. The pure devotee does not render service unto the Lord for such exchange, and therefore the full mercy of the Lord is open for him. Suffering and needy men, inquisitive persons, or philosophers make temporary connections with the Lord to serve a particular purpose. When the purpose is served, there is no more relation with the Lord. A suffering man, if he is pious at all, prays to the Lord for his recovery. But as soon as the recovery is over, in most cases the suffering man no longer cares to keep any connection with the Lord. The mercy of the Lord is open for him, but he is reluctant to receive it. That is the difference between a pure devotee and a mixed devotee. Those who are completely against the service of the Lord are considered to be in abject darkness, those who ask for the Lord's favor only at the time of necessity are partial recipients of the mercy of the Lord, and those who are cent-percent engaged in the service of the Lord are full recipients of the mercy of the Lord. Such partiality in receiving the Lord's mercy is relative to the recipient, and it is not due to the partiality of the all-merciful Lord.

When the Lord descends on this material world by His all-merciful energy, He plays like a human being, and therefore it appears that the Lord is partial to His devotees only, but that is not a fact. Despite such an apparent manifestation of partiality, His mercy is equally distributed.

In the Battlefield of Kurukṣetra all persons who died in the fight before the presence of the Lord got salvation without the necessary qualifications, because death before the presence of the Lord purifies the passing soul from the effects of all sins, and therefore the dying man gets a place somewhere in the transcendental abode. Somehow or other if someone puts himself open in the sun rays, he is sure to get the requisite benefit both by heat and by ultraviolet rays. Therefore, the conclusion is that the Lord is never partial. It is wrong for the people in general to think of Him as partial.

The Lord says in *Bhagavad-gītā* (4.8):

paritrāṇāya sādhūnāṁ
vināśāya ca duṣkṛtām
dharma-saṁsthāpanārthāya
sambhavāmi yuge yuge

"In order to deliver the pious and to annihilate the miscreants, as well as to reestablish the principles of religion, I advent Myself millennium after millennium."

When God incarnates, He has two missions – to vanquish the demons and deliver the *sādhus*, the faithful devotees. The word *sādhūnām*, which means "saintly persons," refers to devotees. It has nothing to do with worldly honesty or dishonesty, morality or immorality; it has nothing to do with material activities. Sometimes we may think that the word *sādhu* refers to a person who is materially good or moral, but actually the word *sādhu* refers to one who is on the transcendental platform. A *sādhu*, therefore, is a devotee, because one who engages in devotional service is transcendental to material qualities (*sa guṇān samatītyaitān*).

Now, the Lord comes to deliver the devotees (*paritrāṇāya sādhūnām*), but it is clearly stated in *Bhagavad-gītā* (14.26) that a devotee transcends the material qualities (*sa guṇān samatītyaitān*). A devotee is in a transcendental position because he is no longer under the control of the three material modes of nature – goodness, passion, and ignorance. But if a *sādhu* is already delivered, being on the transcendental platform, then where is the necessity of delivering him? This question may arise. The Lord comes to deliver the devotee, but the devotee is already delivered. Therefore the word *viḍambanam,* meaning "bewildering," is used in this verse because this appears contradictory.

The answer to this contradiction is that a *sādhu,* a devotee, does not require deliverance, but because he is very much anxious to see the Supreme Lord face to face, Kṛṣṇa comes not to deliver him from the clutches of matter, from which he has already been delivered, but to satisfy his inner desire. Just as a devotee wants to satisfy the Lord in all respects, the Lord even more wants to satisfy the devotee. Such are the exchanges of loving affairs. Even in our ordinary dealings, if we love someone we want to satisfy him or her, and he or she also wants to reciprocate. So if the reciprocation of loving affairs exists in this material world, in what an elevated way must it exist in the spiritual world. There is a verse in which the Lord says, "The *sādhu* is My heart, and I am also the *sādhu's* heart." The *sādhu* is always thinking of Kṛṣṇa, and Kṛṣṇa is always thinking of the *sādhu,* His devotee.

The appearance and disappearance of the Lord within this material world are called *cikīrṣitam,* pastimes. It is Kṛṣṇa's pastime that He comes. Of course, when the Lord comes He has some work to perform – to protect the *sādhu* and kill those who are against the *sādhu* – but both of these activities are His pastimes.

The Lord is not envious. The killing of the demons is also a display of His affection. Sometimes we may punish our children by giving them a very strong slap because of love. Similarly, when Kṛṣṇa kills a demon this killing is not on the platform of material jealousy or envy, but on the platform of affection. Therefore it is mentioned in the *śāstras,* the Vedic literatures, that even the demons killed by the Lord attain immediate salvation. Pūtanā, for example, was a demoniac witch who wanted to kill Kṛṣṇa. When Kṛṣṇa was performing pastimes as a small child, she coated the nipple of her breast with poison and approached Kṛṣṇa's home to offer the milk of her breast. "When Kṛṣṇa sucks my nipple," she thought, "the child will immediately die." But that was not possible. Who can kill Kṛṣṇa? Instead she herself was killed, for Kṛṣṇa sucked the nipple and also sucked out her life altogether. But what was the result? Kṛṣṇa took the bright side. "This demoniac woman came to kill Me," He thought, "but somehow or other I have sucked her breast milk, so she is My mother." Thus Pūtanā attained the position of Kṛṣṇa's mother in the spiritual world. This is explained in the *Śrīmad-Bhāgavatam,* where Uddhava says to Vidura that Kṛṣṇa is so kind, God is so kind, that even the witch who wanted to kill Him with poison was accepted as His mother. "Since Kṛṣṇa is such a kind God," he said, "whom else shall I worship but Kṛṣṇa?"

Kuntīdevī says, *na yasya kaścid dayitaḥ.* The word *dayita* means "favorite." Kṛṣṇa favors no one. *Dveṣyaś ca:* and no one is His enemy. We expect some benediction or profit from a friend and harmful activities from an enemy, but Kṛṣṇa is so perfect that no one can harm Him nor can anyone give Him anything. So who can be His friend or enemy? *Na yasya kaścid dayito 'sti:* He doesn't need anyone's favor. He is complete. I may be a very poor man, and therefore I may expect some favor from a friend, but that is because I am imperfect. Because I am not full, because I am deficient in so many ways, I am always needy, and therefore I want to create some friend, and similarly I hate an enemy. But since Kṛṣṇa is the Supreme, no one can harm Kṛṣṇa, nor can anyone give Kṛṣṇa anything.

Why then are we worshiping Kṛṣṇa in the temple by offering Kṛṣṇa so many comforts, dressing Him, decorating Him, and giving Him nice food? We should try to understand that Kṛṣṇa does not need our offerings of nice garments, flowers, or food, but if we give such offerings to Kṛṣṇa, we shall benefit. Thus it is Kṛṣṇa's favor that He accepts such offerings. If one decorates oneself, one's reflection in a mirror will also appear decorated. Similarly, since we are reflections of Kṛṣṇa, if we decorate Kṛṣṇa we also shall be decorated. In the Bible it is said that man was made in the image of God, and this means that we are reflections of God's image. It is not that we invent or imagine some form of God according to our own form. Those who adhere to the Māyāvāda philosophy of anthropomorphism say, "The Absolute Truth is impersonal, but because we are persons we imagine that the Absolute Truth is also a person." This is a mistake, and in fact just the opposite is true. We have two hands, two legs, and a head because God Himself has these same features. We have personal forms because we are reflections of God. Furthermore, we should philosophically understand that if the original person benefits, the reflection also benefits. So if we decorate Kṛṣṇa, we also shall be decorated. If we satisfy Kṛṣṇa, we shall become satisfied. If we offer nice food to Kṛṣṇa, we shall also eat the same food. Those who live outside the temples of Kṛṣṇa consciousness may never have imagined such palatable food as the food we are offering to Kṛṣṇa, but because it is being offered to Kṛṣṇa, we also have the opportunity to eat it. So we should try to satisfy Kṛṣṇa in all respects, and then we shall be satisfied in all respects.

Kṛṣṇa does not need our service, but He kindly accepts it. When Kṛṣṇa asks us to surrender unto Him (*sarva-dharmān parityajya mām ekaṁ śaraṇaṁ vraja*), this does not mean that Kṛṣṇa is lacking servants and that if we surrender He will profit. Kṛṣṇa can create millions of servants by His mere desire. So that is not the point. But if we surrender to Kṛṣṇa, we shall be saved, for Kṛṣṇa says, *ahaṁ tvāṁ sarva-pāpebhyo mokṣayiṣyāmi:* "I shall free you from all sinful reactions." We are suffering here in this material world without any shelter. We even see many people loitering in the street, with no aim in life. When we go walking by the beach in the early morning, we see many young people sleeping or loitering there, aimless, confused, and not knowing what to do. But if we take shelter of Kṛṣṇa, then we shall know, "Oh, now I have found shelter." Then there will be no more confusion, no more hopelessness. I receive so many letters daily from people expressing how they have found hope in Kṛṣṇa consciousness. Therefore, it is not a fact that Kṛṣṇa descended here merely to collect some servants. Rather, He descended for our benefit.

Unfortunately, however, instead of becoming Kṛṣṇa's servants, we are becoming servants of so many other things. We are servants of our senses and the sensual activities of lust, anger, greed, and illusion. Actually the whole world is serving in this way. But if we engage our senses in the service of Kṛṣṇa, we shall no longer be servants of the senses, but masters of the senses. When we have the strength to refuse to allow our senses to be engaged other than in the service of Kṛṣṇa, then we shall be saved.

Here Kuntīdevī says, "Your appearance in this material world is misleading, bewildering." We think, "Kṛṣṇa has some mission, some purpose, and therefore He has appeared." No, it is for His pastimes that He appears. For example, sometimes a governor goes to inspect a prison. He gets reports from the prison superintendent, so he has no business going there, but still he sometimes goes, thinking, "Let me see how they are doing." This may be called a pastime because he is going by his free will. It is not that he has become subject to the laws of the prison. But still a foolish prisoner may think, "Oh, here the governor is also in prison. So we are equal. I am also governor." Rascals think like that. "Because Kṛṣṇa has descended as an *avatāra,*" they say, "I am also an *avatāra.*" So here it is said, *na veda kaścid bhagavaṁś cikīrṣitam:* "No one knows the purpose of Your appearance and disappearance." *Tavehamānasya nṛṇāṁ viḍambanam:* the Lord's pastimes are bewildering. No one can understand their real purpose.

The real purpose of the Lord's pastimes is His free will. He thinks, "Let Me go and see." He doesn't need to come to kill the demons. He has so many agents in the material nature that can kill them. For example, in a moment He can kill thousands of demons merely by a strong wind. Nor does He need to come to give protection to the devotees, for He can do everything simply by His will. But He descends to enjoy pleasure pastimes. "Let Me go and see."

Sometimes Kṛṣṇa even wants to enjoy the pleasure pastimes of fighting. The fighting spirit is also in Kṛṣṇa, otherwise wherefrom have we gotten it? Because we are part and parcel of Kṛṣṇa, all the qualities of Kṛṣṇa are present in minute quantity within us. We are samples of Kṛṣṇa. Wherefrom do we get the fighting spirit? It is present in Kṛṣṇa. Therefore, just as a king sometimes engages a wrestler to fight with him, Kṛṣṇa also engages living entities to engage in fighting. The wrestler is paid to fight with the king. He is not the king's enemy; rather, he gives pleasure to the king by mock fighting. But when Kṛṣṇa wants to fight, who will fight with Him? Not anyone ordinary. If a king wants to practice mock fighting, he will engage some very qualified wrestler. Similarly, Kṛṣṇa does not fight with anyone ordinary, but rather with some of His great devotees. Because Kṛṣṇa wants to fight, some of His devotees come down to this material world to become His enemies and fight with Him. For example, the Lord descended to kill Hiraṇyakaśipu and Hiraṇyākṣa. Should we think that these were ordinary living entities? No, they were the great devotees Jaya and Vijaya, who came to this world because Kṛṣṇa wanted to fight. In the Vaikuṇṭha world, the spiritual world, there is no possibility of fighting, because everyone there engages in Kṛṣṇa's service. With whom will He fight? Therefore He sends some devotee in the garb of an enemy and comes here to this material world to fight with him. At the same time, the Lord teaches us that becoming His enemy is not very profitable and that it is better to become His friend. Kuntīdevī therefore says, *na veda kaścid bhagavaṁś cikīrṣitam:* "No one knows the purpose of Your appearance and disappearance." *Tavehamānasya nṛṇāṁ viḍambanam:* "You are in this world just like an ordinary human being, and this is bewildering."

Because Kṛṣṇa sometimes appears like an ordinary man, people sometimes cannot believe or understand His activities. They wonder, "How can God become an ordinary person like us?" But although Kṛṣṇa sometimes plays like an ordinary person, in fact He is not ordinary, and whenever necessary He displays the powers of God. When sixteen thousand girls were kidnapped by the demon Bhaumāsura, they prayed to Kṛṣṇa, and therefore Kṛṣṇa went to the demon's palace, killed the demon, and delivered all the girls. But according to the strict Vedic system, if an unmarried girl leaves her home even for one night, no one will marry her. Therefore when Kṛṣṇa told the girls, "Now you can safely return to your fathers' homes," they replied, "Sir, if we return to the homes of our fathers, what will be our fate? No one will marry us, because this man kidnapped us."

"Then what do you want?" Kṛṣṇa asked. The girls replied, "We want You to become our husband." And Kṛṣṇa is so kind that He immediately said yes and accepted them.

Now, when Kṛṣṇa brought the girls back home to His capital city, it is not that each of the sixteen thousand wives had to wait sixteen thousand nights to meet Kṛṣṇa. Rather, Kṛṣṇa expanded Himself into sixteen thousand forms, constructed sixteen thousand palaces, and lived in each palace with each wife.

Although this is described in *Śrīmad-Bhāgavatam,* rascals cannot understand this. Instead they criticize Kṛṣṇa. "He was very lusty," they say. "He married sixteen thousand wives." But even if He is lusty, He is *unlimitedly* lusty. God is unlimited. Why sixteen thousand? He could marry sixteen million and still not reach the limits of His perfection. That is Kṛṣṇa. We cannot accuse Kṛṣṇa of being lusty or sensuous. No. There are so many devotees of Kṛṣṇa, and Kṛṣṇa shows favor to all of them. Some ask Kṛṣṇa to become their husband, some ask Kṛṣṇa to become their friend, some ask Kṛṣṇa to become their son, and some ask Kṛṣṇa to become their playmate. In this way, there are millions and trillions of devotees all over the universe, and Kṛṣṇa has to satisfy them all. He does not need any help from these devotees, but because they want to serve Him in a particular way, the Lord reciprocates. These sixteen thousand devotees wanted Kṛṣṇa as their husband, and therefore Kṛṣṇa agreed.

Thus Kṛṣṇa may sometimes act like a common man, but as God He expanded Himself into sixteen thousand forms. Once the great sage Nārada went to visit Kṛṣṇa and His wives. "Kṛṣṇa has married sixteen thousand wives," he thought. "Let me see how He is dealing with them." Then he found Kṛṣṇa living differently in each of the sixteen thousand palaces. In one palace He was talking with His wife, in another He was playing with His children, in another He was arranging for the marriage of His sons and daughters, and in this way He was engaged in varied pastimes in all of the sixteen thousand palaces. Similarly, in His childhood Kṛṣṇa played just like an ordinary child, but when His mother, Yaśodā, wanted Him to open His mouth so that she could see whether He had eaten dirt, within His mouth He showed her all the universes. This is Kṛṣṇa. Although He plays just like an ordinary human being, when there is need He shows His nature as God. To give another example, Kṛṣṇa acted as the chariot driver of Arjuna, but when Arjuna wanted to see Kṛṣṇa's universal form, Kṛṣṇa immediately showed him a cosmic form with thousands and millions of heads, legs, arms, and weapons. This is Kṛṣṇa.

Kṛṣṇa is completely independent, and He has no friends or enemies, but He plays for the benefit of both His friends and enemies, and when He acts for the benefit of either, the result is the same. That is Kṛṣṇa's absolute nature.

13

The Vital Force of the Universe

janma karma ca viśvātmann
ajasyākartur ātmanaḥ
tiryaṅ-nṝṣiṣu yādaḥsu
tad atyanta-viḍambanam

Of course it is bewildering, O soul of the universe, that You work, though You are inactive, and that You take birth, though You are the vital force and the unborn. You Yourself descend among animals, men, sages, and aquatics. Verily, this is bewildering.

Śrīmad-Bhāgavatam 1.8.30

The transcendental pastimes of the Lord are not only bewildering but also apparently contradictory. In other words, they are all inconceivable to the limited thinking power of the human being. The Lord is the all-prevailing Supersoul of all existence, and yet He appears in the form of a boar among the animals, in the form of a human being as Rāma, Kṛṣṇa, etc., in the form of a *ṛṣi* like Nārāyaṇa, and in the form of an aquatic like a fish. Yet it is said that He is unborn, and He has nothing to do. In the *śruti-mantra* it is said that the Supreme Brahman has nothing to do. No one is equal to or greater than Him. He has manifold energies, and everything is performed by Him perfectly by automatic knowledge, strength, and activity. All these statements prove without any question that the Lord's activities, forms, and deeds are all inconceivable to our limited thinking power, and because He is inconceivably powerful, everything is possible in Him. Therefore no one can calculate Him exactly; every action of the Lord is bewildering to the common man. He cannot be understood by the Vedic knowledge, but He can be easily understood by the pure devotees because they are intimately related with Him. The devotees therefore know that although He appears among the animals, He is not an animal or a man or a *ṛṣi* or a fish. He is eternally the Supreme Lord, in all circumstances.

Kuntī addresses Kṛṣṇa as *viśvātman,* the vital force of the universe. In everyone's body there is a vital force. That vital force is the *ātmā* – the living being, the living entity, the soul. It is because of the presence of that vital force, the soul, that the whole body works. Similarly, there is a supreme vital force. That supreme vital force is Kṛṣṇa, the Supreme Personality of Godhead. Therefore, where is the question of His taking birth? In *Bhagavad-gītā* (4.9) the Lord says:

janma karma ca me divyam
evaṁ yo vetti tattvataḥ
tyaktvā dehaṁ punar janma
naiti mām eti so 'rjuna

"One who knows the transcendental nature of My appearance and activities does not, upon leaving the body, take his birth again in this material world, but attains My eternal abode, O Arjuna."

In this verse the word *divyam* especially indicates that the Lord's appearance and activities are spiritual. And elsewhere in the *Bhagavad-gītā* it is said, *ajo 'pi sann avyayātmā*. The word *aja* means "unborn," and *avyayātmā* means "not subject to destruction." This is the nature of Kṛṣṇa, whose transcendental nature is further described by Kuntīdevī in her prayers to the Lord.

In the beginning of her prayers, Kuntīdevī said to the Lord, "You are within, and You are without, but still You are invisible." Kṛṣṇa is within everyone's heart (*īśvaraḥ sarva-bhūtānāṁ hṛd-deśe 'rjuna tiṣṭhati, sarvasya cāhaṁ hṛdi sanniviṣṭaḥ*). Indeed, He is within everything, even within the atom (*aṇḍāntara-stha-paramāṇu-cayāntara-stham*). Kṛṣṇa is within and He is also without. Thus Kṛṣṇa showed Arjuna His external feature as the *viśva-rūpa*, the gigantic cosmic manifestation.

This external body of Kṛṣṇa is described in the *Śrīmad-Bhāgavatam*. There the hills and mountains are described as the bones of the Lord. Similarly, the great oceans have been described as different holes in the Lord's universal body, and the planet known as Brahmaloka has been described as the upper portion of His skull. Those who cannot see God have thus been advised to see Him in many ways in terms of the material cosmic manifestation, according to the instructions given in the Vedic literature.

There are those who can simply think of God as being great but do not know how great He is. When they think of greatness, they think of very high mountains, the sky, and other planets. Therefore the Lord has been described in terms of such material manifestations so that while thinking of these different manifestations one can think of the Lord. That is also Kṛṣṇa consciousness. If one thinks, "This mountain is the bone of Kṛṣṇa," or if one thinks of the vast Pacific Ocean as Kṛṣṇa's navel, one is in Kṛṣṇa consciousness. Similarly, one may think of the trees and plants as the hairs on Kṛṣṇa's body, one may think of Brahmaloka as the top of Kṛṣṇa's skull, and one may think of the Pātāla-loka planetary system as the soles of Kṛṣṇa's feet. Thus one may think of Kṛṣṇa as greater than the greatest (*mahato mahīyān*).

Similarly, one may think of Kṛṣṇa as smaller than the smallest. That is also a kind of greatness. Kṛṣṇa can manufacture this gigantic cosmic manifestation, and He can also manufacture a small insect. In a book one may sometimes find a small running insect smaller than a period. This is Kṛṣṇa's craftsmanship. *Aṇor aṇīyān mahato mahīyān* (*Kaṭha Upaniṣad* 1.2.20): He can create something greater than the greatest and smaller than the smallest. Now human beings have manufactured the 747 airplane, which according to their conception is very big. But can they produce an airplane as small as a flying insect? That is not possible. Actual greatness, however, is not one-sided. One who is actually great can become greater than the greatest and smaller than the smallest.

But even the great things men can manufacture in the modern age are still not the greatest things man has created. We have information from the *Śrīmad-Bhāgavatam* that Kardama Muni, the father of the great sage Kapiladeva, manufactured a huge plane that resembled a great city. It included lakes, gardens, streets, and houses, and the whole city was able to fly all over the universe. In that plane, Kardama Muni traveled with his wife and showed her all the planets. He was a great *yogī*, and his wife, Devahūti, was the daughter of Svāyambhuva Manu, a great king. Kardama Muni had desired to marry, and Devahūti told her father, "My dear father, I want to marry that sage." Thus Svāyambhuva Manu brought his daughter to Kardama Muni and said, "Sir, here is my daughter. Please accept her as your wife." She was a king's daughter and was very opulent, but when she joined her austere husband, she had to serve so much that she became lean and thin. In fact, even with insufficient food she was working day and night. Thus Kardama Muni became compassionate. "This woman who has come to me is a king's daughter," he thought, "but under my protection she is not receiving any comfort. So I shall give her some comfort." Thus he asked his wife, "What will make you comfortable?" A woman's nature, of course, is that she wants a good house, good food, fine garments, good children, and a good husband. These are a woman's ambitions. Thus Kardama Muni proved to her that she had received the best husband. By yogic powers he created for her this great airplane and gave her a big house with maidservants and all opulences. Kardama Muni was merely a human being, but he could perform such wonderful things by yogic powers.

Kṛṣṇa, however, is Yogeśvara, the master of all yogic powers. If we get a little mystic power we become important, but Kṛṣṇa is the master of all mystic powers. In *Bhagavad-gītā* it is said that wherever there is

Yogeśvara, Kṛṣṇa, the Supreme Personality of Godhead, the master of all mystic powers, and wherever there is Arjuna, who is also known as Pārtha or Dhanur-dhara, everything is present.

We should always remember that if we can keep ourselves always in company with Kṛṣṇa, we shall attain all perfection. And especially in this age, Kṛṣṇa has incarnated as the holy name (*kali-kāle nāma-rūpe kṛṣṇa-avatāra, Caitanya-caritāmṛta, Ādi* 17.22). Therefore Caitanya Mahāprabhu says:

nāmnām akāri bahudhā nija-sarva-śaktis
tatrārpitā niyamitaḥ smaraṇe na kālaḥ

"My dear Lord, You are so kind that You are giving me Your association in the form of Your holy name, and this holy name can be chanted in any situation." There are no hard and fast rules for chanting Hare Kṛṣṇa. One can chant Hare Kṛṣṇa anywhere. Children, for example, also chant and dance. It is not at all difficult. While walking, our students take their beads with them and chant. Where is the loss? But the gain is very great, for by chanting we associate with Kṛṣṇa personally. Suppose we were to associate personally with the President. How proud we would feel. "Oh, I am with the President." So should we not feel very much proud if we were to associate with the supreme president, who is able to create many millions of presidents like those of this world? This chanting is our opportunity to do so. Therefore Caitanya Mahāprabhu says, *etādṛśī tava kṛpā bhagavan mamāpi:* "My dear Lord, You are so kind to me that You are always prepared to give me Your association." *Durdaivam īdṛśam ihājani nānurāgaḥ:* "But I am so unfortunate that I do not take advantage of this opportunity."

Our Kṛṣṇa consciousness movement is simply requesting people, "Chant Hare Kṛṣṇa." There was a cartoon in some newspaper that depicted an old lady and her husband sitting face to face. The lady is requesting her husband, "Chant, chant, chant." And the husband is answering, "Can't, can't, can't." So in this same way, we are requesting everyone, "Please chant, chant, chant." But they are replying, "Can't, can't, can't." This is their misfortune.

Still, it is our duty to make all such unfortunate creatures fortunate. That is our mission. Therefore we go into the street and chant.

Although they say "Can't," we go on chanting. That is our duty. And if somehow or other we place some literature in someone's hand, he becomes fortunate. He would have squandered his hard-earned money in so many nasty, sinful ways, but if he purchases even one book, regardless of the price, his money is properly utilized. This is the beginning of his Kṛṣṇa consciousness. Because he gives some of his hard-earned money for the Kṛṣṇa consciousness movement, he gets some spiritual profit. He is not losing; rather, he is gaining some spiritual profit. Therefore our business is somehow or other to bring everyone to this Kṛṣṇa consciousness movement so that everyone may spiritually profit.

When Kṛṣṇa appeared on earth, not everyone knew that He was the Supreme Personality of Godhead. Although when there was need He proved Himself the Supreme Godhead, He generally appeared to be just like an ordinary human being. Therefore Śukadeva Gosvāmī, while describing how Kṛṣṇa played as one of the cowherd boys, points out Kṛṣṇa's identity. Who is this cowherd boy? Śukadeva Gosvāmī says, *itthaṁ satāṁ brahma-sukhānubhūtyā*. The impersonalists meditate upon the impersonal Brahman and thus feel some transcendental bliss, but Śukadeva Gosvāmī points out that the source of that transcendental bliss is here – Kṛṣṇa.

Kṛṣṇa is the source of everything (*ahaṁ sarvasya prabhavaḥ*), and therefore the transcendental bliss that the impersonalists try to experience by meditating on the impersonal Brahman in fact comes from Kṛṣṇa. Śukadeva Gosvāmī says, "Here is the person who is the source of *brahma-sukha,* the transcendental bliss that comes from realization of Brahman."

A devotee is always prepared to render service to the Lord (*dāsyaṁ gatānāṁ para-daivatena*), but for those who are under the spell of illusory energy, He is an ordinary boy (*māyāśritānāṁ nara-dārakeṇa*). *Ye yathā māṁ prapadyante tāṁs tathaiva bhajāmy aham:* Kṛṣṇa deals with different living entities according to their conceptions. For those who regard Kṛṣṇa as an ordinary human being, Kṛṣṇa will deal like an ordinary human being, whereas devotees who accept Kṛṣṇa as the Supreme Personality of Godhead will enjoy the association of the Supreme Personality of Godhead. Of course, the object of the impersonalist is the *brahma-jyotir,* the impersonal effulgence of the Supreme, but Kṛṣṇa is the source of that effulgence. Therefore Kṛṣṇa is everything (*brahmeti paramātmeti bhagavān iti śabdyate*).

Yet the cowherd boys are able to play with that same Kṛṣṇa, the exalted Personality of Godhead. How have they become so fortunate that they are able to play with Him?

itthaṁ satāṁ brahma-sukhānubhūtyā
dāsyaṁ gatānāṁ para-daivatena
māyāśritānāṁ nara-dārakeṇa
sārdhaṁ vijahruḥ kṛta-puṇya-puñjāḥ
(*Bhāgavatam* 10.12.11)

The cowherd boys playing with Kṛṣṇa are also not ordinary, for they have attained the highest perfection of being able to play with the Supreme Personality of Godhead. How did they achieve this position? *Kṛta-puṇya-puñjāḥ:* by many, many lives of pious activities. For many, many lives these boys underwent austerities and penances to achieve the highest perfection of life, and now they have the opportunity to play with Kṛṣṇa personally on an equal level. They do not know that Kṛṣṇa is the Supreme Personality of Godhead, for that is the nature of *vṛndāvana-līlā,* Kṛṣṇa's pastimes in the village of Vṛndāvana.

Not knowing Kṛṣṇa's identity, the cowherd boys simply love Kṛṣṇa, and their love is unending. This is true of everyone in Vṛndāvana. For example, Yaśodāmātā and Nanda Mahārāja, Kṛṣṇa's mother and father, love Kṛṣṇa with parental affection. Similarly Kṛṣṇa's friends love Kṛṣṇa, Kṛṣṇa's girlfriends love Kṛṣṇa, the trees love Kṛṣṇa, the water loves Kṛṣṇa, the flowers, the cows, the calves – everyone loves Kṛṣṇa. That is the nature of Vṛndāvana. So if we simply learn how to love Kṛṣṇa, we can immediately transform this world into Vṛndāvana.

This is the only central point – how to love Kṛṣṇa (*premā pum-artho mahān*). People are generally pursuing *dharma, artha, kāma, mokṣa* – religiosity, economic development, sense gratification, and liberation. But Caitanya Mahāprabhu disregarded these four things. "These are not what is to be achieved in life," He said. The real goal of life is love of Kṛṣṇa.

Of course, human life does not actually begin until there is some conception of religion (*dharma*). But in the present age, Kali-yuga, *dharma* is practically nil – there is no religion or morality, and there are no pious activities – and therefore according to Vedic calculations the present human civilization does not even consist of human beings. Formerly people would care about morality and immorality, religion and irreligion, but with the progress of Kali-yuga this is all being vanquished, and people can do anything, without caring what it is. *Śrīmad-Bhāgavatam* says, and we can actually see, that in Kali-yuga about eighty percent of the people are sinful. Illicit sex life, intoxication, meat-eating, and gambling are the four pillars of sinful life, and therefore we request that one first break these four pillars, so that the roof of sinful life will collapse. Then by chanting Hare Kṛṣṇa one can remain established in a transcendental position. It is a very simple method.

One cannot realize God if one's life is sinful. Therefore Kṛṣṇa says:

yeṣāṁ tv anta-gataṁ pāpaṁ
janānāṁ puṇya-karmaṇām
te dvandva-moha-nirmuktā
bhajante māṁ dṛḍha-vratāḥ

"Persons who have acted piously in previous lives and in this life, whose sinful actions are completely eradicated, and who are freed from the duality of delusion engage themselves in My service with determination." (*Bhagavad-gītā* 7.28)

The word *anta-gatam* means "finished." One can engage in devotional service if one has finished with his sinful life. Who can finish with sinful life? Those who engage in pious activities. One must have activities, and if one engages in pious activities one's sinful activities will naturally vanish. On one side, one should voluntarily try to break the pillars of sinful life, and on another side one must engage himself in pious life.

If one has no pious engagement, it is not that one can become free from sinful activities simply by theoretical understanding. For example, the American government is spending millions of dollars to stop the use of LSD and other such intoxicants, but the government has failed. How is it that simply by passing laws or giving lectures one can make people give up these things? It is not possible. One must give people good

His Divine Grace A. C. Bhaktivedanta Swami Prabhupāda
Founder-*Ācārya* of the International Society for Krishna Consciousness

For years Duryodhana had tormented Queen Kuntī's family, but Kṛṣṇa had protected them at every turn – and now He was going away. (p. 7)

Queen Kuntī recalls how although Duryodhana had tried to kill her family by setting fire to a house of lac, she and her sons excavated a tunnel beneath the palace and escaped. (p. 46)

One who sees the Supersoul accompanying the individual soul in all bodies, and who understands that neither the soul nor the Supersoul is ever destroyed, actually sees and gradually advances toward spiritual perfection. (p. 82)

Even a great devotee like Queen Kuntī could not fully fathom Kṛṣṇa's humanlike pastimes and relationships with His most intimate associates. (p. 105)

Because Queen Kuntī knew Kṛṣṇa's supreme position, she was amazed that although He was feared by fear personified, He appeared to be afraid of His mother, who wanted to punish Him just like an ordinary child. (pp. 112–13)

Vasudeva and Devakī were in Kaṁsa's prison when Kṛṣṇa appeared in His Viṣṇu form as their son. After receiving prayers from them, the Supreme Personality of Godhead transformed Himself into His original form as a small human child. (p. 133)

Just to enchant the hearts of pure devotees like Queen Kuntī, Kṛṣṇa enacted His delightful childhood pastimes in Vṛndāvana, such as stealing butter. (pp. 209–210)

engagements, and then they will automatically give up the bad ones. For example, we instruct our students, "No intoxication," and they immediately give it up, even though the government has failed to stop them. This is practical.

Paraṁ dṛṣṭvā nivartate. If someone isn't given good engagement, his bad engagements cannot be stopped. That is not possible. Therefore we have two sides – prohibition of sinful activities, and engagement in good activities. We don't simply say, "No illicit sex," "No intoxication," and so on. Mere negativity has no meaning; there must be something positive, because everyone wants engagement. That is because we are living entities, not dead stones. By meditation the impersonalist philosophers try to become dead stones: "Let me think of something void or impersonal." But how can one artificially make oneself void? The heart and mind are full of activities, so these artificial methods will not help human society.

Methods of so-called *yoga* and meditation are all rascaldom because they provide one no engagement. But in Kṛṣṇa consciousness there is adequate engagement for everyone. Everyone rises early in the morning to offer worship to the Deities. The devotees prepare nice food for Kṛṣṇa, they decorate the temple, make garlands, go out chanting, and sell books. They are fully engaged twenty-four hours a day, and therefore they are able to give up sinful life. If a child has in his hands something that he is eating but we give him something better, he will throw away the inferior thing and take the better thing. So in Kṛṣṇa consciousness we offer better engagement, better life, better philosophy, better consciousness – everything better. Therefore those who engage in devotional service can give up sinful activities and promote themselves to Kṛṣṇa consciousness.

Activities intended to promote all living entities to Kṛṣṇa consciousness are going on not only in human society but even in animal society also. Because all living entities here are part and parcel of Kṛṣṇa but are rotting in this material world, Kṛṣṇa has a plan, a big plan to deliver them. Sometimes He comes to this world personally, and sometimes He sends His very confidential devotees. Sometimes He leaves instructions like those of *Bhagavad-gītā*. Kṛṣṇa's incarnation appears everywhere, and He appears among animals, men, sages, and even aquatics (*tiryaṅ-nṛṣiṣu yādaḥsu*). For example, Kṛṣṇa even appeared as a fish incarnation.

Thus Kṛṣṇa's birth, appearance, and disappearance are all bewildering (*tad atyanta-viḍambanam*). We conditioned living entities transmigrate from one body to another because we are forced to do so by the laws of nature, but Kṛṣṇa does not appear because He is forced. That is the difference. Those who are foolish rascals think, "I have taken my birth in this world, and Kṛṣṇa has taken birth here also. Therefore I am also God." They do not know that they will have to take birth again by the force of the laws of nature.

One may have been given the chance to have a very beautiful body in a country where one can live in opulence and receive a good education. But if one misuses all this, one will get another body according to one's mentality. For example, at the present moment, despite so many arrangements by the government for good schools and universities, the civilized countries of the world are producing hippies, young people who are so frustrated that they even worship hogs. But if one associates with the qualities of the hogs, one will actually become a hog in one's next birth. *Prakṛteḥ kriyamāṇāni guṇaiḥ karmāṇi sarvaśaḥ*. Nature will give one a full opportunity: "All right, sir, become a hog." Such are nature's arrangements. *Prakṛti,* nature, has three modes, and if one associates with one type of mode, one will receive his next body accordingly.

Kṛṣṇa's appearance and disappearance are meant to put an end to the living entities' transmigration from one body to another, and therefore one should understand the greatness of the plan behind Kṛṣṇa's appearance and disappearance. It is not that Kṛṣṇa comes whimsically. He has a great plan, otherwise why should He come here? He is very much eager to take us back home, back to Godhead. That is Kṛṣṇa's business. Therefore He says:

sarva-dharmān parityajya
mām ekaṁ śaraṇaṁ vraja
ahaṁ tvāṁ sarva-pāpebhyo
mokṣayiṣyāmi mā śucaḥ

"Abandon all varieties of religion and just surrender unto Me. I shall deliver you from all sinful reaction. Do not fear." (*Bhagavad-gītā* 18.66) All of us are children of Kṛṣṇa, God, and since we are unhappy because of taking material bodies for repeated birth, death, old age, and disease,

He is more unhappy than we are. Our situation in the material body is not at all comfortable, but we are such foolish rascals that we do not care to do anything about this. We are busy trying to arrange for temporary comforts in this life, but we are neglecting the real discomforts of birth, death, old age, and disease. This is our ignorance and our foolishness, and therefore Kṛṣṇa comes to wake us up from this ignorance and take us back home, back to Godhead.

14

Lord Kṛṣṇa's Wonderful Activities

gopy ādade tvayi kṛtāgasi dāma tāvad
yā te daśāśru-kalilāñjana-sambhramākṣam
vaktraṁ ninīya bhaya-bhāvanayā sthitasya
sā māṁ vimohayati bhīr api yad bibheti

My dear Kṛṣṇa, Yaśodā took up a rope to bind You when You committed an offense, and Your perturbed eyes overflooded with tears, which washed the mascara from Your eyes. And You were afraid, though fear personified is afraid of You. This sight is bewildering to me.

Śrīmad-Bhāgavatam 1.8.31

Here is another explanation of the bewilderment created by the pastimes of the Supreme Lord. The Supreme Lord is the Supreme in all circumstances, as already explained. Here is a specific example of the Lord's being the Supreme and at the same time a plaything in the presence of His pure devotee. The Lord's pure devotee renders service unto the Lord out of unalloyed love only, and while discharging such devotional service the pure devotee forgets the position of the Supreme Lord. The Supreme Lord also accepts the loving service of His devotees more relishably when the service is rendered spontaneously out of pure affection, without anything of reverential admiration. Generally the Lord is worshiped by the devotees in a reverential attitude, but the Lord is meticulously pleased when the devotee, out of pure affection and love, considers the Lord to be less important than himself. The Lord's pastimes in the original abode, Goloka Vṛndāvana, are exchanged in that spirit. The friends of Kṛṣṇa consider Him one of them. They do not consider Him to be of reverential importance. The parents of the Lord (who are all pure devotees) consider Him a child only. The Lord accepts the chastisements of the parents more cheerfully than the prayers of the Vedic hymns. Similarly, He accepts the reproaches of His fiancées more palatably than the Vedic hymns. When Lord Kṛṣṇa was present in this material world to manifest His eternal pastimes of the transcendental realm Goloka Vṛndāvana as an attraction for the people in general, He displayed a unique picture of subordination before His foster mother, Yaśodā. The Lord, in His naturally childish playful activities, used to spoil the stocked butter of mother Yaśodā by breaking the pots and distributing the contents to His friends and playmates, including the celebrated monkeys of Vṛndāvana, who took advantage of the Lord's munificence. Mother Yaśodā saw this, and out of her pure love she wanted to make a show of punishment for her transcendental child. She took a rope and threatened the Lord that she would tie Him up, as is generally done in the ordinary household. Seeing the rope in the hands of mother Yaśodā, the Lord bowed down His head and began to weep just like a child, and tears rolled down His cheeks, washing off the black ointment smeared about His beautiful eyes. This picture of the Lord is adored by Kuntīdevī because she is conscious of the Lord's supreme position. He is feared often by fear personified, yet He is afraid of His mother, who wanted to punish Him just in an ordinary manner. Kuntī was conscious of the exalted position of Kṛṣṇa, whereas Yaśodā was not. Therefore Yaśodā's position was more exalted than Kuntī's. Mother Yaśodā got the Lord as her child, and the Lord made her forget altogether that her child was the Lord Himself. If mother Yaśodā had been conscious of the exalted position of the Lord, she would certainly have hesitated to punish the Lord. But she was made to forget this situation because the Lord wanted to make a complete gesture of childishness before the affectionate Yaśodā. This exchange of love between the mother and the son was performed in a natural way, and Kuntī, remembering the scene, was bewildered, and she could do nothing but praise the transcendental filial love. Indirectly mother Yaśodā is praised for her unique position of love, for she could control even the all-powerful Lord as her beloved child.

This pastime presents another opulence of Kṛṣṇa – His opulence of beauty. Kṛṣṇa has six opulences: all wealth, all strength, all influence, all knowledge, all renunciation, and all beauty. The nature of Kṛṣṇa is that He is greater than the greatest and smaller than the smallest (*aṇor aṇīyān mahato mahīyān*). We offer obeisances to Kṛṣṇa with awe and veneration, but no one comes to Kṛṣṇa with a rope, saying, "Kṛṣṇa, You have committed an offense, and now I shall bind You." Yet that is the prerogative of the most perfect devotee, and Kṛṣṇa wants to be approached in that way.

Thinking of Kṛṣṇa's opulence, Kuntīdevī did not dare take the part of Yaśodā, for although Kuntīdevī was Kṛṣṇa's aunt, she did not have the privilege to approach Kṛṣṇa the way He was approached by Yaśodāmayī, who was such an advanced devotee that she had the right to chastise the Supreme Personality of Godhead. That was Yaśodāmayī's special prerogative. Kuntīdevī was simply thinking of how fortunate was Yaśodāmayī that she could threaten the Supreme Personality of Godhead, who is feared even by fear personified (*bhīr api yad bibheti*). Who is not afraid of Kṛṣṇa? No one. But Kṛṣṇa is afraid of Yaśodāmayī. This is the superexcellence of Kṛṣṇa.

To give another example of such opulence, Kṛṣṇa is known as Madana-mohana. *Madana* means Cupid. Cupid enchants everyone, but Kṛṣṇa is known as Madana-mohana because He is so beautiful that He enchants even Cupid. Nonetheless, Kṛṣṇa Himself is enchanted by Śrīmatī Rādhārāṇī, and therefore Śrīmatī Rādhārāṇī is known as Madana-mohana-mohinī, "the enchanter of the enchanter of Cupid." Kṛṣṇa is the enchanter of Cupid, and Rādhārāṇī is the enchanter of that enchanter.

These are very exalted spiritual understandings in Kṛṣṇa consciousness. They are not fictional, imaginary, or concocted. They are facts, and every devotee can have the privilege to understand and indeed take part in Kṛṣṇa's pastimes if he is actually advanced. We should not think that the privilege given to mother Yaśodā is not available to us. Everyone can have a similar privilege. If one loves Kṛṣṇa as one's child, then one will have such a privilege, because the mother has the most love for the child. Even in this material world, there is no comparison to a mother's love, for a mother loves her child without any expectation of return. Of course, although that is generally true, this material world is so polluted that a mother sometimes thinks, "My child will grow up and become a man, and when he earns money, I shall get it." Thus there is still some desire to get something in exchange. But while loving Kṛṣṇa there are no selfish feelings, for that love is unalloyed, free from all material gain (*anyābhilāṣitā-śūnyam*).

We should not love Kṛṣṇa for some material gain. It is not that we should say, "Kṛṣṇa, give us our daily bread, and then I shall love You. Kṛṣṇa, give me this or that, and then I shall love You." There should be no such mercantile exchanges, for Kṛṣṇa wants unalloyed love.

When Kṛṣṇa saw mother Yaśodā coming with a rope to bind Him, He immediately became very much afraid, thinking, "Oh, Mother is going to bind Me." He began to cry, and the tears washed the mascara from His eyes. Looking at His mother with great respect, He appealed to her with feeling, "Yes, Mother, I have offended you. Kindly excuse Me." Then He immediately bowed His head. Kuntīdevī appreciated this scene, for this was another of Kṛṣṇa's perfections. Although He is the Supreme Personality of Godhead, He puts Himself under the control of mother Yaśodā. In *Bhagavad-gītā* (7.7) the Lord says, *mattaḥ parataraṁ nānyat kiñcid asti dhanañjaya:* "My dear Arjuna, there is no one superior to Me." Yet that Supreme Personality of Godhead, to whom no one is superior, bows down to mother Yaśodā, accepting, "My dear Mother, yes, I am an offender."

When mother Yaśodā saw that Kṛṣṇa had become too much afraid of her, she also became disturbed. She did not actually want Kṛṣṇa to suffer by her punishment. That was not her purpose. But it is a system, still current in India, that when a child creates too much of a disturbance, his mother may bind him up in one place. That is a very common system, so mother Yaśodā adopted it.

This scene is very much appreciated by pure devotees, for it shows how much greatness there is in the Supreme Person, who plays exactly like a perfect child. When Kṛṣṇa plays like a child, He plays perfectly, when He plays as the husband of sixteen thousand wives He plays perfectly, when He plays as the lover of the *gopīs* He plays perfectly, and as the friend of the cowherd boys He also plays perfectly.

The cowherd boys all depend on Kṛṣṇa. Once they wanted to take fruit from a forest of palm trees, but there was a demon named Gardabhāsura who would not allow anyone to enter that forest. Therefore Kṛṣṇa's cowherd boyfriends said to Kṛṣṇa, "Kṛṣṇa, we want to taste that fruit, if You can arrange for it." Kṛṣṇa immediately said yes, and He and Balarāma went to the forest where that demon was living with other demons, who had all taken the shape of asses. When the ass demons came to kick Kṛṣṇa and Balarāma with their hind legs, Balarāma caught one of them and threw him into the top of a tree, and the demon died. Then Kṛṣṇa and Balarāma killed the other demons the same way. Thus Their cowherd friends were very much obliged to Them.

On another occasion, the cowherd boys were surrounded by fire. Not knowing anyone else but Kṛṣṇa, they immediately called for Him, and Kṛṣṇa was ready: "Yes." Thus Kṛṣṇa immediately swallowed the whole fire. There were many demons that attacked the boys, and every day the boys would return to their mothers and say, "Mother, Kṛṣṇa is so wonderful," and they would explain what had happened that day. And the mothers would say, "Yes, our Kṛṣṇa is wonderful." They did not know that Kṛṣṇa is God, the Supreme Person. They only knew that Kṛṣṇa is wonderful, that's all. And the more they perceived Kṛṣṇa's wonderful activities, the more their love increased. "Perhaps He may be a demigod," they thought. When Nanda Mahārāja, Kṛṣṇa's father, talked among his friends, the friends would talk about Kṛṣṇa and say, "Oh, Nanda Mahārāja, your child Kṛṣṇa is wonderful." And Nanda Mahārāja would respond, "Yes, I see that. Maybe He is some demigod." And even that was not certain – "maybe."

Thus the inhabitants of Vṛndāvana do not care who is God, and who is not. They love Kṛṣṇa, that's all. Those who think of first analyzing Kṛṣṇa to determine whether He is God are not first-class devotees. The first-class devotees are those who have spontaneous love for Kṛṣṇa. How can we analyze Kṛṣṇa? He is unlimited, and therefore it is impossible. We have limited perception, and our senses have limited potency, so how can we study Kṛṣṇa? It is not possible at all. Kṛṣṇa reveals Himself to a certain extent, and that much is sufficient.

We should not be like the Māyāvādī philosophers, who try to find God by speculative deduction. "*Neti neti,*" they say. "God is not this, and God is not that." But what God *is* they do not know. Materialistic scientists also try to find the ultimate cause, but their process is the same: "Not this, not that." As much as they advance, they will always find "Not this, not that." But what the ultimate cause is, they will never find. That is not possible.

What to speak of finding Kṛṣṇa, materialistic scientists cannot properly understand even material objects. They are trying to go to the moon, but actually they do not know what it is. If they understand what the moon is, why do they come back here? If they knew perfectly what the moon is, they would have resided there by now. They have been trying for the last twenty years to go there and stay, but they are simply seeing, "Not this, not that. There are no living entities, and there is no possibility of our living here." Thus they can report on what is *not* on the moon, but do they know what *is* there? No, they do not know. And this is only one planet or one star.

According to the Vedic literature, the moon is regarded as a star. The scientists say that the stars are all suns, but according to *Bhagavad-gītā* the stars are of the same nature as the moon. In *Bhagavad-gītā* (10.21) Lord Kṛṣṇa says, *nakṣatrāṇām ahaṁ śaśī:* "Of stars I am the moon." Thus the moon is just like the many stars. What is the nature of the moon? It is bright because it reflects light from the sun. Therefore although the scientists say that the stars are many suns, we do not agree. According to the Vedic calculation, there are innumerable suns, but in every universe there is only one.

What we see in this universe we are seeing imperfectly, and our knowledge is not perfect. We cannot count how many stars or planets there are. We cannot fully understand the material things existing all around us, and therefore how can we understand the Supreme Lord who created this universe? That is not possible. Therefore in the *Brahma-saṁhitā* (5.34) it is said:

panthās tu koṭi-śata-vatsara-sampragamyo
vāyor athāpi manaso muni-puṅgavānām
so 'py asti yat-prapada-sīmny avicintya-tattve
govindam ādi-puruṣaṁ tam ahaṁ bhajāmi

Space is unlimited, and the *Brahma-saṁhitā* suggests: Suppose one travels by spacecraft for millions of years at the velocity of the wind or even the speed of mind. Everyone knows that the mind is so swift that in even one ten-thousandth of a second it can take us millions of miles. If we have seen something millions of miles away, the mind can go there immediately. But even if we can travel at that speed on a spacecraft manufactured by *muni-puṅgavānām,* the greatest scientists and most thoughtful men, will that be perfection? No. The *Brahma-saṁhitā* says, *so 'py asti yat-prapada-sīmny avicintya-tattve:* still this creation will remain inconceivable to our understanding. And Kṛṣṇa has created all these things, so how can we study Kṛṣṇa? If we cannot understand the things Kṛṣṇa has created, how can we understand Kṛṣṇa? It is not possible at all.

Therefore the mentality of Vṛndāvana is the perfect status of mind for devotees. The inhabitants of Vṛndāvana have no concern with understanding Kṛṣṇa. Rather, they want to love Kṛṣṇa unconditionally. It is not that they think, "Kṛṣṇa is God, and therefore I love Him." In Vṛndāvana Kṛṣṇa does not play as God; He plays there as an ordinary cowherd boy, and although at times He proves that He is the Supreme Personality of Godhead, the devotees there do not care to know it.

Kuntīdevī, however, was not an inhabitant of Vṛndāvana. She was an inhabitant of Hastināpura, which is outside Vṛndāvana. The devotees outside Vṛndāvana study how great the inhabitants of Vṛndāvana are, but the inhabitants of Vṛndāvana don't care to know how great Kṛṣṇa is. That is the difference between them. So our concern should be simply to love Kṛṣṇa. The more we love Kṛṣṇa, the more we shall become perfect. It is not necessary to understand Kṛṣṇa and how He creates. Kṛṣṇa explains Himself in *Bhagavad-gītā,* and we should not try to understand much more. We should not bother very much to know Kṛṣṇa. That is not possible. We should simply increase our unalloyed love for Kṛṣṇa. That is the perfection of life.

15

Beyond Birth and Death

kecid āhur ajaṁ jātaṁ
puṇya-ślokasya kīrtaye
yadoḥ priyasyānvavāye
malayasyeva candanam

Some say that the Unborn is born for the glorification of pious kings, and others say that He is born to please King Yadu, one of Your dearest devotees. You appear in his family as sandalwood appears in the Malaya Hills.

Śrīmad-Bhāgavatam 1.8.32

Because the Lord's appearance in this material world is bewildering there are different opinions about the birth of the Unborn. In the *Bhagavad-gītā* the Lord says that He takes His birth in the material world, although He is the Lord of all creations and He is unborn. So there cannot be any denial of the birth of the Unborn, because He Himself establishes the truth. But still there are different opinions as to why He takes His birth. That is also declared in the *Bhagavad-gītā*. He appears by His own internal potency to reestablish the principles of religion and to protect the pious and annihilate the impious. That is the mission of the appearance of the Unborn. Still, it is said that the Lord is there to glorify the pious King Yudhiṣṭhira. Lord Śrī Kṛṣṇa certainly wanted to establish the kingdom of the Pāṇḍavas for the good of all in the world. When there is a pious king ruling over the world, the people are happy. When the ruler is impious, the people are unhappy. In the age of Kali in most cases the rulers are impious, and therefore the citizens are also continuously unhappy. But in the case of democracy, the impious citizens themselves elect their representative to rule over them, and therefore they cannot blame anyone for their unhappiness. Mahārāja Nala was also celebrated as a great pious king, but he had no connection with Lord Kṛṣṇa. Therefore Mahārāja Yudhiṣṭhira is meant here to be glorified by Lord Kṛṣṇa, who had also glorified King Yadu by taking birth in his family. He is known as Yādava, Yaduvīra, Yadunandana, etc., although the Lord is always independent of such obligations. He is just like the sandalwood that grows in the Malaya Hills. Trees can grow anywhere and everywhere, yet because the sandalwood trees grow mostly in the area of the Malaya Hills, the name sandalwood and the Malaya Hills are interrelated. Therefore, the conclusion is that the Lord is ever unborn like the sun, and yet He appears as the sun rises on the eastern horizon. As the sun is never the sun of the eastern horizon, so the Lord is no one's son, but is the father of everything that be.

In the *Bhagavad-gītā* (4.6) the Lord says:

ajo 'pi sann avyayātmā
bhūtānām īśvaro 'pi san
prakṛtiṁ svām adhiṣṭhāya
sambhavāmy ātma-māyayā

"Although I am unborn and My transcendental body never deteriorates, and although I am the Lord of all sentient beings, I still appear in every millennium in My original, transcendental form."

Kṛṣṇa is unborn, and we are also unborn, but the difference is that unlike the Lord we have been entangled in a material body. Therefore we cannot keep our position as unborn, but have to take birth and transmigrate from one body to another, with no guarantee of what kind of body we shall receive next. Even in this life, we are obliged to accept one body after another. A child gives up his childhood body and accepts the body of a boy, and the boy gives up his boyhood body to accept a youthful body, which he then gives up for an old body. Therefore it is natural to conclude that when one gives up one's old body, one will have to accept another body; again one will accept the body of a child.

This is a natural cycle of this material world. It is similar to changes of season. After spring comes summer, and after summer comes fall and then winter, and then spring again. Similarly, after day comes night, and after night comes day. And just as these cyclic changes take place one after another, we change from one body to another, and it is natural to conclude that after leaving the present body we shall receive another body (*bhūtvā bhūtvā pralīyate*).

This conclusion is very logical, it is supported by the *śāstra,* the Vedic literature, and it is also affirmed by the greatest authority, Kṛṣṇa Himself. Therefore why should we not accept it? If one does not accept this – if one thinks that there is no life after death – one is foolish.

There is life after death, and there is also the chance to free oneself from the cycle of repeated birth and death and attain a life of immortality. But because we have been accustomed to accepting one body after another since time immemorial, it is difficult for us to think of a life that is eternal. And the life of material existence is so troublesome that one may think that if there is an eternal life, that life must be troublesome also. For example, a diseased man who is taking very bitter medicine and who is lying down in bed, eating there and passing stool and urine there, unable to move, may find his life so intolerable that he thinks, "Let me commit suicide." Similarly, materialistic life is so miserable that in desperation one sometimes takes to a philosophy of voidism or impersonalism to try to negate his very existence and make everything zero.

Actually, however, becoming zero is not possible, nor is it necessary. We are in trouble in our material condition, but when we get out of our material condition we can find real life, eternal life.

Because we are part and parcel of Kṛṣṇa, who is *aja,* beyond birth and death, we are also *aja.* How could we be otherwise? If my father is happy and I am the son of my father, why should I be unhappy? I can naturally conclude that I shall enjoy my father's property just as my father is enjoying it. Similarly, God, Kṛṣṇa, is all-powerful, all-beautiful, all-knowledgeable, and complete in everything, and although I may not be complete, I am part and parcel of God, and therefore I have all the qualities of God to a partial extent.

God does not die, so I also shall not die. That is my position. That is explained in *Bhagavad-gītā* (2.20): *na jāyate mriyate vā kadācit.* Describing the soul, Kṛṣṇa says that the soul is never born (*na jāyate*), and if one is not born how can he die? There is no question of death (*mriyate vā*). Death is for one who has taken birth, and if one has no birth he can also have no death.

Unfortunately, however, we do not know this. We are conducting scientific research, but we do not know that every living entity is a spiritual soul, with no birth and no death. This is our ignorance. The soul is eternal, everlasting, and primeval (*nityaḥ śāśvato 'yaṁ purāṇo*). The soul does not die with the annihilation of the body (*na hanyate hanyamāne śarīre*). But although the soul does not die, it accepts another body, and this is called *bhava-roga,* the material disease.

Since Kṛṣṇa is the supreme living entity (*nityo nityānāṁ cetanaś cetanānām*),we are exactly like Kṛṣṇa, the difference being that Kṛṣṇa is *vibhu,* unlimited, whereas we are *aṇu,* limited. Qualitatively, we are as good as Kṛṣṇa. Therefore whatever propensities Kṛṣṇa has, we have also. For example, Kṛṣṇa has the propensity to love someone of the opposite sex, and therefore we have this same propensity. The beginning of love is present in the eternal love between Rādhā and Kṛṣṇa. We are also seeking eternal love, but because we are conditioned by the material laws, our love is interrupted. But if we can transcend this interruption, we can take part in loving affairs similar to those of Kṛṣṇa and Rādhārāṇī. Our aim should therefore be to go back home, back to Kṛṣṇa, because since Kṛṣṇa is eternal, we shall there receive an eternal body.

Kuntī says, *kecid āhur ajaṁ jātam:* the supreme eternal, the supreme unborn, has now taken His birth. But although Kṛṣṇa takes birth, His birth is not like ours. That we should know. The Lord says in *Bhagavad-gītā* (4.9):

janma karma ca me divyam
evaṁ yo vetti tattvataḥ
tyaktvā dehaṁ punar janma
naiti mām eti so 'rjuna

"One who knows the transcendental nature of My appearance and activities does not, upon leaving the body, take his birth again in this material world, but attains My eternal abode, O Arjuna."

It is described in *Śrīmad-Bhāgavatam* that when Kṛṣṇa first appeared, He did not take birth from the womb of Devakī; rather, He first appeared in the majestic four-armed form of Viṣṇu, and then He became a small child on Devakī's lap. Therefore Kṛṣṇa's birth is transcendental, whereas our birth takes place by force, by the laws of nature. Kṛṣṇa is not under the laws of nature; the laws of nature work under Him (*mayādhyakṣeṇa prakṛtiḥ sūyate sa-carācaram*). *Prakṛti,* nature, works under the order of Kṛṣṇa, and we work under the order of nature. Kṛṣṇa is the master of nature, and we are servants of nature. Therefore Kuntīdevī says, *kecid āhuḥ:* "Someone may *say* that the unborn has taken birth." It may appear that He has taken birth just like us, but in fact He has not. Kuntīdevī distinctly says, *kecid āhuḥ:* "some foolish persons may say that He has taken birth." Kṛṣṇa Himself also says in *Bhagavad-gītā* (9.11), *avajānanti māṁ mūḍhā mānuṣīṁ tanum āśritam:* "Because I have appeared just like a human being, those who are rascals think that I am also just like an ordinary human." *Paraṁ bhāvam ajānantaḥ:* "They do not know the mystery behind God's taking birth like a human being."

Kṛṣṇa is everywhere. The Lord is situated in everyone's heart (*īśvaraḥ sarva-bhūtānāṁ hṛd-deśe 'rjuna tiṣṭhati*). And since He is within us and is all-powerful, why should it be difficult for Him to appear before us? When the great devotee Dhruva Mahārāja was engaged in meditation on the four-handed form of Viṣṇu, all of a sudden his meditation broke, and he immediately saw before him the same form upon which he had been meditating. Was it very difficult for Kṛṣṇa to appear in this way? Of course not. Similarly it was not difficult for Him to appear before Devakī in the same four-handed form. Therefore Kṛṣṇa says, *janma karma ca me divyam:* "One must understand My transcendental birth and activities." Kuntīdevī has this understanding. She knows that although to some fools Kṛṣṇa appears to take birth, in fact He is unborn.

But why should Kṛṣṇa perform the pastime of taking birth? Kuntīdevī replies, *puṇya-ślokasya kīrtaye:* to glorify those who are very pious and very much advanced in spiritual understanding. Kṛṣṇa comes as the son of Devakī to glorify His devotee Devakī. Kṛṣṇa becomes the son of Yaśodā to glorify Yaśodā. Similarly, Kṛṣṇa appears in the dynasty of Mahārāja Yadu, His great devotee, just to glorify Mahārāja Yadu. Thus Kṛṣṇa is still known as Yādava, the descendant of Mahārāja Yadu. Kṛṣṇa has no obligation to take His birth in a particular family or country, but He takes birth to glorify a certain person or a certain family because of their devotion. Therefore His birth is called *divyam,* transcendental.

The Lord is not obliged to take birth, but we are obliged to do so. That is the distinction between our birth and the birth of Kṛṣṇa. If by our *karma,* or activities, we are fit to take birth in a good family in human society or demigod society, we shall do so, but if our activities are low like those of animals, we shall have to take birth in a family of animals. That is the force of *karma. Karmaṇā daiva-netreṇa jantor dehopapattaye* (*Bhāgavatam* 3.31.1). We develop a certain type of body according to our *karma.*

The human form of life is meant for understanding the Supreme, the Absolute Truth (*athāto brahma jijñāsā*). But if we do not endeavor for this, if we misuse this opportunity and simply remain like animals, we shall return to an animal form of life. Therefore the Kṛṣṇa consciousness movement is trying to save people from going down to animal life.

The appearance of Lord Kṛṣṇa is compared to the growth of sandalwood trees in the Malaya Hills (*malayasyeva candanam*). There are two Malayas – the Malaya Hills and the part of the world now known as Malaysia. The *candana* tree, or sandalwood tree, can grow anywhere – there is no rule that it has to grow in Malaysia or the Malaya Hills – but because this sandalwood grows in large quantities in those parts of the world, it is known as *malaya-candana.* In the Western countries there is scented water known as eau de cologne. It can be manufactured anywhere, but because it was originally manufactured in the city of Cologne, it is known as eau de cologne. Similarly, sandalwood can grow anywhere, but because it was originally very prominent in Malaysia and the Malaya Hills, it is known as Malayan sandalwood. Kuntī offered this prayer five thousand years ago, and this indicates that sandalwood was growing five thousand years ago in Malaysia. Malaysia is not a new name; it was known thousands and thousands of years ago to the followers of the Vedic culture. Nowadays, of course, Malaysia is growing rubber trees because there is a good demand for rubber, but formerly Malaysia grew sandalwood on a large scale because there was a great demand for sandalwood, especially in India.

Because India is a tropical country and sandalwood is very cooling people in India use sandalwood pulp as a cosmetic. Even now, during the very warm days of the summer season, those who can afford to do so apply sandalwood pulp to their bodies and feel cool all day. In India it was the system that after bathing and sanctifying the body by applying marks of *tilaka,* one would offer obeisances to the Deity, take some *candana-prasāda* from the room of the Deity, and apply it as a cosmetic to the body. This was called *prasādhana.* But it is said that in Kali-yuga, the present age, *snānam eva prasādhanam* (*Bhāgavatam* 12.2.5): if one can even bathe nicely, that is *prasādhana.* In India even the poorest man will take an early morning bath every day, but when I came to America I saw that even taking one's daily bath may be a difficult thing and is often not the practice. In India we are accustomed to see people bathe thrice in a day, but in New York I have seen that one may have to go to a friend's house to bathe because one may not have facilities to do so at home. These are symptoms of Kali-yuga. *Snānam eva prasādhanam.* In the Kali-yuga it will be very difficult even to take a bath.

Another symptom of Kali-yuga is *dākṣyaṁ kuṭumba-bharaṇam* (*Bhāgavatam* 12.2.7): one will be famous for his pious activities simply if he can maintain his family. The word *dākṣyam,* meaning "famous for pious activities," comes from *dakṣa,* which means "expert." In Kali-yuga one will be considered expert if he can maintain a family consisting of himself, his wife, and one or two children. In India, of course, the traditional family is the joint family, consisting of a man and his wife, their parents and children, their in-laws, and so on. But in Kali-yuga it will be difficult to maintain a simple family of oneself, one's wife, and a few children. When I was living in New York, among the people coming to our classes was an old lady who had a grown son. I asked her, "Why doesn't your son get married?" She replied, "Yes, he can marry when he can maintain a family." I did not know that maintaining a family was such a difficult job here. But this is described in the *Bhāgavatam:* if one can maintain a family, he will be considered a very glorious man, and if a girl has a husband she will be considered very fortunate.

It is not our business to criticize, but the symptoms of Kali-yuga are very severe, and they will grow more severe. The duration of Kali-yuga is 432,000 years, and although 5000 years of it have passed, already we find so many difficulties, and the more we grow into this Kali-yuga, the more the times will be difficult. The best course, therefore, is to complete our Kṛṣṇa consciousness and return home, back to Godhead. That will save us. Otherwise, if we come back again for another life in Kali-yuga, we shall find difficult days ahead, and we shall have to suffer more and more.

16

Returning to Our Natural Consciousness

apare vasudevasya
devakyāṁ yācito 'bhyagāt
ajas tvam asya kṣemāya
vadhāya ca sura-dviṣām

Others say that since both Vasudeva and Devakī prayed for You, You have taken Your birth as their son. Undoubtedly You are unborn, yet You take Your birth for their welfare and to kill those who are envious of the demigods.

Śrīmad-Bhāgavatam 1.8.33

It is also said that Vasudeva and Devakī, in their previous birth as Sutapā and Pṛśni, underwent a severe type of penance to get the Lord as their son, and as a result of such austerities the Lord appeared as their son. It is already declared in the *Bhagavad-gītā* that the Lord appears for the welfare of all people in the world and to vanquish the *asuras,* or the materialistic atheists.

The Lord says:

yadā yadā hi dharmasya
glānir bhavati bhārata
abhyutthānam adharmasya
tadātmānaṁ sṛjāmy aham

"Whenever and wherever there is a decline in religious practice, O descendant of Bharata, and a predominant rise of irreligion – at that time I descend Myself." (*Bhagavad-gītā* 4.7) The words *dharmasya glāniḥ* mean "irregularities in religion." When there are irregularities, religion becomes polluted.

In human society there must be a proper balance between spirit and matter. We are actually spirit soul, but somehow or other we have been encaged within material bodies, and as long as we have these bodies we have to accept the bodily necessities of eating, sleeping, mating, and defending, although the soul itself does not need these things. The soul does not need to eat anything; whatever we eat is for the upkeep of the body. But a civilization that simply looks after these bodily necessities and does not care for the necessities of the soul is a foolish, unbalanced civilization. Suppose one merely washes one's coat but does not take care of one's body. Or suppose one has a bird in a cage but merely takes care of the cage, not the bird within it. This is foolishness. The bird is crying, "*Ka, ka.* Give me food, give me food." If one only takes care of the cage, how can the bird be happy?

So why are we unhappy? In the Western countries there is no scarcity of wealth, no scarcity of food, no scarcity of cars, and no scarcity of sex. Everything is available in full abundance. Then why is there still a section of people who are frustrated and confused, like the hippies? They are not satisfied. Why? Because there is no balance. We are taking care of the necessities of the body, but we have no information of the soul and its necessities. The soul is the real substance, and the body is only a covering. Therefore neglect of the soul is a form of *dharmasya glāniḥ,* pollution of duty.

The word *dharma* means "duty." Although the word *dharma* is often translated as "religion" and religion is generally defined as a kind of faith, *dharma* is not in fact a kind of faith. *Dharma* means one's actual constitutional duty. It is one's duty to know the needs of the soul, but unfortunately we have no information of the soul and are simply busy supplying the necessities for bodily comfort.

Bodily comfort, however, is not enough. Suppose a man is very comfortably situated. Does it mean he will not die? Of course not. We speak of a struggle for existence and survival of the fittest, but bodily comforts alone cannot enable anyone to exist or survive permanently. Therefore, taking care of the body only is called *dharmasya glāniḥ,* or pollution of one's duty.

One must know the necessities of the body and also the necessities of the soul. The real necessity in life is to supply the comforts of the soul, and the soul cannot be comforted by material adjustments. Because the soul is a different identity, the soul must be given spiritual food, and that spiritual food is Kṛṣṇa consciousness. When one is diseased, he must be given the proper diet and the proper medicine. Both are required. If he is simply given medicine but not a proper diet, the treatment will not be very successful. Therefore the Kṛṣṇa consciousness movement is meant to give both the proper medicine and the proper diet for the soul. The diet is *kṛṣṇa-prasāda,* food that has first been offered to Kṛṣṇa, and the medicine is the Hare Kṛṣṇa *mantra.*

nivṛtta-tarṣair upagīyamānād
bhavauṣadhāc chotra-mano-'bhirāmāt
ka uttamaśloka-guṇānuvādāt
pumān virajyeta vinā paśu-ghnāt
(*Bhāgavatam* 10.1.4)

Parīkṣit Mahārāja said to the great sage Śukadeva Gosvāmī, "The discourses on *Śrīmad-Bhāgavatam* that you are giving me are not ordinary. These *Bhāgavata* discourses are relishable for persons who are *nivṛtta-tṛṣṇa,* free from hankering." Everyone in this material world is hankering for enjoyment, but one who is free from this hankering can taste how relishable the *Bhāgavatam* is. The word *bhāgavata* refers to anything in relationship to Bhagavān, the Supreme Lord, and the Hare Kṛṣṇa *mantra* is also *bhāgavata.* Thus Parīkṣit Mahārāja said that the taste of the *Bhāgavata* can be relished by one who is free from hankering to satisfy material desires. And why should this *Bhāgavata* be tasted? *Bhavauṣadhi:* it is the medicine for our disease of birth and death.

At the present moment, we are in a diseased condition. Materialists do not know what is disease and what is health. They do not know anything, but still they are posing as great scientists and philosophers. They do not inquire, "I do not want to die. Why is death enforced upon me?" Nor do they have any solution to this problem. But still they call themselves scientists. What kind of scientists are they? Advancement in science should bring about knowledge by which misery can be minimized. Otherwise, what is the meaning of science? Scientists may promise that they can help us in the future, but we may ask them, "What are you giving us right now, sir?" A real scientist will not say, "Just go on suffering as you are suffering now, and in the future we shall find some chemicals to help you." No. *Ātyantika-duḥkha-nivṛttiḥ.* The word *ātyantika* means "ultimate," and *duḥkha* means "sufferings." The aim of human life should be to put an end to the ultimate sufferings, but people do not even know what these ultimate sufferings are. These sufferings are pointed out in *Bhagavad-gītā* as *janma-mṛtyu-jarā-vyādhi:* birth, death, old age, and disease. What have we done to nullify these sufferings? There is no remedy for them in the material world. The ultimate way to relinquish all kinds of suffering is stated in *Bhagavad-gītā* (8.15), where the Lord says:

mām upetya punar janma
duḥkhālayam aśāśvatam
nāpnuvanti mahātmānaḥ
saṁsiddhiṁ paramāṁ gatāḥ

"After attaining Me, the great souls, who are *yogīs* in devotion, never return to this temporary world, which is full of miseries, because they have attained the highest perfection."

Thus the Lord says that one should approach Him and go back to Him, back home, back to Godhead. But unfortunately people have no knowledge of what God is, whether one can go back home to Him or not, and whether or not it is practical. Because they have no knowledge, they are simply like animals. They pray, "O God, give us our daily bread." But now suppose we ask them, "What is God?" Can they explain? No. Then whom are they asking? Are they merely praying into the air? If I submit some petition, there must be some person to whom the petition is submitted. But they do not know who that person is or where the petition is to be submitted. They say that God is in the sky. But there are also so many birds in the sky. Are they God? People have imperfect knowledge or no knowledge at all. Nonetheless, they pose as scientists, philosophers, writers, and great thinkers, although their ideas are all rubbish.

The only truly worthwhile books are those like *Śrīmad-Bhāgavatam* and *Bhagavad-gītā*. In the *Bhāgavatam* (1.5.10–11) it is said:

na yad vacaś citra-padaṁ harer yaśo
jagat-pavitraṁ pragṛṇīta karhicit
tad vāyasaṁ tīrtham uśanti mānasā
na yatra haṁsā niramanty uṣik-kṣayāḥ

"Those words which do not describe the glories of the Lord, who alone can sanctify the atmosphere of the whole universe, are considered by saintly persons to be like unto a place of pilgrimage for crows. Since the all-perfect persons are inhabitants of the transcendental abode, they do not derive any pleasure there."

tad-vāg-visargo janatāgha-viplavo
yasmin prati-ślokam abaddhavaty api
nāmāny anantasya yaśo-'ṅkitāni yat
śṛṇvanti gāyanti gṛṇanti sādhavaḥ

"On the other hand, that literature which is full of descriptions of the transcendental glories of the name, fame, forms, pastimes, etc., of the unlimited Supreme Lord is a different creation, full of transcendental words directed toward bringing about a revolution in the impious lives of this world's misdirected civilization. Such transcendental literatures, even though imperfectly composed, are heard, sung, and accepted by purified men who are thoroughly honest."

Any literature that has no connection with God is just like a place where crows take enjoyment. Where do crows enjoy? In a filthy place. But white swans take pleasure in nice clear waters surrounded by gardens. So even among animals there are natural divisions. The crows will not go to the swans, and the swans will not go to the crows. Similarly, in human society there are men who are like crows and men who are like swans. The swanlike men will come to centers of Kṛṣṇa consciousness, where everything is clear, where there is good philosophy, good transcendental food, good education, good intelligence – everything good – whereas crowlike men will go to clubs, parties, naked dance shows, and so many other such things.

So the Kṛṣṇa consciousness movement is meant for swanlike men, not for men who are like crows. But we can convert the crows into swans. That is our philosophy. Those who were crows are now swimming like swans. That is the benefit of Kṛṣṇa consciousness.

The material world is the world where swans have become crows. In the material world the living entity is encaged in a material body, and he tries to gratify his senses in one body after another. But the reestablishment of *dharma* will gradually turn crows into swans. For example, a man may be illiterate and uncultured, but he can be converted into an educated, cultured man by training.

This training is possible in the human form of life. I cannot train a dog to become a devotee. That is difficult. Of course, that also can be done, although I may not be powerful enough to do it. When Lord Caitanya Mahāprabhu was traveling through the jungles of Jhārikhaṇḍa the tigers, the snakes, the deer, and all the other animals became devotees. This was possible for Caitanya Mahāprabhu because He is God Himself and can therefore do anything. But although we cannot do that, we can work in human society. Regardless of how fallen a man is, if he follows the instructions of Kṛṣṇa consciousness he can return to his original position. Of course, there are degrees of understanding, but one's original position is that one is part and parcel of God. Understanding of this position is called Brahman realization, spiritual realization, and it is this realization that Kṛṣṇa Himself comes to this world to reestablish.

Lord Kṛṣṇa came to this world at the request of His devotees Vasudeva and Devakī (*vasudevasya devakyāṁ yācito 'bhyagāt*). Although in their former lives Vasudeva and Devakī were married, they did not have any children. They engaged themselves in severe austerities, and when Kṛṣṇa came before them and asked them what they wanted, they said, "We want a son like You. That is our desire." But how is it possible for there to be another God? Kṛṣṇa is God, and God is one; He cannot be two. So how could there be another God to become the son of Vasudeva and Devakī? Kṛṣṇa therefore said, "It is not possible to find another God, so I Myself shall become your son." So some people say that it is because Vasudeva and Devakī wanted Kṛṣṇa as their son that He appeared.

Although Kṛṣṇa actually comes to satisfy His devotees like Vasudeva and Devakī, when He comes He performs other activities also. *Vadhāya ca sura-dviṣām.* The word *vadhāya* means "killing," and *sura-dviṣām* refers to the demons, who are always envious of the devotees. Kṛṣṇa comes to kill these demons.

An example of a demon is Hiraṇyakaśipu. Because Prahlāda Mahārāja was a devotee, his father, Hiraṇyakaśipu, was so envious that he was prepared to kill his own son, although the little boy's only fault was that he was chanting Hare Kṛṣṇa. This is the nature of demons. Jesus Christ also was killed by the *sura-dviṣām,* those who were envious of him. What was his fault? His only fault was that he was preaching about God. Yet he had so many enemies, who cruelly crucified him. Therefore Kṛṣṇa comes to kill such *sura-dviṣām.*

This killing of the envious, of course, can be done without the presence of Kṛṣṇa. By setting to work the natural forces of war, pestilence, famine, and so on, Kṛṣṇa can kill millions of people. He does not need to come here to kill these rascals, for they can be killed simply by His direction, or nature's law. *Sṛṣṭi-sthiti-pralaya-sādhana-śaktir ekā* (*Brahma-saṁhitā* 5.44). Nature has so much power that it can create, maintain, and annihilate everything. *Sṛṣṭi* means "creation," *sthiti* means "maintenance," and *pralaya* means "destruction." Nature can create, maintain, and also destroy. This material cosmic manifestation is being maintained by the mercy of nature, by which we are getting sunlight, air, and rain by which to grow our food so that we can eat and grow nicely. But nature is so powerful that at any time it can destroy everything simply by one strong wind. Nature is working under the direction of Kṛṣṇa (*mayādhyakṣeṇa prakṛtiḥ sūyate sa-carācaram*). Therefore, if Kṛṣṇa wants demons killed, He can kill millions of them with merely one strong blast of nature's wind.

So to kill the demons Kṛṣṇa does not need to come. When He comes, He does so because He is requested by His devotees like Vasudeva and Devakī, as Kuntīdevī indicates by using the word *yācitaḥ,* meaning "being prayed for." Therefore the real cause of His coming is at the request of His devotees, but when He comes He simultaneously shows that He is prepared to kill anyone who is envious of His devotees. Of course, His killing and maintaining are the same because He is absolute. Those who are killed by Kṛṣṇa immediately attain salvation, which generally takes millions of years to get.

So people may say that Kṛṣṇa has come for this purpose or that purpose, but actually Kṛṣṇa comes for the benefit of His devotees. He always looks after the welfare of the devotees, and so from this instruction of Kuntī we should understand that we should always be concerned with how to become devotees. Then all good qualities will come upon us.

yasyāsti bhaktir bhagavaty akiñcanā
sarvais gunaiṣ tatra samāsate surāḥ
(*Bhāgavatam* 5.18.12)

If one simply develops one's dormant, natural devotion for Kṛṣṇa, one will develop all good qualities.

Our devotion for Kṛṣṇa is natural. Just as a son has natural devotion to his father and mother, we have natural devotion to Kṛṣṇa. When there is danger, even materialistic scientists pray to God. Of course, when they are not in danger they defy God, and therefore danger is required in order to teach these rascals that there is God. *Jīvera svarūpa haya—kṛṣṇera 'nitya-dāsa'*. Our natural position is to be dependent on God. Artificially we are trying to banish God, saying, "God is dead," "There is no God," or "I am God." But when we give up this rascaldom, Kṛṣṇa will give us all protection.

17
Lightening the Burden of the World

bhārāvatāraṇāyānye
bhuvo nāva ivodadhau
sīdantyā bhūri-bhāreṇa
jāto hy ātma-bhuvārthitaḥ

Others say that the world, being overburdened like a boat at sea, is much aggrieved, and that Brahmā, who is Your son, prayed for You, and so You have appeared to diminish the trouble.

Śrīmad-Bhāgavatam 1.8.34

Brahmā is directly the son of the Supreme Lord, the supreme father, and was not put into the womb of a mother. Therefore he is known as *ātma-bhū*. This Brahmā is in charge of further creations in the universe, secondarily reflected by the potency of the Omnipotent. Within the halo of the universe there is a transcendental planet known as Śvetadvīpa, which is the abode of the Kṣīrodaka-śāyī Viṣṇu, the Paramātmā feature of the Supreme Lord. Whenever there is trouble in the universe that cannot be solved by the administrative demigods, they approach Brahmājī for a solution, and if it is not to be solved even by Brahmājī, then Brahmājī consults with and prays to the Kṣīrodaka-śāyī Viṣṇu for an incarnation and solution to the problems. Such a problem arose when Kaṁsa and others were ruling over the earth and the earth became too much overburdened by the misdeeds of the *asuras*. Brahmājī, along with other demigods, prayed at the shore of the Kṣīrodaka Ocean, and they were advised of the descent of Kṛṣṇa as the son of Vasudeva and Devakī. So some people say that the Lord appeared because of the prayers of Brahmājī.

Kuntīdevī is describing the different statements of different persons about why Kṛṣṇa appears. Some say that He appeared at the request of Vasudeva and Devakī, and some say He appeared at the request of Brahmā. *Bhārāvatāraṇāyānye bhuvo nāva ivodadhau:* "Some say that He appeared just to reduce the burden of the world, which was overburdened like a boat at sea." When the world is overburdened, there must be war, pestilence, famine, epidemics, and so on. This is nature's law.

The earth floats in space among many millions of other planets, all of them bearing huge mountains and oceans. It floats because Kṛṣṇa enters into it, as stated in *Bhagavad-gītā* (*gām āviśya*), just as He enters the atom. The earth is certainly not weightless; rather, it is very heavy. But it floats because the Supreme Spirit is within it.

Everything is lightened by the presence of spirit. One's body will float in water as long as one is alive, but as soon as the spirit soul leaves, the body immediately sinks. As long as a child is alive we can take it along by one hand, but when the child is dead it is heavy. So now we are heavy, but when we are spiritually advanced we will be free from impediments. Now we cannot fly in the air, but the spirit soul is so light that when freed from the body it can go within a second to Vaikuṇṭhaloka, the spiritual world (*tyaktvā dehaṁ punar janma naiti mām eti*).

Why then does the world become overloaded? It becomes overloaded due to the presence of demons, those who are against devotional service. When mother earth feels this load to be too heavy, Kṛṣṇa comes just to unburden the earth. If a ship is overloaded, its position is very dangerous, for it may sink at any moment. Therefore when mother earth felt too uncomfortable because of being overloaded with demons (*sīdantyā bhūri-bhāreṇa*), she approached Brahmā, the chief living being within this universe. When there is a need, the chief personalities in the universe approach Brahmā, who approaches Viṣṇu to ask that He reduce whatever the burden is. Then Viṣṇu or Kṛṣṇa appears as an incarnation, as stated in *Bhagavad-gītā* (4.7):

yadā yadā hi dharmasya
glānir bhavati bhārata
abhyutthānam adharmasya
tadātmānaṁ sṛjāmy aham

"Whenever and wherever there is a decline in religious practice, O descendant of Bharata, and a predominant rise of irreligion – at that time I descend Myself."

When there is too much lawlessness and there are too many criminals, the state becomes overburdened and disturbed, and the state administrators are puzzled about what to do. Similarly, when the world is overrun by demons and atheists, they create a burden, and the demigods, the pious administrators of the universe, become perplexed. When the people of a state abide by the laws, administration is easy, but if people are criminals they overburden the state administrators. A similar situation sometimes upsets the balance of the cosmic affairs of this material world. Both the demons and the demigods always exist, but when the demoniac power increases, the world is overburdened. It is then that the demigods approach Lord Brahmā for assistance.

Lord Brahmā is one of the twelve authorities known as *dvādaśa-mahājana* (*svayambhūr nāradaḥ śambhuḥ kaumāraḥ kapilo manuḥ/ prahlādo janako bhīṣmo balir vaiyāsakir vayam, Bhāgavatam* 6.3.20). We have to follow the *mahājanas,* the great authorities, if we want to receive transcendental knowledge. The Vedic injunction is, *tad-vijñānārthaṁ sa gurum evābhigacchet:* if one wants to be in knowledge of everything, one must approach a *guru,* a bona fide authority, a spiritual master. The original *guru* is Kṛṣṇa. As Kṛṣṇa taught Arjuna, He also taught Brahmā, as stated in *Śrīmad-Bhāgavatam* (*tene brahma hṛdā ya ādi-kavaye*).

The *Śrīmad-Bhāgavatam* describes the original source of the creation, and this should be the actual subject matter of our research work. What is the original source of creation? *Janmādy asya yataḥ:* the original source of everything is the source of *janma, sthiti,* and *pralaya* – creation, maintenance, and dissolution. Our body has taken birth at a certain date, it lasts for some years – ten years, twenty years, fifty years, or whatever, according to the body – and then it will be finished. Where did this body come from, and when it is destroyed where will it go? There are scientific laws concerning the conservation of energy. What is the source of that energy? There is a source (*yato vā imāni bhūtāni jāyante*), and that source is identified in the *Śrīmad-Bhāgavatam.*

That source is not blind. Rascals think that everything has come from nothing. But how can something come out of nothing? There is no proof that such a thing happens, but fools claim that it does, and therefore they are blind. What is the nature of the original source from whom everything has come, in whom everything exists, and within whom everything will enter? The *Bhāgavatam* (1.1.1) says, *janmādy asya yato 'nvayād itarataś cārtheṣv abhijñaḥ.* The word *abhijñaḥ* indicates that the source of everything is completely conscious.

The word *jña* means "knowledge," and *abhi* means "specific." We have inadequate knowledge of where we have come from and where we shall go after death, and therefore we are not *abhijña,* supremely conscious. But the supreme source is *abhijña.* He is not a stone or a void. How could He be? The creation itself is evidence of the consciousness of the Supreme. Everyone can appreciate the cosmic manifestation and how nicely it is working. The sun and moon rise exactly on time, without deviating even one ten-thousandth of a second, and the seasons change in the same way, bringing with them fruits and flowers. In this way the entire cosmic manifestation is going on in a very orderly, systematic way. So unless there is some *abhijña* – some very clever intelligence who knows everything – how could all this have been created? Some people say that all this has come from nothing. What is this nonsense? Can such a creation come from nothing? Does this idea show very good reasoning? The *Bhāgavatam* says no.

The *Bhāgavatam* tells us that everything comes from the person who is *abhijña,* very intelligent and experienced, and that original intelligent person transmitted knowledge to *ādi-kavi,* the original created being, Lord Brahmā (*tene brahma hṛdā ya ādi-kavaye*). Brahmā, the original created being, has an original source, and he is in contact with that source. We understand that we get knowledge from another person with whom we are face to face. But when Brahmā was created he was alone. Therefore, how did he receive knowledge? That is explained in the *Bhāgavatam: tene brahma hṛdā.* The word *hṛdā* means "through the heart." The Supreme Person, Paramātmā, is within the heart of every living being, including Brahmā. Therefore although Brahmā was alone, he received knowledge dictated by the Supreme. The word *brahma* means "Vedic knowledge." Thus the Vedic knowledge was given first to Lord Brahmā.

The Vedic knowledge is given to everyone because Kṛṣṇa is within everyone's heart (*sarvasya cāhaṁ hṛdi sanniviṣṭaḥ*), but one must be qualified to receive that knowledge. Kṛṣṇa helps us by giving us knowledge both from within as the Supersoul (*caitya-guru*) and from without as the spiritual master.

Brahmā receives knowledge from Kṛṣṇa and distributes that Vedic knowledge, and therefore he is an authority. There are four *sampradāyas,* or chains of disciplic succession, through which Vedic knowledge is distributed – one from Brahmā, one from Lakṣmī, one from Lord Śiva, and one from the four Kumāras. We have to approach an authoritative representative of Kṛṣṇa appearing in one of these *sampradāyas,* and then we can receive real knowledge. Thus the earth personified approached Brahmā, who prayed to the Supreme Personality of Godhead, "The world is now overburdened with demons, and therefore I request You to appear." Some say, therefore, that the Lord appeared at the request of Brahmā that He lighten the burden of the world.

When Kṛṣṇa appears, He protects the devotees and kills the demons. Therefore Kṛṣṇa in His Nārāyaṇa form has four hands. In two hands

He holds a disc and club with which to kill the demons, and in the other two hands He holds the conchshell and lotus with which to bless and protect the devotees. The Lord says, *kaunteya pratijānīhi na me bhaktaḥ praṇaśyati.* Thus Kṛṣṇa bugles with His conchshell, "My devotees will never be vanquished." And with the lotus flower He extends His blessings. The lotus flower, which sometimes also appears in the hand of Lakṣmī, is a symbol of blessings.

Now some may say that Kṛṣṇa appeared for this purpose or that purpose, but the real conclusion is that Kṛṣṇa appears for His own pleasure, not because He is bound by any other cause. We take our birth because we are bound by our *karma,* but Kṛṣṇa, being fully independent, does not come because of someone else's request or because of *karma.* Rather, He comes by His own free will (*ātma-māyayā*). We are compelled to take birth because of Kṛṣṇa's external, material energy, but Kṛṣṇa is not controlled by the *māyā,* or energy, of anyone else, and therefore He does not take birth in such a condition. *Māyā,* the illusory energy, is under the control of Kṛṣṇa, so how could *māyā* control Him? One who thinks that Kṛṣṇa, like us, is controlled by *māyā* is described in *Bhagavad-gītā* as *mūḍha,* a fool (*avajānanti māṁ mūḍhā mānuṣīṁ tanum āśritam*).

Kṛṣṇa is the original Nārāyaṇa, the original source of the entire cosmic manifestation. Brahmā, or the first living being born just after the creation, is the direct son of Nārāyaṇa, who as Garbhodaka-śāyī Viṣṇu first entered the material universe. Without spiritual contact, matter cannot create. Those who are seeking the original cause of the material creation should know that the creation takes place when the spirit soul is present. Matter is activated by the spirit soul; it is not that the soul is created by matter.

According to the Buddhist theory, the living force – the living energy we all have – is created by material conditions. At the present moment, the entire world is influenced by this Buddhist theory. The actual fact, however, is that matter develops because of the presence of the living force. We can understand this very easily. After a child is born, he grows, and his body develops, but if the child is born dead – if the spirit soul is not present – the body will not develop. Therefore the spirit is the basis for the development of matter, and not vice versa. Why does a dead child not grow? Because the spirit is not present. A tree grows as long as there is life in it. If we sow the small seed of a banyan tree in good soil and favor it with water, it will grow because the spirit soul is present. But if we were to fry such a seed in fire and then sow it, it would fail to grow because the spirit soul would not be there.

Matter grows and develops because of the presence of the spirit soul, and this principle has been followed from the very beginning of the creation. At the beginning of creation the Supreme Spirit entered the universe, and the first living being, Brahmā, was born on a lotus flower grown from the transcendental abdomen of Viṣṇu. Accepting that the lotus on which Brahmā was born is matter, we should understand that it is also grown from spirit. Therefore spirit is the basis of creation.

Because the lotus flower on which Lord Brahmā is born is grown from the navel of Viṣṇu, Lord Viṣṇu is known as Padmanābha. Brahmā is known as *ātma-bhū* because he was begotten directly from the father, Nārāyaṇa, or Viṣṇu, without the contact of mother Lakṣmījī. Lakṣmījī was present near Nārāyaṇa, engaged in the service of the Lord, but still, without contact with Lakṣmījī, Nārāyaṇa begot Brahmā. That is the omnipotency of the Lord. When we want to beget a child, we need the help of a wife because we cannot beget a child alone. But Kṛṣṇa, Lord Viṣṇu, produced Lord Brahmā without the help of His wife, Lakṣmī, although she was present, because He is not dependent on anything. One who foolishly considers Nārāyaṇa to be like other living beings should take a lesson from this.

The Vedic literature forbids one to think that other living beings are on an equal level with Nārāyaṇa.

yas tu nārāyaṇaṁ devaṁ
brahma-rudrādi-daivataiḥ
samatvenaiva vīkṣeta
sa pāṣaṇḍī bhaved dhruvam

Someone has invented the word *daridra-nārāyaṇa,* trying to show that Nārāyaṇa has become poor and that the beggar who comes to my door to beg is also Nārāyaṇa. This is not authorized in the Vedic literature. Nārāyaṇa is the master of Lakṣmī, the goddess of fortune, and only fools think that He somehow becomes poverty-stricken. Rascals say that Nārāyaṇa, Brahmā, Śiva, all the demigods, you, I, and everyone else are all on the same level. This is foolishness. Nārāyaṇa is *asamaurdhva*. This means that no one can be equal to or greater than Him. Therefore Kṛṣṇa Himself, the original Nārāyaṇa, says in *Bhagavad-gītā, mattaḥ parataraṁ nānyat:* "There is no one superior to Me." Nor is anyone equal to Him. The word *asama* means that no one is equal to Him, and *anūrdhva* means that no one is greater than Him. This is the position of the Lord.

Nārāyaṇa is not an ordinary living being. He is the Personality of Godhead Himself, and He has all the potencies of all the senses in all parts of His transcendental body. An ordinary living being begets a child by sexual intercourse and has no other means to beget a child than the one designed for him. But Nārāyaṇa is all-powerful, and therefore He can beget a child from His navel. Every part of His body has full potency, as explained in the *Brahma-saṁhitā* (5.32), *aṅgāni yasya sakalendriya-vṛttimanti*. For example, I can see with my eyes, but Kṛṣṇa can also eat with His eyes. Foolish rascals will say, "You are offering food to Kṛṣṇa, but what has He eaten? It is still here. He has not eaten anything." Such people do not know that Kṛṣṇa can eat just by seeing, for He can do anything with any part of His transcendental body. When a washerman refused to supply cloth to Kṛṣṇa in Mathurā, Lord Kṛṣṇa displayed His transcendental potency by cutting off the man's head with His hand. How was this possible? It was possible by the Lord's omnipotence.

The Lord is complete and independent to do anything and everything by His various potencies. This is explained in the beginning of *Śrīmad-Bhāgavatam* by the words *abhijñaḥ sva-rāṭ*. The word *sva-rāṭ* indicates that He is self-sufficient, not dependent on anyone. That is the qualification of God. Nowadays there are so many self-proclaimed incarnations of God, but as soon as they have some toothache they immediately say, "*Ooooooh,* doctor, help me. Save me." If you are God, save yourself. Why go to a doctor? Such people are rascals, and they make it very difficult to spread Kṛṣṇa consciousness. The whole world is now overburdened by such rascals and demons, and therefore the atom bomb is waiting for them by the will of the Supreme.

18

Liberation from Ignorance and Suffering

bhave 'smin kliśyamānānām
avidyā-kāma-karmabhiḥ
śravaṇa-smaraṇārhāṇi
kariṣyann iti kecana

And yet others say that You appeared to rejuvenate the devotional service of hearing, remembering, worshiping, and so on, in order that the conditioned souls suffering from material pangs might take advantage and gain liberation.

Śrīmad-Bhāgavatam 1.8.35

In the *Śrīmad Bhagavad-gītā* the Lord asserts that He appears in every millennium just to reestablish the way of religion. The way of religion is made by the Supreme Lord. No one can manufacture a new path of religion, as is the fashion for certain ambitious persons. The factual way of religion is to accept the Lord as the supreme authority and thus render service unto Him in spontaneous love. A living being cannot help but render service because he is constitutionally made for that purpose. The only function of the living being is to render service to the Lord. The Lord is great, and living beings are subordinate to Him. Therefore, the duty of the living being is just to serve Him only. Unfortunately the illusioned living beings, out of misunderstanding only, become servants of the senses by material desire. This desire is called *avidyā,* or nescience. And out of such desire the living being makes different plans for material enjoyment centered about a perverted sex life. He therefore becomes entangled in the chain of birth and death by transmigrating into different bodies on different planets under the direction of the Supreme Lord. Unless, therefore, one is beyond the boundary of this nescience, one cannot get free from the threefold miseries of material life. That is the law of nature.

The Lord, however, out of His causeless mercy, because He is more merciful to the suffering living beings than they can expect, appears before them and renovates the principles of devotional service, comprised of hearing, chanting, remembering, serving, worshiping, praying, cooperating, and surrendering unto Him. Adoption of all the above-mentioned items, or any one of them, can help a conditioned soul get out of the tangle of nescience and thus become liberated from all material sufferings created by the living being illusioned by the external energy. This particular type of mercy is bestowed upon the living being by the Lord in the form of Lord Śrī Caitanya Mahāprabhu.

In this very important verse the words *bhave 'smin* mean "in this material world." The word *bhava* also means "grow," and it refers to that which has taken birth. In the material world there are six kinds of changes. First there is birth, then growth, and then that which has been born and has grown stays for some time, produces some by-products, and then dwindles and finally vanishes. These six changes are called *ṣaḍ-vikāra.* The body, for example, takes birth at a certain date, and then it grows and stays for some time. From the body come so many by-products in the form of sons and daughters, and then the body becomes old and weak, and finally when it is very old it dies.

But when the body is finished, I am not finished. When the gross body comes to an end, I am still present within the subtle body of mind, intelligence, and false ego, and this subtle body carries me to another gross body. Although everyone has to accept a subtle body, the scientists and medical men cannot see it. I have a mind, and you have a mind, but I cannot see your mind, and you cannot see mine. I have intelligence, and you have intelligence, but you cannot see my intelligence, nor can I see yours, because they are very subtle. Similarly, the spirit soul is still more subtle, so what will the materialistic scientists see of it? They cannot see the mind, intelligence, or false ego, what to speak of the soul. Therefore they say, "The body is everything, and there is nothing more." Actually, however, that is not a fact.

The fact is that the spirit soul is very, very small. *Bālāgra-śata-bhāgasya śatadhā kalpitasya ca* (*Śvetāśvatara Upaniṣad* 5.9). The soul is one ten-thousandth the size of the tip of a hair. Suppose we were to take a hair and divide it into a hundred parts. Could we do it? No. That is not possible. But if we could do it and then divide it again into another one hundred parts, each part would be the size of the spirit soul.

Of course, this is not possible to understand by experimental knowledge, so how can it be learned? One must learn of this from an authority. Our knowledge is so imperfect that it cannot deal with such subtle affairs, and because rascals cannot deal with such things, they think that matter is the cause of life. Nonetheless, they have not been able to demonstrate that life comes from matter. Let them take chemicals in their laboratory and produce even a small insect with hands, legs, and eyes. Every night we see many of such small insects with legs and eyes with which they approach the light. From such small insects up to Brahmā there are 8,400,000 different forms of life, among which we are traveling from body to body, leaving one body and entering another, as stated by Kṛṣṇa in *Bhagavad-gītā* (*tathā dehāntara-prāptiḥ*). Therefore, either we must reject Kṛṣṇa's word or reject all the so-called scientific theories that life comes from matter. But we are pledged to Kṛṣṇa consciousness, and therefore we cannot reject Kṛṣṇa's word. We accept Kṛṣṇa when He says that we have to travel from one body to another.

Every living entity within this material world is under the influence of *avidyā,* ignorance. *Avidyā-karma-saṁjñānyā tṛtīyā śaktir iṣyate.* God, Kṛṣṇa, has many millions of potencies (*parāsya śaktir vividhaiva śrūyate*), and they have been summarized into three categories – the external potency, the internal potency, and the marginal potency. The marginal potency and the internal potency are of the same spiritual quality, but the third potency, the external potency, is inferior.

viṣṇu-śaktir parā proktā
kṣetrajñākhyā tathā parā
avidyā-karma-saṁjñānyā
tṛtīyā śaktir iṣyate
(*Viṣṇu Purāṇa* 6.7.61)

In this material world, everyone is in ignorance (*avidyā*). Even Brahmā was ignorant until he was given knowledge by Kṛṣṇa. Therefore no one should be proud of his knowledge. Everyone in this material world is a rascal. A particular living entity desires, "If I can get the opportunity to obtain the post of Brahmā, then I can create a big universe." Thus he receives the body of Brahmā. And the small insect thinks, "If I can create a small hole within this room, then I can live very peacefully and eat." Thus Brahmā desires to create a universe, we desire to create a skyscraper, and an ant desires to create a hole in a room, but the quality of the work is the same. We are all fools, however, because we do not realize that because these things are material they will not last. Because of ignorance we think, "This will be very nice. That will be very nice." *Kāma-karmabhiḥ.* We create some desire (*kāma*), and then we work accordingly. This results in so many difficulties (*kliśyanti*). To become Brahmā is not a very easy thing. Brahmā is such a big post, and it is given to a very qualified living entity who is highly advanced in austerities and penance. But he is also a living entity like us. In America there are many citizens, and President Ford is also a citizen, but by dint of his ardent labor and diplomacy he captured the post. Still, he is an ordinary citizen. President Nixon, for example, has now been dragged down and is no longer President. This is because he was an ordinary citizen. Similarly, if we like, we may also become Brahmā. Therefore Bhaktivinoda Ṭhākura says:

kīṭa-janma hao yathā tuyā dāsa
bahirmukha brahma-janme nāhi āśā

"Let me become an insect in a place where Your devotee is present, because if I fall down in the dust of the feet of a devotee my life will be successful." Bhaktivinoda Ṭhākura says, *bahirmukha brahma-janme nāhi āśā:* "I would not want to be a Brahmā and not be a devotee of Kṛṣṇa."

Because we are in ignorance, *māyā,* at any time we may forget Kṛṣṇa. Therefore we must always engage in Kṛṣṇa consciousness so that we shall not forget Him. That is indicated by Kuntīdevī by the words *śravaṇa-smaraṇārhāṇi.* The word *śravaṇa* means "hearing," *smaraṇa* means "remembering," and *arhaṇa* means "worshiping the Deity of Kṛṣṇa." One should always engage oneself in hearing about, remembering, and worshiping Kṛṣṇa. All the centers of the Kṛṣṇa consciousness movement are opened only for this purpose – to facilitate chanting, dancing, and worshiping so that we shall not forget Kṛṣṇa. *Sadā tad-bhāva-bhāvitaḥ:* if we always think of Kṛṣṇa, there is a chance that we shall remember Kṛṣṇa at the end of life (*ante nārāyaṇa-smṛtiḥ*).

Everything takes practice. For example, if one wants to dance on the stage, one has to perform many rehearsals to practice how to dance. Then if one becomes an expert dancer, when one dances on stage one will receive acclaim: "Ah, a very good dancer." But one cannot say, "I shall go immediately to the stage and become a good dancer." That is not possible. One may say, "No, no, no. I shall not attend the rehearsal. Just give me the stage, and I shall perform." But the director will not allow this, for one cannot become a good dancer without practice. The real purpose of life is to remember Kṛṣṇa when one's life comes to an end (*ante nārāyaṇa-smṛtiḥ*). If at the time of death one can remember Kṛṣṇa, one's life is successful.

In this material world one must suffer from material miseries, but rascals do not care to understand this, for they are absorbed in ignorance. A smuggler may go on with his work, even though he knows that he will be arrested and punished. A thief may know that he will be arrested and punished for criminal acts, and he may even have been punished several times, but still he will commit the same crime again (*punaḥ punaś carvita-carvaṇānām*). Why? Ignorance. He is so much absorbed in ignorance that he does not think, "I am repeatedly stealing and being repeatedly arrested and sent to jail to be punished. Why am I doing this? The result is not good." A person who is too much sexually inclined may suffer many times from venereal disease and have to undergo treatment, but still he will go to a prostitute again. This is *avaidha-strī-saṅga,* illegitimate sex. But even legitimate sex involves so many difficulties. After sex, a woman becomes pregnant and has to suffer for ten months, and at the time of delivery there is also sometimes very great danger. And the father, after the child is born, must take care of the child and work hard to provide for its education. Therefore the Vedic literature says, *bahu-duḥkha-bhājaḥ:* after sex, legitimate or illegitimate, there are so many troubles. *Tṛpyanti neha kṛpaṇāḥ:* but one who is an ignorant rascal will not be satisfied. Instead, he will do the same things again and again (*punaḥ punaś carvita-carvaṇānām*). This is called *bhava-roga,* the disease of material existence.

yan maithunādi-gṛhamedhi-sukhaṁ hi tucchaṁ
kaṇḍūyanena karayor iva duḥkha-duḥkham
(*Bhāgavatam* 7.9.45)

In the Vedic civilization, therefore, small boys are trained to remain *brahmacārī,* celibate, and not involve themselves in the troubles of sex. But if one is unable to remain *brahmacārī,* he is allowed to marry. After being trained in the beginning as a *brahmacārī,* he will not stay for many years in family life, but will very soon become *vānaprastha* (retired) and then accept *sannyāsa,* the renounced order of life.

In this material world everyone is suffering – the birds, the beasts, the trees, the animals, the plants, and even Brahmā and Indra. Indra is also not safe; he is always in anxiety about competitors who may come.

tat sādhu manye 'sura-varya dehināṁ
sadā samudvigna-dhiyām asad-grahāt
(*Bhāgavatam* 7.5.5)

Why is everyone in this material world always in anxiety? *Avidyā-kāma-karmabhiḥ:* because they are rascals. Therefore Kṛṣṇa stresses, "You rascal, give up all your nonsense and surrender unto Me." This is Kṛṣṇa's very good mercy. He is the supreme father. Therefore He directly says, *sarva-guhyatamam:* "This is the most confidential knowledge." *Sarva-dharmān parityajya mām ekaṁ śaraṇaṁ vraja:* "You rascal, give up everything and simply surrender unto Me."

Therefore Kuntī says, "You have come to teach rascals like this and engage them in hearing, remembering, and worship." This is *bhakti. Śravaṇaṁ kīrtanaṁ viṣṇoḥ:* one should hear and chant about Viṣṇu, Kṛṣṇa. But as soon as devotees begin to hear and chant about Viṣṇu, some rascal *svāmī* will say, "No, hearing or chanting any name will do. Why Viṣṇu? Why not Kālī?" In Bengal there is a group of people who have invented *"kālī-kīrtana,"* chanting the name of the demigoddess Kālī. What is this nonsense? In the Vedic literature there is no such thing as *"kālī-kīrtana."* Kīrtana means *śravaṇaṁ kīrtanaṁ viṣṇoḥ* – hearing and chanting about Viṣṇu, Kṛṣṇa. The Vedic literature recommends *harer nāma,* chanting of the holy name of Hari, Kṛṣṇa, and no one else.

This *śravaṇaṁ kīrtanam,* hearing and chanting, was described very nicely by Śukadeva Gosvāmī in the Second Canto of *Śrīmad-Bhāgavatam* (2.4.15). He said:

yat-kīrtanaṁ yad-smaraṇaṁ yad-īkṣaṇaṁ
yad-vandanaṁ yat-śravaṇaṁ yad-arhaṇam
lokasya sadyo vidhunoti kalmaṣaṁ
tasmai subhadra-śravase namo namaḥ

Before speaking *Śrīmad-Bhāgavatam,* Śukadeva Gosvāmī offered his obeisances to Kṛṣṇa with this verse. He said, "I offer my obeisances unto Him, for simply hearing of Him is *subhadra,* auspicious." The entire *Bhāgavatam* is glorification of Kṛṣṇa, and this is glorification by Śukadeva Gosvāmī. He says that one can be perfectly purified if one either glorifies Kṛṣṇa, meditates upon Him, or simply sits before the Deity of Kṛṣṇa and sees Him, thinking, "How nicely dressed is Kṛṣṇa. How nicely dressed is Rādhārāṇī." If one has no ability to chant or if one's mind is so disturbed that one cannot fix it upon Kṛṣṇa, one is given this chance: "Here is the Deity. Simply see Him." If one is engaged in the service of the Deity, there is a good chance of always seeing Him, twenty-four hours a day. While cleansing the floor of the temple, while dressing the Deity, while bathing the Deity, or while offering Him food, one will always see Him. This is the process of devotional service, but people are such fallen rascals that they do not even go see the Deity. "Oh," they think, "what is this Deity worship? It is idol worship." They may worship the statue of Gandhi or someone else, but when asked to come see the worship of the Deity they will say, "No, this is idol worship."

I have seen that in Calcutta in Chaurangi Square there is a statue of Sir Asutosa Mukherji. Throughout the year the crows pass stool on his face, and the stool becomes caked on. So on one day a year the ordinary sweepers cleanse the statue with their brush in the morning, and in the evening some big men come and garland him with flowers. Then after that evening they go away, and again the next morning the crows come to pass stool on his face. So this kind of worship is accepted – sweeping the face of Sir Asutosa Mukherji with the municipal brush – but if we install the Deity of Kṛṣṇa and worship Him nicely, people will say that this is idol worship.

So people are embarrassed by being entangled in *avidyā,* ignorance, and the method by which to educate them and rescue them from the clutches of this ignorance is devotional service. As explained by Śukadeva Gosvāmī, one may chant the name of Kṛṣṇa or meditate upon Kṛṣṇa, or if one cannot meditate one may simply sit down and see Kṛṣṇa. Even a child can see, "Here is Kṛṣṇa. Here is Rādhārāṇī." Even a small child or even an animal can do this and benefit, or if one is more intelligent one may offer prayers, and if one is expert and has been trained by a spiritual master one may perform appropriate worship.

Christians and Muslims are also Vaiṣṇavas, devotees, because they offer prayers to the Lord. "O God," they say, "give us our daily bread." Those who offer this prayer may not know very much and may be at a lower stage, but this is a beginning, because they have approached God. Going to a church or mosque is also pious (*catur-vidhā bhajante māṁ janāḥ sukṛtino 'rjuna*). Therefore those who begin in this way will one day become pure Vaiṣṇavas. But the atheistic propaganda that one should not go to a church, temple, or mosque is very dangerous to human society.

One may not be very advanced, but one should try at least to do something to understand God. A child is sent to school, and although he may simply learn ABCD, if he is interested he may one day become a very good scholar. Similarly, one day a pious man may become a pure devotee. Why should one give up religion altogether, become completely secular, and simply open a factory in which to manufacture nuts and bolts and work very hard and drink, and eat meat? What kind of civilization is this? It is because of this so-called civilization that people are suffering.

It is by ignorance that people think that by opening factories they will be happy. Why should they open factories? There is no need. There is so much land, and one can produce one's own food grains and eat sumptuously without any factory. Milk is also available without a factory. The factory cannot produce milk or grains. The present scarcity of food in the world is largely due to such factories. When everyone is working in the city to produce nuts and bolts, who will produce food grains? Simple living and high thinking is the solution to economic problems. Therefore the Kṛṣṇa consciousness movement is engaging devotees in producing their own food and living self-sufficiently so that rascals may see how one can live very peacefully, eat the food grains one has grown oneself, drink milk, and chant Hare Kṛṣṇa.

The process of Kṛṣṇa consciousness should be very vigorously propagated all over the world. Simply by seeing the Deity or simply by joining in chanting of the Hare Kṛṣṇa *mantra,* people will derive tremendous benefit. If one performs *kīrtana,* chanting, one will be able to think of Kṛṣṇa. One may think, "I danced for two hours and chanted Hare Kṛṣṇa. What is the meaning of this?" This is *smaraṇa,* thinking of Kṛṣṇa. One may even think, "I foolishly chanted 'Kṛṣṇa, Kṛṣṇa' for two hours." But that also is *smaraṇa.* Because the Kṛṣṇa consciousness movement is spreading, people are purchasing our books about Kṛṣṇa. Because they are curious they say, "What is this Kṛṣṇa? Let us see the book." Then they immediately see a picture of Rādhā and Kṛṣṇa, and if they open the book they will see more. In the book there are many prayers glorifying Kṛṣṇa. So some will hear about Kṛṣṇa, and others will read, and if they are fortunate enough they will become Kṛṣṇa conscious and engage in the worship of the Deity. These methods of devotional service – hearing, chanting, remembering Kṛṣṇa, and so on – are so perfect that as soon as one takes to them (either all of them, some of them, or even one of them) one becomes purified. Therefore Śukadeva Gosvāmī prays, "I offer my worship to the Supreme Personality of Godhead, for simply by remembering Him, simply by glorifying Him, or simply by seeing Him, so many benefits follow."

Śukadeva Gosvāmī is one of twelve important spiritual authorities, and these are the authorities we must follow (*mahājano yena gataḥ sa panthāḥ*). He affirms that by performing these methods of devotional service one will be cleansed of material contamination. When? *Sadyaḥ:* immediately, without waiting. This is the great benefit of the Kṛṣṇa consciousness movement.

19

Crossing Beyond Illusion's Currents

śṛṇvanti gāyanti gṛṇanty abhīkṣṇaśaḥ
smaranti nandanti tavehitaṁ janāḥ
ta eva paśyanty acireṇa tāvakaṁ
bhava-pravāhoparamaṁ padāmbujam

O Kṛṣṇa, those who continuously hear, chant, and repeat Your transcendental activities, or take pleasure in others' doing so, certainly see Your lotus feet, which alone can stop the repetition of birth and death.

Śrīmad-Bhāgavatam 1.8.36

The Supreme Lord, Śrī Kṛṣṇa, cannot be seen by our present conditional vision. In order to see Him, one has to change his present vision by developing a different condition of life, full of spontaneous love of Godhead. When Śrī Kṛṣṇa was personally present on the face of the globe, not everyone could see Him as the Supreme Personality of Godhead. Materialists like Rāvaṇa, Hiraṇyakaśipu, Kaṁsa, Jarāsandha, and Śiśupāla were highly qualified personalities by acquisition of material assets, but they were unable to appreciate the presence of the Lord. Therefore, even though the Lord may be present before our eyes, it is not possible to see Him unless we have the necessary vision. This necessary qualification is developed by the process of devotional service only, beginning with hearing about the Lord from the right sources. The *Bhagavad-gītā* is one of the popular literatures which are generally heard, chanted, repeated, etc., by the people in general, but in spite of such hearing, etc., sometimes it is experienced that the performer of such devotional service does not see the Lord face to face. The reason is that the first item, *śravaṇa,* is very important. If hearing is from the right sources, it acts very quickly. Generally people hear from unauthorized persons. Such unauthorized persons may be very learned by academic qualifications, but because they do not follow the principles of devotional service, hearing from them becomes a sheer waste of time. Sometimes the texts are interpreted fashionably to suit their own purposes. Therefore, first one should select a competent and bona fide speaker and then hear from him. When the hearing process is perfect and complete, the other processes become automatically perfect in their own way.

There are different transcendental activities of the Lord, and each and every one of them is competent to bestow the desired result, provided the hearing process is perfect. In the *Bhāgavatam* the activities of the Lord begin from His dealings with the Pāṇḍavas. There are many other pastimes of the Lord in connection with His dealings with the *asuras* and others. And in the Tenth Canto the sublime dealings with His conjugal associates, the *gopīs,* as well as with His married wives at Dvārakā are mentioned. Since the Lord is absolute, there is no difference in the transcendental nature of each and every dealing of the Lord. But sometimes people, in an unauthorized hearing process, take more interest in hearing about His dealings with the *gopīs*. Such an inclination indicates the lusty feelings of the hearer, so a bona fide speaker of the dealings of the Lord never indulges in such hearings. One must hear about the Lord from the very beginning, as in the *Śrīmad-Bhāgavatam* or any other scriptures, and that will help the hearer attain perfection by progressive development. One should not, therefore, consider that His dealings with the Pāṇḍavas are less important than His dealings with the *gopīs*. We must always remember that the Lord is always transcendental to all mundane attachment. In all the above-mentioned dealings of the Lord, He is the hero in all circumstances, and hearing about Him or about His devotees or combatants is conducive to spiritual life. It is said that the *Vedas* and *Purāṇas*, etc., are all made to revive our lost relation with Him. Hearing of all these scriptures is essential.

In the previous verses, Kuntīdevī has explained that those who have come to this material world are working very hard like asses and have such a hard burden that they cannot bear it. Because their lusty desires have created heavy work that puts them always in trouble, Kṛṣṇa comes to introduce the system by which one can get relief from this continuously troublesome life.

Religion consists of the laws of God. People who do not know this think that religion means faith. But although you may have faith in something and I may have faith in something, and although I may believe you and you may or may not believe me, that is not religion. There is even a supposedly religious mission that says, "You can manufacture your own way." *Yata mata tata patha:* "Whatever you think is right, that is right." This is their philosophy. But that is not science. Suppose I am a madman. Is whatever I think all right? How could this be? "Two plus two equals four" is science. If I believe that two plus two equals five or three, does it become true? No. So there are laws of God, and when there is *dharmasya glāniḥ,* deviation from these laws, we suffer. Just as we might suffer by violating the laws of the state, as soon as we violate the laws of God we are subjected to so many tribulations.

Now, how are we to get free from these tribulations? Kṛṣṇa comes to free us from them by giving us *bhakti-yoga*. Kṛṣṇa recommends, "Do this," and if we do it we shall get relief. Prahlāda Mahārāja mentions that this *bhakti-yoga* consists of nine items:

śravaṇaṁ kīrtanaṁ viṣṇoḥ
smaraṇaṁ pāda-sevanam
arcanaṁ vandanaṁ dāsyaṁ
sakhyam ātma-nivedanam

iti puṁsārpitā viṣṇau
bhaktiś cen nava-lakṣaṇā
kriyeta bhagavaty addhā
tan manye 'dhītam uttamam

"Hearing and chanting about the transcendental holy name, form, qualities, paraphernalia, and pastimes of Lord Viṣṇu, remembering them, serving the lotus feet of the Lord, offering the Lord respectful worship, offering prayers to the Lord, becoming His servant, considering the Lord one's best friend, and surrendering everything unto Him (in other words, serving Him with the body, mind, and words) – these nine processes are accepted as pure devotional service. One who has dedicated his life to the service of Kṛṣṇa through these nine methods should be understood to be the most learned person, for he has acquired complete knowledge." (*Bhāgavatam* 7.5.23–24)

"Hearing" means hearing about someone's activities, form, qualities, entourage, and so on. If I want to hear about someone, he must have some activities. We hear about history, and what is history? It is but the record of the activities of different persons in different ages. As soon as there is a question of hearing, we must ask what subject matter we should hear about. *Śravaṇaṁ kīrtanaṁ viṣṇoḥ:* we should hear about the activities of Lord Viṣṇu, or Lord Kṛṣṇa, not about the news in the newspaper. *Brahma-jijñāsā:* we should inquire and hear about Brahman, the Supreme. These are the statements of the *Vedas*. In our Kṛṣṇa consciousness movement, we also hear and chant, but what is the subject matter? The subject matter is Kṛṣṇa. We are not hearing about market reports and the price of this share or that share. No. We are hearing about Kṛṣṇa.

And when there is hearing, there must also be speaking or chanting. So we speak and chant about Kṛṣṇa (*śravaṇaṁ kīrtanaṁ viṣṇoḥ*). And as soon as one becomes expert in hearing and chanting, the next stage is *smaraṇam,* thinking or meditation. Whatever we speak or hear we shall later contemplate or meditate upon. First one must begin with *śravaṇam,* hearing, otherwise how can there be meditation? If one does not know the subject matter of meditation, where is the question of meditation? Therefore there must be hearing and chanting about Lord Viṣṇu (*śravaṇaṁ kīrtanaṁ viṣṇoḥ*).

Actual meditation in *yoga* aims at seeing the four-armed Viṣṇu *mūrti,* which is the form of the Lord within the heart. That is real meditation. Now rascals have manufactured other methods they call meditation, but these are not actually meditation. The senses are very restless, going this way and that way with the mind, but by the *aṣṭāṅga-yoga* system, which regulates one's sitting posture, one's breath, and so on, one can control the senses and concentrate the mind on the form of Viṣṇu. This concentration is called *samādhi,* and it is the real goal of *yoga.* Thus the *aṣṭāṅga-yoga* system aims at coming to the point of *smaraṇam,* or remembering the Supreme Lord.

The next process of devotional service is *arcanam,* worship of the Deity, the form of Kṛṣṇa in the temple.

śrī-vigrahārādhana-nitya-nānā-
śṛṅgāra-tan-mandira-mārjanādau
(*Śrī Gurv-aṣṭaka* 3)

It is not that one should worship Kṛṣṇa once a week or once a month. Rather, one should worship Kṛṣṇa twenty-four hours a day (*nitya*). The Deity should have a new dress every day or twice or four times a day – as many times as possible. This is called *śṛṅgāra.* Kṛṣṇa is the most opulent enjoyer, and we should supply Him things by which He can enjoy. For instance, if someone gives me new clothing, I say, "Oh, this new clothing is very nice," and this is my enjoyment. Similarly, we should try to satisfy Kṛṣṇa every day with gorgeous clothing. The dress for the Deity should be first class, the food offered to Him must be first class, and the place where He is situated in the temple must be first class or even more than first class. Furthermore, the temple should always be as clean as glass. Everyone remarks that the temples of the Kṛṣṇa consciousness movement are very clean, and they *must* be very clean. The more one cleanses the temple, the more one's heart becomes cleansed. This is the process of devotional service. The more we dress Kṛṣṇa, the more satisfied we become. At the present moment we are accustomed to seeing and appreciating our own clothing. I think, "What costly clothing I have," and in this way I become satisfied. But when we dress Kṛṣṇa we shall feel spiritual satisfaction.

yuktasya bhaktāṁś ca niyuñjato 'pi
vande guroḥ śrī-caraṇāravindam
(*Śrī Gurv-aṣṭaka* 3)

It is the duty of the spiritual master to engage his disciples always in worshiping the Deity in this way, and it is to such a *guru*, or spiritual master, that we offer our obeisances.

By the word *śṛṇvanti* Kuntīdevī indicates that our first concern should be to hear about Kṛṣṇa. One must be eager to hear. Why do we pay a college fee and go to college? To hear. By sitting down and hearing from the learned professor, we get knowledge. Therefore a devotee always engages in hearing about Kṛṣṇa. For those who are cultivating Kṛṣṇa consciousness, the first business is hearing.

And if one has actually heard about Kṛṣṇa, one's next engagement in *bhakti-yoga* will be to chant (*gāyanti*). The preachers of the Kṛṣṇa consciousness movement go from town to town, village to village. Why? What is their purpose? To preach, to chant, so that people may get the opportunity to hear this philosophy and take it seriously (*gṛṇanti*). The word *abhīkṣṇaśaḥ* indicates that these engagements should go on continuously, twenty-four hours a day without stopping. Caitanya Mahāprabhu therefore recommends, *kīrtanīyaḥ sadā hariḥ:* one should engage in chanting twenty-four hours a day. That is the business of Kṛṣṇa conscious devotees.

One may perform all the methods of devotional service or may accept only one. Simply hearing is enough. Parīkṣit Mahārāja did not do anything else but sit down before Śukadeva Gosvāmī and hear for the last seven days of his life. If one simply hears, without doing anything else, if one simply sits down in the temple and whenever there is talk of *Bhagavad-gītā* one goes on hearing, that will be enough.

Even if you do not understand, please hear. The vibration, the *mantra,* will help you. Grammatical or scholarly understanding is not very important. One may not know Sanskrit grammar, but *bhakti* is *apratihatā,* unimpedable. Nothing can check the progress of *bhakti.* Therefore one should simply adopt this process of hearing, as recommended by Caitanya Mahāprabhu.

After Caitanya Mahāprabhu accepted the renounced order of life, he was criticized by Sārvabhauma Bhaṭṭācārya, whose father had been a schoolfriend of Nīlāmbara Cakravartī, the father-in-law of Caitanya Mahāprabhu's father, Jagannātha Miśra. By this relationship, Sārvabhauma Bhaṭṭācārya was on the level of Caitanya Mahāprabhu's grandfather. Thus he said to Caitanya Mahāprabhu, "You are a boy only twenty-four years old, and now You have taken *sannyāsa. Sannyāsa* is very difficult to keep, because for a young man the world has so many attractions. So You should hear *Vedānta-sūtra.*" Sārvabhauma Bhaṭṭācārya belonged to the Māyāvāda school, and this indicates that hearing is important even among the Māyāvādīs, who stress the importance of hearing *Vedānta-sūtra.* The Vaiṣṇavas, the devotees of Kṛṣṇa, also hear *Vedānta-sūtra,* but not from the Māyāvādīs, who falsely interpret it and spoil the process of hearing. The Vaiṣṇavas actually hear *Vedānta-sūtra,* because they do not interpret it. When Kṛṣṇa says, "I am the Supreme," the Vaiṣṇavas accept it, and that is the proper way of hearing. If one speculatively interprets the *Vedānta-sūtra* or *Bhagavad-gītā,* saying, "The word *kṛṣṇa* means this, and *kurukṣetra* means that," one is simply wasting one's time. One should hear this literature as it is.

Thus although Caitanya Mahāprabhu agreed to hear *Vedānta* from Sārvabhauma Bhaṭṭācārya, He simply went on hearing it for many days but did not ask any questions. Finally Sārvabhauma Bhaṭṭācārya said to Him, "My dear boy, You are hearing, but You do not ask any questions. Why is this? Is it that You can't understand? What is the reason You are silent?" Caitanya Mahāprabhu answered, "Yes, I understand. But I am silent because You are explaining the *Vedānta-sūtra* in a speculative way. Therefore I am simply listening to the verses of *Vedānta-sūtra* but not actually listening to you." Thus He indirectly said, "You are explaining the meaning foolishly." Later He said, "The verses of *Vedanta-sutra* are just like sunshine, but your explanations are like clouds that cover them."

No one needs a lamp to see the sun. Everyone can see it. But if the sun is covered by a cloud, it is very difficult to see. Similarly, the *Vedānta-sūtra* is like the sun, but the Māyāvāda interpretations cover the real meaning. The Māyāvādīs never accept the direct meaning. Even big political leaders who are influenced by the Māyāvāda philosophy cover the meaning of the Vedic literature by speculating, "*Kurukṣetra* means this, and *dharma-kṣetra* means that." Our policy, therefore, should be to hear the original, as it is. Then it will be effective. *Śravaṇaṁ kīrtanaṁ viṣṇoḥ:* Viṣṇu should be heard as He is. Then one can meditate upon Viṣṇu and remember Him (*smaranti*). In this way one becomes jubilant (*nandanti*). The word *nandana* means "pleasing," and one comes in touch with the reservoir of pleasure in this way.

Therefore those who are cultivating Kṛṣṇa consciousness have to hear about Kṛṣṇa, speak about Kṛṣṇa, and deal only in relationship with Kṛṣṇa. "By this process," Kuntīdevī tells the Lord, "one will one day come to see You." And when one sees God, Kṛṣṇa, what is the effect? *Bhava-pravāhoparamam.* The word *pravāha* means "current." When there are very forceful currents in the river and some animal is thrown in, it will be washed away. Similarly, we are being washed away by the currents of material nature, which come one after another like big waves in the Pacific Ocean. Because we are under the grip of the three modes of material nature (*prakṛteḥ kriyamāṇāni guṇaiḥ karmāṇi sarvaśaḥ*), we are being washed away. Therefore Bhaktivinoda Ṭhākura says, *māyāra vaśe yaccha bhese':* "You are being washed away, carried away, by the currents of material nature." These are the currents of hunger and thirst, of birth, death, and old age, the currents of illusion. We are spirit souls, but because we have been put into the material ocean, the currents are carrying us away. However, if we engage twenty-four hours a day in hearing, chanting, and seriously serving Kṛṣṇa, the current will stop.

Where will the current stop? Kuntīdevī says to the Lord, *padām-bujam:* "It will stop at Your lotus feet." One has to learn how to see Kṛṣṇa's lotus feet and offer a little *tulasī* and sandalwood pulp at the lotus feet of the Lord, and then this current of material life will stop.

There may be currents in the ocean, but if one gets a good boat, one can cross over these currents very nicely. As mentioned in another verse of *Śrīmad-Bhāgavatam* (10.14.58), *samāśritā ye pada-pallava-plavam.* A lotus petal is something like a small boat, and therefore this verse says that if one takes shelter of the petal boat of the lotus feet of Kṛṣṇa, the great ocean of birth and death becomes as insignificant as the water contained in the hoofprint of a calf. In India during the rainy season the roads become muddy, and when the cows and calves walk they create holes in which water collects. But of course one can easily jump over a dozen of such puddles at any time. Similarly, although for others the world of birth and death is like a great ocean, for a devotee it is like such a puddle (*bhavāmbudhir vatsa-padam*), and he can jump over it very easily. In this way the devotee attains *paraṁ padam,* the supreme abode. Then what about this material world? *Padaṁ padaṁ yad vipadām:* this is a place not for devotees but for people who are suffering. Therefore Kuntīdevī suggests, "This Kṛṣṇa consciousness is the medicine for your suffering. Take it and be happy."

20
Full Surrender

apy adya nas tvaṁ sva-kṛtehita prabho
jihāsasi svit suhṛdo 'nujīvinaḥ
yeṣāṁ na cānyad bhavataḥ padāmbujāt
parāyaṇaṁ rājasu yojitāṁhasām

O my Lord, You have executed all duties Yourself. Are You leaving us today, though we are completely dependent on Your mercy and have no one else to protect us, now when all kings are at enmity with us?

Śrīmad-Bhāgavatam 1.8.37

The Pāṇḍavas are most fortunate because with all good luck they were entirely dependent on the mercy of the Lord. In the material world, to be dependent on the mercy of someone else is the utmost sign of misfortune, but in the case of our transcendental relation with the Lord, it is the most fortunate case when we can live completely dependent on Him. The material disease is due to thinking of becoming independent of everything. But the cruel material nature does not allow us to become independent. The false attempt to become independent of the stringent laws of nature is known as material advancement of experimental knowledge. The whole material world is moving on this false attempt at becoming independent of the laws of nature. Beginning from Rāvaṇa, who wanted to prepare a direct staircase to the planets of heaven, down to the present age, they are trying to overcome the laws of nature. They are trying now to approach distant planetary systems by electronic mechanical power. But the highest goal of human civilization is to work hard under the guidance of the Lord and become completely dependent on Him. The highest achievement of perfect civilization is to work with valor but at the same time depend completely on the Lord. The Pāṇḍavas were the ideal executors of this standard of civilization. Undoubtedly they were completely dependent on the good will of Lord Śrī Kṛṣṇa, but they were not idle parasites of the Lord. They were all highly qualified both by personal character and by physical activities. Still they always looked for the mercy of the Lord because they knew that every living being is dependent by constitutional position. The perfection of life is, therefore, to become dependent on the will of the Lord, instead of becoming falsely independent in the material world. Those who try to become falsely independent of the Lord are called *anātha,* or without any guardian, whereas those who are completely dependent on the will of the Lord are called *sanātha,* or those having someone to protect them. Therefore we must try to be *sanātha,* so that we can always be protected from the unfavorable condition of material existence. By the deluding power of the external, material nature we forget that the material condition of life is the most undesirable perplexity. The *Bhagavad-gītā* (7.19) therefore directs us that after many, many births one fortunate person becomes aware of the fact that Vāsudeva, Kṛṣṇa, is all in all and that the best way of leading one's life is to surrender unto Him completely.

That is the sign of a *mahātmā*. All the members of the Pāṇḍava family were *mahātmās* in household life. Mahārāja Yudhiṣṭhira was the head of these *mahātmās,* and Queen Kuntīdevī was the mother. The lessons of the *Bhagavad-gītā* and all the *Purāṇas,* specifically the *Bhāgavata Purāṇa,* are therefore inevitably connected with the history of the Pāṇḍava *mahātmās.* For them, separation from the Lord was just like the separation of a fish from water. Śrīmatī Kuntīdevī, therefore, felt such separation like a thunderbolt, and the whole prayer of the Queen is to try to persuade the Lord to stay with them. After the Battle of Kurukṣetra, although the inimical kings were killed, their sons and grandsons were still there to deal with the Pāṇḍavas. It is not only the Pāṇḍavas who were put into the condition of enmity; all of us are always in such a condition, and the best way of living is to become completely dependent on the will of the Lord and thereby overcome all difficulties of material existence.

After the Battle of Kurukṣetra ended and the Pāṇḍavas were established in their kingdom, Kṛṣṇa, before going back home to Dvārakā, was taking leave of His aunt and bidding her farewell. It was at that time that Kuntī offered this prayer. Now she directly asks, "Is it a fact that after finishing Your duty You are going away and leaving us alone?" This is the devotee's position. Kuntīdevī says, *yeṣāṁ na cānyad bhavataḥ padāmbujāt:* "We have no means of protection other than Your lotus feet." This is full surrender.

In the process of surrender (*śaraṇāgati*) there are six items. The first is that one should completely depend on Kṛṣṇa, and the next is that one should accept everything favorable for Kṛṣṇa's service (*ānukūlyasya saṅkalpaḥ*). *Ānukūlyena kṛṣṇānuśīlanaṁ bhaktir uttamā:* a symptom of first-class *bhakti,* devotional service, is that one accepts everything favorable for that service. Another item of surrender is *prātikūlyasya varjanam,* rejecting everything unfavorable to the procedures of Kṛṣṇa consciousness. Sometimes the spiritual master says, "Don't do this," forbidding something unfavorable, and he also recommends that which is favorable: "Do this. Chant Hare Kṛṣṇa." Full surrender, therefore, entails giving up unfavorable things and accepting that which is favorable (*ānukūlyasya saṅkalpaḥ prātikūlyayasya varjanam*). Furthermore, one should believe with full faith, "Kṛṣṇa will give me protection," and one should count oneself as one of the servants of Kṛṣṇa. These are some of the items of *śaraṇāgati,* full surrender.

Now Kuntīdevī says, "My dear Kṛṣṇa, if You think that we are well established now that we have our kingdom back, and if You therefore want to leave us, that is not a very good proposal. We are not free yet. Because we have killed so many kings, all their friends and relatives are planning to come fight with us again. So don't think that we are free from all dangers. We are not. And we have no protection other than Your lotus feet. That is our position." Thus she indirectly says to Kṛṣṇa, "Do not leave us. Don't think that we are now safe. Without Your protection, we are always unsafe."

This should be the position of a devotee. We should know that we are actually in danger in this material world. *Māyā,* illusion, may catch us at any time, as soon as we are a little inattentive, thinking, "Now I have done my duty. Let me take a little rest." No, there is no rest. We must be always alert.

There is a verse in which Śrīla Rūpa Gosvāmī says, *avyartha-kālatvam:* a devotee should be very much careful to see whether his time is being spent unnecessarily. He should ask himself, "Am I now engaged in *māyā's* service or Kṛṣṇa's service?" This is a symptom of an advanced devotee. *Nāma-gāne sadā ruciḥ:* such a devotee is never tired of chanting, singing, or dancing. The word *sadā* means "always," and *ruci* means "taste." A devotee always has a taste for chanting Hare Kṛṣṇa: "Oh, very nice. Hare Kṛṣṇa, Hare Kṛṣṇa, Kṛṣṇa Kṛṣṇa, Hare Hare/ Hare Rāma, Hare Rāma, Rāma Rāma, Hare Hare." This is taste. Of course, this taste takes time to awaken, but when Rūpa Gosvāmī was chanting he was thinking, "I have only one tongue and two ears. What can I appreciate of chanting? If I could have millions of tongues and trillions of ears, then I could relish something by chanting and hearing." Of course, we should not imitate him, but the devotees of the Kṛṣṇa consciousness movement must at least be very careful to complete their sixteen rounds, their minimum amount of prescribed chanting. *Nāma-gāne sadā ruciḥ:* we have to increase our taste for singing and chanting Hare Kṛṣṇa.

Furthermore, we should also increase our inclination to live in a place where Kṛṣṇa lives (*prītis tad-vasati-sthale*). In the vision of higher devotees, Kṛṣṇa actually lives everywhere, but because we are in a lower condition, we should know that for us Kṛṣṇa lives in the temple. Because we do not see Kṛṣṇa everywhere, we should come to the temple to see Kṛṣṇa, who kindly appears there, by His mercy, in a manner in which we can see Him.

Kṛṣṇa has a completely spiritual body (*sac-cid-ānanda-vigraha*), but we do not have the eyes to see what that spiritual body is. We are accustomed to seeing material, gross things (*jaḍa*). We can see stone, metal, wood, and other elements, and because Kṛṣṇa is everything, to be visible to our imperfect eyes He appears in a form of these elements. It is not that Kṛṣṇa is stone or that we are worshiping stone. We are worshiping Kṛṣṇa, but because we cannot see anything except material elements like stone, Kṛṣṇa kindly appears in a form carved from stone. Therefore one should be very much inclined to live within the circle of a temple environment in which the form of Kṛṣṇa is worshiped.

Moreover, one should always think oneself dependent on Kṛṣṇa. This is Kṛṣṇa consciousness. One should always think, "Without Kṛṣṇa my life is useless, and I am in danger." Therefore, while offering her prayers to Kṛṣṇa, Kuntī says, "Kṛṣṇa, You are thinking that now we are safe, but I don't think we are safe. We are always in danger. If You think we are safe, who will give us protection? We have no protection other than Your lotus feet. We are encircled by so many enemies because the sons of those who have died in the fight are now preparing to fight with us."

Now, although Kṛṣṇa had come to Kuntīdevī to take the dust of the feet of His superior, His aunt, Kuntīdevī addresses Him as Prabhu, the Lord, not as her beloved nephew. She knows, "Although Kṛṣṇa is playing the part of my nephew, my brother's son, He is still the supreme master."

The symptoms of a really Kṛṣṇa conscious person are that he knows that Kṛṣṇa is the supreme master, he always thinks himself in danger without Kṛṣṇa, and by taking shelter of Kṛṣṇa's lotus feet he always feels safe. Kṛṣṇa says, *kaunteya pratijānīhi na me bhaktaḥ praṇaśyati:* "You may declare to the world that My devotee is never vanquished." (*Bhagavad-gītā* 9.31) If one becomes a pure devotee of Kṛṣṇa, there is no question of danger. Of course, Kṛṣṇa gives protection to everyone, for without His protection no one can live even for a single moment. But one should not think, "If Kṛṣṇa is giving protection to everyone, what is the use of becoming a devotee?" A king gives protection to every one of his citizens, for that is his duty, but he especially protects his own circle of men. This is not unnatural. If one directly engages in the service of the President, when one is in some difficulty he is especially protected. Although the President gives protection to all the citizens, those who personally associate with him, giving him service, receive special consideration. That is not actually partiality. That is natural. When a gentleman loves all children but has special love for his own children, no one will say, "Oh, why are you loving your own children more than others?" No, that is natural. Similarly, Kṛṣṇa says in *Bhagavad-gītā, samo 'haṁ sarva-bhūteṣu:* "I am equal to everyone." Kṛṣṇa, being God, loves everyone because everyone is part of Him. Nonetheless, He takes special care of His devotees. Therefore He says, *kaunteya pratijānīhi na me bhaktaḥ praṇaśyati:* "My devotee will never be vanquished."

Kṛṣṇa always sees to the comforts of His devotees, and the devotees are always busy seeing that Kṛṣṇa is satisfied. The devotees dress Kṛṣṇa, supply Him food, and always engage in serving Him, and similarly Kṛṣṇa always sees to the happiness of His devotees. This is the intimate relationship between the devotee and Kṛṣṇa. Every living entity has a relationship with Kṛṣṇa, but when one becomes a devotee the relationship becomes intimate. Therefore Kuntīdevī says to Kṛṣṇa, "How can You leave us? We are Your intimate friends. We are simply living by Your care, by Your mercy. Don't think that we are safe and that You can therefore leave us. Our life is always under Your mercy, for we have no shelter other than Your lotus feet. Kindly don't leave us." This is Kuntī's prayer. Similarly, Narottama dāsa Ṭhākura sings:

hā hā prabhu nanda-suta vṛṣabhānu-sutā-yuta
karuṇā karaha ei-bāra

"Kṛṣṇa, Nanda-suta, You are present with Rādhārāṇī, the daughter of King Vṛṣabhānu. Now I fully surrender unto You. Please show me Your mercy."

Without Kṛṣṇa consciousness one thinks, "I shall protect myself, or my society, community, or state will give me protection. I have so many protectors. Why should I care for God? Why shall I go to Kṛṣṇa? Those rascals who have no protection can go to Kṛṣṇa." But the fact is that unless Kṛṣṇa gives one protection one cannot be protected. This is stated in the *Śrīmad-Bhāgavatam* (7.9.19): *bālasya neha śaraṇaṁ pitarau nṛsiṁha.* When Prahlāda Mahārāja offered prayers to Kṛṣṇa as Nṛsiṁha-deva, he said, "My dear Lord, one should not think that because a child has a father and mother he has full protection." If Kṛṣṇa did not protect a child, the child could not be protected, even if he were to have thousands of fathers and mothers. Prahlāda also says, *nārtasya cāgadam udanvati majjato nauḥ:* "It is not that a good physician or good medicine can protect one from disease." Suppose a rich man is suffering from some disease and he hires a first-class physician and takes first-class medicine. Does it mean that his life is guaranteed? No. If Kṛṣṇa does not give him protection, despite good medical treatment and a good supply of medicine he will die. "Similarly," Prahlāda continues, "one may have a good boat, but this does not guarantee that he will not drown in the ocean. If You do not protect him he may drown at any moment." Nature offers so many difficulties, and although scientists may try to invent something to check these difficulties in the struggle for existence, unless Kṛṣṇa gives one protection one's inventions will be of no use.

Kuntīdevī knows this, and therefore although she is the mother of the great warriors Arjuna and Bhīma, she still thinks, "Although my sons are great warriors, they are not sufficient to give us protection. Nothing can give us protection but Your lotus feet." This verse illustrates the position of a surrendered soul seeking the protection of Kṛṣṇa. If we remain in this position, knowing that our only protector is Kṛṣṇa and that our only duty is to serve Kṛṣṇa, then our life is successful.

21

What Is Our Actual Value?

ke vayaṁ nāma-rūpābhyāṁ
yadubhiḥ saha pāṇḍavāḥ
bhavato 'darśanaṁ yarhi
hṛṣīkāṇām iveśituḥ

As the name and fame of a particular body is finished with the disappearance of the living spirit, similarly, if You do not look upon us, all our fame and activities, along with the Pāṇḍavas and Yadus, will end at once.

Śrīmad-Bhāgavatam 1.8.38

Kuntīdevī is quite aware that the existence of the Pāṇḍavas is due to Śrī Kṛṣṇa only. The Pāṇḍavas are undoubtedly well established in name and fame and are guided by the great King Yudhiṣṭhira, who is morality personified, and the Yadus are undoubtedly great allies, but without the guidance of Lord Kṛṣṇa all of them are nonentities, as much as the senses of the body are useless without the guidance of consciousness. No one should be proud of his prestige, power, and fame without being guided by the favor of the Supreme Lord. The living beings are always dependent, and the ultimate dependable object is the Lord Himself. We may, therefore, invent by our advancement of material knowledge all sorts of counteracting material resources, but without being guided by the Lord all such inventions end in fiasco, however strong and stout the reactionary elements may be.

As soon as an important man dies, his name and form become unimportant, even though he may have been a big scientist, politician, or philosopher. As long as we are alive our name, form, and activities are glorious, but as soon as the life is gone the body is but a lump of matter. When an important man is alive he may have so many guards, and no one can go before him or touch him, but when the same man is dead and lying on the floor, one may kick him in the face, and practically no one will care. After the disappearance of the soul, the body of the important man has no value. And what is that soul? It is the energy of Kṛṣṇa, and therefore it is part and parcel of Kṛṣṇa. So when the energy is withdrawn – that is, when Kṛṣṇa is not there – the body becomes unimportant.

Kṛṣṇa's energy and Kṛṣṇa Himself are not different (*śakti-śakti-mator abhedaḥ*). The sun, for example, is energetic, and the sunshine is energy. As long as the sunshine is present the sun is present, and if the sun were not present the sun's energy would also not be there. The energy and the energetic must both exist. Although the Māyāvādī philosophers do not accept the energetic but only the impersonal energy, we must accept both the energy and the energetic.

While the energy works, the energetic remains aloof, just as the sunshine spreads everywhere while the sun itself remains apart. Similarly, there is energy working throughout the cosmic manifestation. The cosmic manifestation consists of earth, water, fire, air, ether, mind, intelligence, and false ego. These eight material elements are separated material energies (*me bhinnā prakṛtir aṣṭadhā*), and we can understand that behind these energies there must be an energetic source. For example, we are using electric power, but behind this power are the powerhouse and the engineer. Rascals do not understand this. They simply see the power of this cosmic manifestation, but they do not understand that behind this power is the powermaker, the source of power. Therefore Kṛṣṇa comes and says, "I am the powermaker. I am behind this power."

Kṛṣṇa Himself personally comes because we do not have the eyes to see Kṛṣṇa and cannot understand Him. When we contemplate the form of God, we think that because God created millions and millions of years ago, He must be a very old man. Therefore God personally comes before us so that we can see what He is. This is His kindness. The Lord says in *Bhagavad-gītā* (4.7):

yadā yadā hi dharmasya
glānir bhavati bhārata
abhyutthānam adharmasya
tadātmānaṁ sṛjāmy aham

"Whenever and wherever there is a decline in religious practice, O descendant of Bharata, and a predominant rise of irreligion – at that time I descend Myself."

God comes to this world in person, He leaves behind His instructions like those of *Bhagavad-gītā,* and He leaves behind His devotees who can explain who God is, but still we are so stubborn that we do not accept God. This is foolishness. In *Bhagavad-gītā* those who do not accept God are called *mūḍhāḥ* – rascals and fools.

God exists, and God's energy also exists, so if we cannot see God we can at least see His energy. We may not see the electric powerhouse and the engineer within it generating power, but we use electricity in so many ways. Therefore we should inquire where this electricity comes from. This is intelligence, and if one inquires in this way he will eventually find the powerhouse itself. Similarly, if one studies further to find out who is running the powerhouse, one will find a human being. Although the electricity is impersonal and even the powerhouse is impersonal, the man behind everything is a person. Similarly, God is a person. This is a logical conclusion. How can He be impersonal? That which is impersonal has no intelligence. We have invented so many very wonderful machines, but the machines are not intelligent. The intelligence belongs to the operator. Therefore Kṛṣṇa says, *mayādhyakṣeṇa prakṛtiḥ sūyate sa-carācaram:* "You are seeing the energy displayed in the wonderful actions and reactions of this material cosmic manifestation, but don't think that they are working independently. No, I am behind them."

Kṛṣṇa further says:

mayā tatam idaṁ sarvaṁ
jagad avyakta-mūrtinā
mat-sthāni sarva-bhūtāni
na cāhaṁ teṣv avasthitaḥ

"By Me, in My unmanifested form, this entire universe is pervaded. All beings are in Me, but I am not in them." (*Bhagavad-gītā* 9.4) That which is *avyakta,* unmanifested, also has *mūrti,* a form. The sky, for example, is *avyakta,* unmanifest, but it also has a form – the round form of the universe. If we go to the ocean, there also we shall find a form, like that of a big circle. Without form there is nothing; everything has form, even that which is supposedly impersonal.

Therefore the idea that everything is zero or impersonal is foolish. Behind the impersonal feature and the so-called voidness is the supreme form – Kṛṣṇa. *Īśvaraḥ paramaḥ kṛṣṇaḥ sac-cid-ānanda-vigrahaḥ.* The word *īśvara* means "controller." Nature is not controlling itself; the real controller is Kṛṣṇa. *Icchānurūpam api yasya ca ceṣṭate sā.* The *Brahma-saṁhitā* (5.44) says that Prakṛti, or Durgā – the deity of material nature – is working under the direction of Govinda, Kṛṣṇa. How is she working? Just like a shadow. Below our hand is its shadow, and as our hand moves, the shadow moves. Behind all manifestations there is motion. I have sometimes given the example of the shunting of the big cars in a railway line. The engine gives the motion and pushes one car, which then pushes another and another, and so on. Similarly, who set up the motion of the cosmic manifestation? That original motion-giver is Kṛṣṇa.

Now Kuntīdevī says, "We Pāṇḍavas have become famous, and people say that we are very important. Why? Because You are our friend." Kṛṣṇa was the friend of the Pāṇḍavas and specifically the friend of Arjuna, and therefore Arjuna was a great and valorous warrior. But Kuntīdevī knew, "People say, 'Oh, the Pāṇḍavas are such great warriors and heroes,' but what is the value of my sons, the Pāṇḍavas?" Similarly, the Yadu dynasty was famous because Kṛṣṇa took His birth in that family. But Kuntīdevī says, *ke vayam:* "What are we? What is our value?" *Ke vayaṁ nāma-rūpābhyām:* "We have our name and form, but without You it is all useless. It has no value."

People do not understand this. They are very proud of having a nice body and a nice name. They think, "I am American," "I am Indian," "I am German," and so on. But what is all this? These are simply bogus names and bogus forms with no value.

If we subtract Kṛṣṇa, everything is zero. This is a fact, but people are such rascals that they do not understand this fact. But who can deny it? The American body or Indian body may have a good name, but if it has no consciousness, what is its value? No value. Therefore it is said:

bhagavad-bhakti-hīnasya
jātiḥ śāstraṁ japas tapaḥ
aprāṇasyeva dehasya
maṇḍanaṁ loka-rañjanam

"For a person devoid of devotional service to Kṛṣṇa, his birth in a great family or nation, his knowledge of revealed scripture, his performance of austerities and penance, and his chanting of Vedic *mantras* are all like ornaments on a dead body. Such ornaments simply serve the concocted pleasures of the general populace." (*Hari-bhakti-sudhodaya* 3.11)

We all have consciousness, but what is this consciousness? It is Kṛṣṇa consciousness. We have forgotten Kṛṣṇa, and therefore we simply say "consciousness," but really "consciousness" means Kṛṣṇa consciousness, because without Kṛṣṇa we cannot have consciousness. Without the sun, how can there be sunshine? Therefore we say "sunshine," and not just "shine." Similarly, "consciousness" means Kṛṣṇa consciousness. This requires a little intelligence to understand, but devotees like Kuntī have this intelligence and understanding. Therefore Kuntī says, "The Pāṇḍavas and Yadus are so important, but what is actually our value?"

Because Kṛṣṇa is bidding farewell, Kuntī laments, "You will go, and we shall not be able to see You. What then will be the value of our name and fame?" *Bhavato 'darśanaṁ yarhi hṛṣīkāṇām iveśituḥ.* She gives the example that without Kṛṣṇa they would be like the senses without life. In this material world we desire sense enjoyment, but without Kṛṣṇa or without Kṛṣṇa consciousness there is no possibility of sense enjoyment. We may have strong arms and legs, but when there is no consciousness – when there is no Kṛṣṇa consciousness – we cannot even utilize them. An intelligent person, therefore, knows that without Kṛṣṇa his senses have no value, and therefore he becomes a devotee. He rightly concludes that because there is an intimate relationship between the senses and Kṛṣṇa, as long as the senses are active it is one's duty to use the senses in the service of Kṛṣṇa. This is *bhakti.*

To use an example I have given many times, suppose in an assembly one finds a hundred-dollar note that has fallen from someone's pocket. If one takes that note and puts it in one's own pocket, one is a thief because that note does not belong to him. This is called *bhoga,* false enjoyment. Then again, someone else may think, "Oh, why shall I touch it? It belongs to someone else. Let it remain there. I have nothing to do with it." This is called *tyāga,* renunciation. So although the hundred-dollar note is the same, one person is trying to enjoy it while another is trying to give it up. But both of them – the *bhogī* and the *tyāgī* – are fools.

The *bhogīs* are the *karmīs,* those who are working very hard to exploit the resources of the material nature, like the scientists, for example, who are doing research to further such exploitation. Their intention, actually, is to steal. On the other hand, the *tyāgīs,* those who are unable to steal, have a "sour grapes" philosophy: "Oh, these things are useless. There is no need of them." Mostly, of course, people are *bhogīs;* that is, they are trying to use everything to enjoy sense gratification. But still there are those who are baffled in sense gratification and who therefore say, "No, no, we don't need these things."

Continuing the example, however, when a hundred-dollar note is found, the person who acts most properly is the one who takes it and says, "Someone has lost this note. Let me find its owner." Upon returning that note, one renders real service. One who takes the note for himself and one who leaves the note where it is are both useless. Similarly, the *bhogī* and *tyāgī* are both useless. But the *bhakta,* the devotee, knows that everything belongs to Kṛṣṇa and should therefore be offered to Kṛṣṇa. This is real service.

Everything belongs to Kṛṣṇa. What is the body? It is a combination of material elements – earth, water, fire, air, and the subtle, psychological elements mind, intelligence, and false ego. Kṛṣṇa claims, "All these eight elements are My separated energy." Then how are the body and mind ours? Although I claim that the body is mine, I do not even know how it is working. A tenant in an apartment may pay rent and somehow or other occupy the apartment and enjoy its utilities, although he may not actually know how the heat and tap water are working. Similarly, although we do not know the details of how the body works, we are using this body, which actually belongs not to us but to Kṛṣṇa. This is the real fact. The body consists of the senses and the mind, and therefore the senses and mind also belong to Kṛṣṇa.

I am a spiritual soul, but I have been given the opportunity to utilize a certain type of material body. Because I wanted it, Kṛṣṇa is so kind that He has given it to me. *Ye yathā māṁ prapadyante tāṁs tathaiva bhajāmy aham.* If one wants the body of a king, Kṛṣṇa will give it; if one follows the prescribed method, one will get the body of a king. And if one wants the body of a hog so that one may eat stool, Kṛṣṇa will give one that kind of body also. But now, in the human form of life, one should understand, "Everything belongs to Kṛṣṇa, so why am I hankering to satisfy this body which is supposedly mine? Rather, now that I have this body, let me serve Kṛṣṇa." This is intelligence, and this is *bhakti.*

Hṛṣīkeṇa hṛṣīkeśa-sevanaṁ bhaktir ucyate: bhakti means to use *hṛṣīka,* the senses, in the service of Hṛṣīkeśa, Kṛṣṇa, the master of the senses (*tvayā hṛṣīkeśena hṛdi sthitasya yathā karomi*). Because I wanted some sense gratification, forgetting that everything actually belongs to Kṛṣṇa, I have been given this body, which is a facility for sense gratification. But the senses have no value without Kṛṣṇa, and therefore the natural conclusion is that the senses belong to Kṛṣṇa. Therefore, since I have these senses, why not use them for Kṛṣṇa's satisfaction? This is *bhakti.*

22

Beauty in Kṛṣṇa's Presence

neyaṁ śobhiṣyate tatra
yathedānīṁ gadādhara
tvat-padair aṅkitā bhāti
sva-lakṣaṇa-vilakṣitaiḥ

O Gadādhara [Kṛṣṇa], our kingdom is now being marked by the impressions of Your feet, and therefore it appears beautiful. But when You leave, it will no longer be so.

Śrīmad-Bhāgavatam 1.8.39

There are certain particular marks on the feet of the Lord which distinguish the Lord from others. The marks of a flag, thunderbolt, and instrument to drive an elephant, and also an umbrella, lotus, disc, etc., are on the bottom of the Lord's feet. These marks are impressed upon the soft dust of the land where the Lord traverses. The land of Hastināpura was thus marked while Lord Śrī Kṛṣṇa was there with the Pāṇḍavas, and the kingdom of the Pāṇḍavas thus flourished by such auspicious signs. Kuntīdevī points out these distinguished features and is afraid of ill luck in the absence of the Lord.

In the *cāṇakya-śloka,* the instructions of the great moralist Cāṇakya Paṇḍita, there is this very nice verse:

pṛthivī-bhūṣaṇaṁ rājā
nārīṇāṁ bhūṣaṇaṁ patiḥ
śarvarī-bhūṣaṇaṁ candro
vidyā sarvasya bhūṣaṇam

Everything looks beautiful when one is intimately related with it. The sky, for example, becomes beautiful in relationship with the moon. The sky is always present, but on the full-moon night, when the moon and stars shine brilliantly, it looks very nice. Similarly, the state looks very well if there is a good government, with a good king or president. Then everyone is happy, and everything goes on well. Also, although girls are naturally beautiful, a girl looks especially beautiful when she has a husband. *Vidyā sarvasya bhūṣaṇam:* but if a person, however ugly, is a learned scholar, that is his beauty. Similarly, everything will look beautiful when Kṛṣṇa is present.

Therefore Kuntīdevī thinks, "As long as Kṛṣṇa is with us, everything in our kingdom and our capital, Hastināpura, is beautiful. But when Kṛṣṇa is absent our kingdom will not be beautiful." She says, "Kṛṣṇa, You are now walking in our kingdom, and the impressions of Your footprints are making everything beautiful. There is sufficient water and fruit, and everything looks beautiful, but when You leave us it will not look beautiful."

It is not that this applied only when Kṛṣṇa was present and Kuntī was speaking. Rather, the truth is always the same. Despite the advancement of our civilization, if we cannot bring Kṛṣṇa and Kṛṣṇa consciousness into the center of everything, our civilization will never become beautiful. Those who have joined the Kṛṣṇa consciousness movement were beautiful before they joined, but now that they have become Kṛṣṇa conscious they look especially beautiful. Therefore the newspapers often describe the devotees as "bright-faced." Their countrymen remark, "How joyful and beautiful these boys and girls have become." At the present time in America, many of the younger generation are confused and hopeless, and therefore they appear morose and black-faced. Why? Because they are missing the point; they have no aim in life. But the devotees, the Kṛṣṇaites, look very beautiful because of the presence of Kṛṣṇa.

Therefore, what was a fact five thousand years ago, during the time of the Pāṇḍavas, is still a fact now. With Kṛṣṇa in the center, everything becomes beautiful, and Kṛṣṇa can become the center at any time. Kṛṣṇa is always present, and we simply have to invite Him, "My Lord, please come and be in the center." That's all. To give the same example I have given before, zero has no value, but if we bring the number one and place it by the side of zero, the zero becomes ten. So one need not stop whatever one is doing. We never say, "Stop everything material." One simply has to add Kṛṣṇa.

Of course, we have to give up anything which is against Kṛṣṇa consciousness. It is not that because we do not stop material duties, we should not stop meat-eating. We must stop it, for this is contrary to advancement in Kṛṣṇa consciousness. One cannot commit sinful activities and at the same time advance in Kṛṣṇa consciousness. But Kṛṣṇa says, *ahaṁ tvāṁ sarva-pāpebhyo mokṣayiṣyāmi:* "Surrender unto Me, and I shall rescue you by giving you liberation from all kinds of sinful reactions."

Every one of us, life after life, is knowingly or unknowingly committing sinful activities. I may knowingly kill an animal, and that is certainly sinful, but even if I do it unknowingly, it is also sinful. While walking on the street we unknowingly kill so many ants, and in the course of our other ordinary dealings – while cooking, while taking water, while using a mortar and pestle to crush spices – we kill so many living beings. Unless we remain Kṛṣṇa conscious, we are liable to be punished for all these unknowingly committed sinful acts.

If a child unknowingly touches fire, does it mean that the fire will excuse the child and not burn? No. Nature's law is so strict, so stringent, that there is no question of an excuse. Even in ordinary law, ignorance is no excuse. If we go to court and say, "I did not know that this action was criminal," this plea does not mean that we shall be excused. Similarly, ignorance is no excuse for transgressing nature's laws. Therefore, if we actually want to be free from the reactions of sinful life, we must be Kṛṣṇa conscious, for then Kṛṣṇa will free us from all sinful reactions. It is therefore recommended, *kīrtanīyaḥ sadā hariḥ* – one should always chant Hare Kṛṣṇa, Hare Kṛṣṇa, Kṛṣṇa Kṛṣṇa, Hare Hare/ Hare Rāma, Hare Rāma, Rāma Rāma, Hare Hare, so that Kṛṣṇa will save us.

We should always keep Kṛṣṇa within our minds, for Kṛṣṇa is like the sun. This is the motto of our *Back to Godhead* magazine:

> *kṛṣṇa—sūrya-sama; māyā haya andhakāra*
> *yāhāṅ kṛṣṇa, tāhāṅ nāhi māyāra adhikāra*
> (*Caitanya-caritāmṛta, Madhya* 22.31)

Kṛṣṇa is just like the brilliant sun, and *māyā,* ignorance, is just like darkness. When the sun is present, there cannot be darkness. So if we keep ourselves in Kṛṣṇa consciousness always, we cannot be influenced by the darkness of ignorance; rather, we shall always walk very freely in the bright sunshine of Kṛṣṇa. Kuntīdevī therefore prays that Kṛṣṇa continue to be present with her and the Pāṇḍavas.

In fact, however, Kṛṣṇa was not leaving the Pāṇḍavas, just as He never left Vṛndāvana. In the *śāstra,* the Vedic literature, it is said, *vṛndāvanaṁ parityajya padam ekaṁ na gacchati:* Kṛṣṇa never goes even one step from Vṛndāvana. He is so much attached to Vṛndāvana. How is it, then, that we see that Kṛṣṇa left Vṛndāvana and went to Mathurā and then far away to Hastināpura and did not return for many years? Actually, Kṛṣṇa did not leave, for all the inhabitants of Vṛndāvana, after Kṛṣṇa left, were always thinking of Him and crying. The only engagement of mother Yaśodā, Nanda Mahārāja, Rādhārāṇī, and all the *gopīs,* cows, calves, and cowherd boys was to think of Kṛṣṇa and cry, and in this way they felt Kṛṣṇa to be present, because Kṛṣṇa's presence can be felt more strongly in separation from Him. That is Caitanya Mahāprabhu's teaching: to love Kṛṣṇa in separation. *Śūnyāyitaṁ jagat sarvaṁ govinda-viraheṇa me.* Caitanya Mahāprabhu thought, "Everything is vacant without Govinda, without Kṛṣṇa." Everything was vacant, but Kṛṣṇa consciousness was there.

When we see everything as nothing, but have only Kṛṣṇa consciousness, we shall have attained the highest perfection. Therefore the *gopīs* are so exalted. Having attained this perfection, they could not forget Kṛṣṇa even for a single moment. When Kṛṣṇa went to the forest with His cows and calves, the minds of the *gopīs* at home were disturbed. "Oh, Kṛṣṇa is walking barefoot," they thought. "There are so many stones and nails on the path, and they must be pricking Kṛṣṇa's lotus feet, which are so soft that we think our breasts hard when Kṛṣṇa puts His lotus feet upon them." Thus they would cry, absorbed in these thoughts. The *gopīs* were so anxious to see Kṛṣṇa back home in the evening that they would stand on the path, looking to see Kṛṣṇa returning with His calves and cows. This is Kṛṣṇa consciousness.

Kṛṣṇa cannot be absent from a devotee when the devotee is intensely absorbed in Kṛṣṇa thought. Here Kuntīdevī is very much anxious, thinking that Kṛṣṇa will be absent, but the actual effect of Kṛṣṇa's physical absence is that He becomes more intensely present within the mind of the devotee. Therefore Caitanya Mahāprabhu, by the example of His actual life, taught *vipralambha-sevā,* service of Kṛṣṇa in separation. Tears would come from His eyes like torrents of rain, for He would feel everything to be vacant for want of Kṛṣṇa.

There are two stages of meeting Kṛṣṇa. Being personally present with Kṛṣṇa, personally meeting Him, personally talking with Him, and personally embracing Him is called *sambhoga,* but there is another way to be with Kṛṣṇa – in separation from Him – and this is called *vipralambha.* A devotee can benefit from Kṛṣṇa's association in both ways.

Because we are now in the material world, we do not see Kṛṣṇa directly. Nonetheless, we can see Him indirectly. For example, if one sees the Pacific Ocean one can remember Kṛṣṇa immediately, if one is advanced in spiritual life. This is called meditation. One may think, "The Pacific Ocean is such a vast mass of water, with many large waves, but although I am standing only a few yards from it, I am confident that I am safe, however powerful this ocean may be and however fearful its waves. I am sure that it will not go beyond its limits. How is this happening? By the order of Kṛṣṇa. Kṛṣṇa orders, 'My dear Pacific Ocean, you may be very big and powerful, but you cannot come beyond this line.'" In this way one can immediately remember Kṛṣṇa, or God, who is so powerful that even the Pacific Ocean abides by His order. In this way one can think of Kṛṣṇa, and that is Kṛṣṇa consciousness.

Similarly, when one sees the sunrise one can immediately remember Kṛṣṇa, for Kṛṣṇa says in *Bhagavad-gītā* (7.8), *prabhāsmi śaśi-sūryayoḥ:* "I am the shining of the sun and the moon." If one has learned how to see Kṛṣṇa, one can see Him in the sunshine. Our scientists have not created the sun, and although they may juggle words, it is beyond their ability to know what the sun actually is. But the *Vedānta-sūtra* (1.1.3) says, *śāstra-yonitvāt:* one can know everything through the *śāstra,* the Vedic literature. For example, if one studies the Vedic literature one can know what the sun is, for the sun is described in the *Brahma-saṁhitā* (5.52):

yac-cakṣur eṣa savitā sakala-grahāṇāṁ
rājā samasta-sura-mūrtir aśeṣa-tejāḥ
yasyājñayā bhramati sambhṛta-kāla-cakro
govindam ādi-puruṣaṁ tam ahaṁ bhajāmi

This verse describes the sun as the eye of all the planets, and if one meditates upon this one can understand that this is a fact, for at night, before the sun rises, one cannot see. The sun is also described as the eye of the Lord. The sun is one of His eyes, and the moon is the other. In the *Upaniṣads,* therefore, it is said that only when Kṛṣṇa sees can we see. The sun is also described as *aśeṣa-tejāḥ,* unlimitedly hot. And what is its function? *Yasyājñayā bhramati sambhṛta-kāla-cakraḥ.* The sun has its orbit. God has ordered the sun, "You just travel within this orbit, and not anywhere else." The scientists say that if the sun were to move a little to one side the whole universe would be ablaze, and if it moved to the other side the whole universe would freeze. But by the order of the Supreme it does not move even one ten-thousandth of an inch from where it should be. It always rises exactly at the correct time. Why? There must be some discipline, some obedience, some order. The *Brahma-saṁhitā* therefore says, *yasyājñayā bhramati sambhṛta-kāla-cakro govindam ādi-puruṣaṁ tam ahaṁ bhajāmi:* "I worship that original person, by whose order the sun moves in its orbit. It is He who gives direction even to the sun, the ocean, and the moon. Everything takes place under His order."

So where is the difficulty in understanding God? There is no difficulty. If one is actually sane, if one has a brain that is not made of stool, one can understand God at every step. The Lord says:

raso 'ham apsu kaunteya
prabhāsmi śaśi-sūryayoḥ
praṇavaḥ sarva-vedeṣu
śabdaḥ khe pauruṣaṁ nṛṣu

"O son of Kuntī [Arjuna], I am the taste of water, the light of the sun and the moon, the syllable *oṁ* in the Vedic *mantras;* I am the sound in ether and ability in man." (*Bhagavad-gītā* 7.8) Why then do people say, "I have not seen God"? Why don't they see God as God directs them to see Him? Why do they manufacture their own way? One cannot see God by one's own way. That is not possible. If one tries to do so, one will always remain blind. At the present moment so-called philosophers and scientists are trying to see God in their own way, but that is not possible. One has to see God by God's way. Then one can see Him. If I want to see the President of the United States, can I see him in my own way? If not, then how can I expect to see God in my own way? Is it not rascaldom? I cannot see even an ordinary man in an important position in my own way; I have to make an appointment with his secretary and make the other appropriate arrangements. But although God is so much greater than ordinary men, rascals support the view that one can see God in one's own way. "As many ways as you invent," they say, "they are all bona fide." This is rascaldom. The world is full of rascals and fools, and therefore God consciousness, Kṛṣṇa consciousness, has become a vague idea. Otherwise, if one wants to see God, if one wants Him to be always present, as Kuntīdevī is requesting that He be, one can keep God always within one's heart.

We simply have to apply our mind and senses in Kṛṣṇa consciousness, as done by Mahārāja Ambarīṣa. *Sa vai manaḥ kṛṣṇa-padāravindayor vacāṁsi vaikuṇṭha-guṇānuvarṇane* (*Bhāgavatam* 9.4.18). First we must fix our minds on the lotus feet of Kṛṣṇa, for the mind is the center of all sensory activities. If the mind were absent, in spite of having eyes we could not see, and in spite of having ears we could not hear. Therefore the mind is considered the eleventh sense. There are ten senses – five working senses and five knowledge-acquiring senses, and the center of the senses is the mind. The *Bhagavad-gītā* (3.42) says:

indriyāṇi parāṇy āhur
indriyebhyaḥ paraṁ manaḥ
manasas tu parā buddhir
yo buddheḥ paratas tu saḥ

In this verse Kṛṣṇa explains that although we consider the senses to be very prominent, beyond the senses is something superior – the mind – beyond the mind is the intelligence, and beyond the intelligence is the soul.

How can we appreciate the existence of the soul if we cannot understand even the psychological movements of the mind? Beyond the mind is the intelligence, and by speculation one can at the utmost approach the intellectual platform. But to understand the soul and God, one must go beyond the intellectual platform. It is possible to understand everything, but we must gain understanding through the right channel. Therefore the Vedic injunction is:

tad-vijñānārthaṁ sa gurum evābhigacchet
samit-pāṇiḥ śrotriyaṁ brahma-niṣṭham

"If one is actually serious about understanding supernatural, transcendental subject matters, one must approach a bona fide spiritual master." (*Muṇḍaka Upaniṣad* 1.2.12)

23
Natural Prosperity

ime jana-padāḥ sv-ṛddhāḥ
supakvauṣadhi-vīrudhaḥ
vanādri-nady-udanvanto
hy edhante tava vīkṣitaiḥ

All these cities and villages are flourishing in all respects because the herbs and grains are in abundance, the trees are full of fruits, the rivers are flowing, the hills are full of minerals, and the oceans full of wealth. And this is all due to Your glancing over them.

Śrīmad-Bhāgavatam 1.8.40

Human prosperity flourishes by natural gifts and not by gigantic industrial enterprises. The gigantic industrial enterprises are products of a godless civilization, and they cause the destruction of the noble aims of human life. The more we go on increasing such troublesome industries to squeeze out the vital energy of the human being, the more there will be unrest and dissatisfaction of the people in general, although a few only can live lavishly by exploitation. The natural gifts such as grains and vegetables, fruits, rivers, the hills of jewels and minerals, and the seas full of pearls are supplied by the order of the Supreme, and as He desires, material nature produces them in abundance or restricts them at times. The natural law is that the human being may take advantage of these godly gifts by nature and satisfactorily flourish on them without being captivated by the exploitative motive of lording it over material nature. The more we attempt to exploit material nature according to our whims of enjoyment, the more we shall become entrapped by the reaction of such exploitative attempts. If we have sufficient grains, fruits, vegetables, and herbs, then what is the necessity of running a slaughterhouse and killing poor animals? A man need not kill an animal if he has sufficient grains and vegetables to eat. The flow of river waters fertilizes the fields, and there is more than what we need. Minerals are produced in the hills, and the jewels in the ocean. If the human civilization has sufficient grains, minerals, jewels, water, milk, etc., then why should we hanker after terrible industrial enterprises at the cost of the labor of some unfortunate men? But all these natural gifts are dependent on the mercy of the Lord. What we need, therefore, is to be obedient to the laws of the Lord and achieve the perfection of human life by devotional service. The indications by Kuntīdevī are just to the point. She desires that God's mercy be bestowed upon them so that natural prosperity be maintained by His grace.

Kuntīdevī mentions that the grains are abundant, the trees full of fruits, the rivers flowing nicely, the hills full of minerals, and the oceans full of wealth, but she never mentions that industry and slaughterhouses are flourishing, for such things are nonsense that men have developed to create problems.

If we depend on God's creation, there will be no scarcity, but simply *ānanda,* bliss. God's creation provides sufficient grains and grass, and while we eat the grains and fruits, the animals like the cows will eat the grass. The bulls will help us produce grains, and they will take only a little, being satisfied with what we throw away. If we take fruit and throw away the skin, the animal will be satisfied with the skin. In this way, with Kṛṣṇa in the center, there can be full cooperation between the trees, animals, human beings, and all living entities. This is Vedic civilization, a civilization of Kṛṣṇa consciousness.

Kuntīdevī prays to the Lord, "This prosperity is due to Your glance." When we sit in the temple of Kṛṣṇa, Kṛṣṇa glances over us, and everything is nice. When sincere souls try to become Kṛṣṇa's devotees, Kṛṣṇa very kindly comes before them in His full opulence and glances upon them, and they become happy and beautiful.

Similarly, the whole material creation is due to Kṛṣṇa's glance (*sa aikṣata*). In the *Vedas* it is said that He glanced over matter, thus agitating it. A woman in touch with a man becomes agitated and becomes pregnant and then gives birth to children. The whole creation follows a similar process. Simply by Kṛṣṇa's glance, matter becomes agitated and then becomes pregnant and gives birth to the living entities. It is simply by His glance that plants, trees, animals, and all other living beings come forth. How is this possible? None of us can say, "Simply by glancing over my wife, I can make her pregnant." But although this is impossible for us, it is not impossible for Kṛṣṇa. The *Brahma-saṁhitā* (5.32) says, *aṅgāni yasya sakalendriya-vṛttimanti:* every part of Kṛṣṇa's body has all the capabilities of the other parts. With our eyes we can only see, but Kṛṣṇa, merely by seeing, can make others pregnant. There is no need of sex, for simply by glancing, Kṛṣṇa can create pregnancy.

In *Bhagavad-gītā* (9.10) Lord Kṛṣṇa says, *mayādhyakṣeṇa prakṛtiḥ sūyate sa-carācaram:* "By My supervision, material nature gives birth to all moving and nonmoving beings." The word *akṣa* means "eyes," so *akṣeṇa* indicates that all living entities take birth because of the Lord's glance. There are two kinds of living entities – the moving beings, like insects, animals, and human beings, and the nonmoving beings, like trees and plants. In Sanskrit these two kinds of living entities are called *sthāvara-jaṅgama,* and they both come forth from material nature.

Of course, what comes from material nature is not the life, but the body. The living entities accept particular types of bodies from material nature, just as a child takes its body from its mother. For ten months the child's body develops from the blood and nutrients of the mother's body, but the child is a living entity, not matter. It is the living entity that has taken shelter in the womb of the mother, who then supplies the ingredients for that living entity's body. This is nature's way. The mother may not know how from her body another body has been created, but when the body of the child is fit, the child takes birth.

It is not that the living entity takes birth. As stated in *Bhagavad-gītā* (2.20), *na jāyate mriyate vā:* the living entity neither takes birth nor dies. That which does not take birth does not die; death is meant for that which has been created, and that which is not created has no death. The *Gītā* says, *na jāyate mriyate vā kadācit.* The word *kadācit* means "at any time." At no time does the living entity actually take birth. Although we may see that a child is born, actually it is not born. *Nityaḥ śāśvato 'yaṁ purāṇaḥ.* The living entity is eternal (*śāśvata*), always existing, and very, very old (*purāṇa*). *Na hanyate hanyamāne śarīre:* don't think that when the body is destroyed the living entity will be destroyed; no, the living entity will continue to exist.

A scientist friend was asking me, "What is the proof of eternity?" Kṛṣṇa says, *na hanyate hanyamāne śarīre:* "The soul is not killed when the body is killed." This statement in itself is proof. This type of proof is called *śruti,* the proof established by that which is heard through the disciplic succession from the Supreme. One form of proof is proof by logic (*nyāya-prasthāna*). One can get knowledge by logic, arguments, and philosophical research. But another form of proof is *śruti,* proof established by hearing from authorities. A third form of proof is *smṛti,* proof established by statements derived from the *śruti.* The *Bhagavad-gītā* and the *Purāṇas* are *smṛti,* the *Upaniṣads* are *śruti,* and the *Vedānta* is *nyāya.* Of these three the *śruti-prasthāna,* or the evidence from the *śruti,* is especially important.

Pratyakṣa, the process of receiving knowledge through direct perception, has no value, because our senses are all imperfect. For example, every day we see the sun to be just like a small disc, perhaps twelve inches in diameter, but in fact it is a hundred times larger than the earth. So what is the value of our direct perception through our eyes? We have so many senses through which we can experience knowledge – the eyes, the ears, the nose, and so on – but because these senses are imperfect, whatever knowledge we get by exercising these senses is also imperfect. Because scientists try to understand things by exercising their imperfect senses, their conclusions are always imperfect. Svarūpa Dāmodara, a scientist among our disciples, inquired from a fellow scientist who says that life comes from matter, "If I give you the chemicals with which to produce life, will you be able to produce it?" The scientist replied, "That I do not know." This is imperfect knowledge. If you do not know, then your knowledge is imperfect. Why then have you become a teacher? That is cheating. Our contention is that to become perfect one must take lessons from the perfect.

Kṛṣṇa is perfect, so we take knowledge from Him. Kṛṣṇa says, *na hanyate hanyamāne śarīre:* "The soul does not die when the body dies." Therefore this understanding that the soul is eternal is perfect.

Kuntīdevī says, *ime jana-padāḥ sv-ṛddhāḥ supakvauṣadhi-vīrudhaḥ:* "The grains are abundant, the trees full of fruits, the rivers flowing, the hills full of minerals, and the ocean full of wealth." What more should one want? The oyster produces pearls, and formerly people decorated their bodies with pearls, valuable stones, silk, gold, and silver. But where are those things now? Now, with the advancement of civilization, there are so many beautiful girls who have no ornaments of gold, pearls, or jewels, but only plastic bangles. So what is the use of industry and slaughterhouses?

By God's arrangement one can have enough food grains, enough milk, enough fruits and vegetables, and nice clear river water. But now I have seen, while traveling in Europe, that all the rivers there have become nasty. In Germany, in France, and also in Russia and America I have seen that the rivers are nasty. By nature's way the water in the ocean is kept clear like crystal, and the same water is transferred to the rivers, but without salt, so that one may take nice water from the river. This is nature's way, and nature's way means Kṛṣṇa's way. So what is the use of constructing huge waterworks to supply water?

Nature has already given us everything. If we want wealth we may collect pearls and become rich; there is no need to become rich by starting some huge factory to produce auto bodies. By such industrial enterprises we have simply created troubles. Otherwise, we need only depend on Kṛṣṇa and Kṛṣṇa's mercy, because by Kṛṣṇa's glance (*tava vīkṣitaiḥ*), everything is set right. So if we simply plead for Kṛṣṇa's glance, there will be no question of scarcity or need. Everything will be complete. The idea of the Kṛṣṇa consciousness movement, therefore, is to depend on nature's gifts and the grace of Kṛṣṇa.

People say that the population is increasing, and therefore they are checking this by artificial means. Why? The birds and bees are increasing their populations and have no contraceptives, but are they in need of food? Do we ever see birds or animals dying for want of food? Perhaps in the city, although not very often. But if we go to the jungle we shall see that all the elephants, lions, tigers, and other animals are very stout and strong. Who is supplying them food? Some of them are vegetarians, and some of them are nonvegetarians, but none of them are in want of food.

Of course, by nature's way the tiger, being a nonvegetarian, does not get food every day. After all, who will face a tiger to become its food? Who will say to the tiger, "Sir, I am a philanthropist and have come to you to give you food, so take my body"? No one. Therefore the tiger has difficulty finding food. And as soon as the tiger is out, there is an animal that follows it and makes a sound like "*fayo, fayo,*" so that the other animals will know, "Now the tiger is out." So by nature's way the tiger has difficulty, but still Kṛṣṇa supplies it food. After about a week, the tiger will get the chance to catch an animal, and because it does not get fresh food daily, it will keep the carcass in some bush and eat a little at a time. Since the tiger is very powerful, people want to become like a lion or a tiger, but that is not a very good proposition, because if one actually becomes like a tiger one won't get food daily, but will have to search for food with great labor. If one becomes a vegetarian, however, one will get food every day. The food for a vegetarian is available everywhere.

Now in every city there are slaughterhouses, but does this mean that the slaughterhouses can supply enough so that one can live by eating only meat? No, there will not be an adequate supply. Even meat-eaters have to eat grains, fruits, and vegetables along with their slice of meat. Still, for that daily slice of meat they kill so many poor animals. How sinful this is. If people commit such sinful activities, how can they be happy? This killing should not be done, and therefore people are unhappy. But if one becomes Kṛṣṇa conscious and simply depends on Kṛṣṇa's glance (*tava vīkṣitaiḥ*), Kṛṣṇa will supply everything, and there will be no question of scarcity.

Sometimes there appears to be scarcity, and sometimes we find that grains and fruits are produced in such a huge quantity that people cannot finish eating them. So this is a question of Kṛṣṇa's glance. If Kṛṣṇa likes, He can produce a huge quantity of grains, fruits, and vegetables, but if Kṛṣṇa desires to restrict the supply, what good will meat do? You may eat me, or I may eat you, but that will not solve the problem.

For real peace and tranquillity and a sufficient supply of milk, water, and everything else we need, we simply have to depend on Kṛṣṇa. This is what Bhaktivinoda Ṭhākura teaches us when he says, *mārabi rākhabi – yo icchā tohārā:* "My dear Lord, I simply surrender unto You and depend on You. Now if You like You may kill me, or else You may give me protection." And Kṛṣṇa says in reply, "Yes. *Sarva-dharmān parityajya mām ekaṁ śaraṇaṁ vraja:* simply surrender exclusively unto Me." He does not say, "Yes, depend on Me, and also depend on your slaughterhouses and factories." No. He says, "Depend only on Me. *Ahaṁ tvāṁ sarva-pāpebhyo mokṣayiṣyāmi:* I will rescue you from the results of your sinful activities."

Because we have lived so many years without being Kṛṣṇa conscious, we have lived only a sinful life, but Kṛṣṇa assures us that as soon as one surrenders to Him He immediately squares all accounts and puts an end to all one's sinful activities so that one may begin a new life. When we initiate disciples we therefore tell them, "Now the account is squared. Now don't commit sinful activities any more."

One should not think that because the holy name of Kṛṣṇa can nullify sinful activities, one may commit a little sinful activity and chant Hare Kṛṣṇa to nullify it. That is the greatest offense (*nāmno balād yasya hi pāpa-buddhiḥ*). The members of some religious orders go to church and confess their sins, but then they again commit the same sinful activities. What then is the value of their confession? One may confess, "My Lord, out of my ignorance I committed this sin," but one should not plan, "I shall commit sinful activities and then go to church and confess them, and then the sins will be nullified, and I can begin a new chapter of sinful life." Similarly, one should not knowingly take advantage of the chanting of the Hare Kṛṣṇa *mantra* to nullify sinful activities so that one may then begin sinful acts again. We should be very careful. Before taking initiation, one promises to have no illicit sex, no intoxicants, no gambling, and no meat-eating, and this vow one should strictly follow. Then one will be clean. If one keeps oneself clean in this way and always engages in devotional service, his life will be a success, and there will be no scarcity of anything he wants.

24

Cutting Off Ties of Affection

atha viśveśa viśvātman
viśva-mūrte svakeṣu me
sneha-pāśam imaṁ chindhi
dṛḍhaṁ pāṇḍuṣu vṛṣṇiṣu

O Lord of the universe, soul of the universe, O personality of the form of the universe, please, therefore, sever my tie of affection for my kinsmen, the Pāṇḍavas and the Vṛṣṇis.

Śrīmad-Bhāgavatam 1.8.41

A pure devotee of the Lord is ashamed to ask anything in self-interest from the Lord. But the householders are sometimes obliged to ask favors from the Lord, being bound by the tie of family affection. Śrīmatī Kuntīdevī was conscious of this fact, and therefore she prayed to the Lord to cut off the affectionate tie from her own kinsmen, the Pāṇḍavas and the Vṛṣṇis. The Pāṇḍavas are her own sons, and the Vṛṣṇis are the members of her paternal family. Kṛṣṇa was equally related to both families. Both the families required the Lord's help because both were dependent devotees of the Lord. Śrīmatī Kuntīdevī wished Śrī Kṛṣṇa to remain with her sons, the Pāṇḍavas, but by His doing so her paternal house would be bereft of the benefit. All these partialities troubled the mind of Kuntī, and therefore she desired to cut off the affectionate tie.

A pure devotee cuts off the limited ties of affection for his family and widens his activities of devotional service for all forgotten souls. The typical example is the band of six Gosvāmīs, who followed the path of Lord Caitanya. All of them belonged to the most enlightened and cultured rich families of the higher castes, but for the benefit of the mass of population they left their comfortable homes and became mendicants. To cut off all family affection means to broaden the field of activities. Without doing this, no one can be qualified as a *brāhmaṇa,* a king, a public leader, or a devotee of the Lord. The Personality of Godhead, as an ideal king, showed this by example. Śrī Rāmacandra cut off the tie of affection for His beloved wife to manifest the qualities of an ideal king.

Such personalities as a *brāhmaṇa,* a devotee, a king, or a public leader must be very broad-minded in discharging their respective duties. Śrīmatī Kuntīdevī was conscious of this fact, and being weak she prayed to be free from such bondage of family affection. The Lord is addressed as the Lord of the universe, or the Lord of the universal mind, indicating His all-powerful ability to cut the hard knot of family affection. Therefore, it is sometimes experienced that the Lord, out of His special affinity toward a weak devotee, breaks the family affection by force of circumstances arranged by His all-powerful energy. By doing so He causes the devotee to become completely dependent on Him and thus clears the path for his going back to Godhead.

Kuntī was the daughter of the Vṛṣṇi family and the wife and mother of the Pāṇḍava family. Generally a woman has affection for both her father's family and husband's family, and therefore Kuntī prays to Kṛṣṇa, "I am a woman, and women are generally attached to their families, so kindly cut off my attachment so that I may be thoroughly attached to You. Without You, both families are zero. I am falsely attached to these families, but my real purpose in life is to be attached to You." This is *bhakti.*

Bhakti involves becoming free from the attachments of this material world and becoming attached instead to Kṛṣṇa. One cannot become unattached, for one must be attached to something, but in order to become attached to Kṛṣṇa or enter into the devotional service of the Lord, one has to become detached from material affection.

People ordinarily go to Kṛṣṇa to maintain their attachment to this material world. "O God," they pray, "give us our daily bread." They have attachment to this material world, and to live in this material world they pray for supplies of material things so that they can maintain their status quo. This is called material attachment. Although in one sense, of course, it is good that people go to God to secure their material position, that is not actually desirable. Rather than worship God to increase one's opulence in the material world, one should become free from material attachment. For *bhakti-yoga,* therefore, we should be detached.

Our suffering is due to our attachment. Because we are materially attached, we desire so many material things, and therefore Kṛṣṇa gives us the opportunity to enjoy whatever material facilities we want. Of course, one must deserve these facilities. First deserve, then desire. Suppose I want to become king. I must have pious activities behind me so that I can become king.

Kṛṣṇa can give us whatever we want, even *mukti,* liberation, but *bhakti* is a special consideration because when He gives someone *bhakti* He becomes purchased by the *bhakta* and becomes a tool in the hands of the *bhakta,* even though He is the supreme powerful. Rādhārāṇī, the symbol of the topmost *bhakti,* is so powerful that She has purchased Kṛṣṇa. Therefore Vaiṣṇavas take shelter of the lotus feet of Rādhārāṇī, for if She recommends, "Oh, here is a nice devotee," Kṛṣṇa must accept him.

To become a devotee of the Lord, one must be completely cleansed of all material attachment. This qualification is called *vairāgya.*

Upon becoming a student of Śrī Caitanya Mahāprabhu, Sārvabhauma Bhaṭṭācārya wrote one hundred verses praising Him. Two of those verses are mentioned in the *Caitanya-caritāmṛta,* and one of them is this statement:

> *vairāgya-vidyā-nija-bhakti-yoga-*
> *śikṣārtham ekaḥ puruṣaḥ purāṇaḥ*
> *śrī-kṛṣṇa-caitanya-śarīra-dhārī*
> *kṛpāmbudhir yas tam ahaṁ prapadye*

"Let me take shelter of the Supreme Personality of Godhead, Śrī Kṛṣṇa, who has descended in the form of Lord Caitanya Mahāprabhu to teach us real knowledge, His devotional service, and detachment from whatever does not foster Kṛṣṇa consciousness. He has descended because He is an ocean of transcendental mercy. Let me surrender unto His lotus feet." (*Caitanya-caritāmṛta, Madhya* 6.254) Sārvabhauma Bhaṭṭācārya thus offered his prayer to the Supreme Personality of Godhead, who had now assumed the form of Caitanya Mahāprabhu just to teach people how to develop knowledge, become detached, and become pure devotees of Kṛṣṇa.

Although when Caitanya Mahāprabhu was only twenty-four or twenty-five years old He had a lovable, beautiful wife and a devoted, affectionate mother, He gave up everything and took *sannyāsa,* the renounced order of life. When Caitanya Mahāprabhu was a *gṛhastha,* a householder, He was so much honored that merely by the direction of His finger He was able to enlist thousands of people to join Him in a civil disobedience movement. In Nadia, the city where He lived, His position was very respectable, and physically He was very beautiful. Yet He gave up His young, faithful, beautiful wife, His affectionate mother, His position, and everything else. This is called *vairāgya,* renunciation.

If someone who has nothing to possess says, "I have renounced everything," what is the meaning of his renunciation? But if one has something and then renounces it, his renunciation is meaningful. So Caitanya Mahāprabhu's renunciation is unique. No one else could give up such a happy home, such honor, and such affection from mother, wife, friends, and students. Even Advaita Prabhu, although the age of

Caitanya Mahāprabhu's father, honored Caitanya Mahāprabhu. Yet still Śrī Caitanya Mahāprabhu gave up everything. Why? Just to teach us (*āpani ācari, prabhu jīvere śikhāya*). He personally taught the whole world how one must detach oneself and become a devotee of Kṛṣṇa. Therefore when Rūpa Gosvāmī resigned his post as a government minister and met Caitanya Mahāprabhu at Prayāga, he fell flat before Śrī Caitanya Mahāprabhu and offered obeisances with this prayer:

namo mahā-vadanyāya
kṛṣṇa-prema-pradāya te
kṛṣṇāya kṛṣṇa-caitanya-
nāmne gaura-tviṣe namaḥ

"You are most magnanimous," he prayed, "for You are distributing love of Kṛṣṇa."

Love of Kṛṣṇa is not an easy thing to obtain, because by this love one can purchase Kṛṣṇa, but Caitanya Mahāprabhu distributed this love of Kṛṣṇa to anyone and everyone, even to the two drunkards Jagāi and Mādhāi. Narottama dāsa Ṭhākura has therefore sung:

dīna-hīna yata chila hari-nāme uddharila,
tā'ra sākṣī jagāi-mādhāi

"Caitanya Mahāprabhu is so magnanimous that He delivered all kinds of sinful men simply by allowing them to chant the Hare Kṛṣṇa *mantra*. The evidence of this is Jagāi and Mādhāi." At that time, of course, there were two Jagāis and Mādhāis, but at the present moment, by the grace of Caitanya Mahāprabhu and His process of teaching, so many Jagāis and Mādhāis are being delivered. If Caitanya Mahāprabhu is pleased, He can give *kṛṣṇa-prema,* love of Kṛṣṇa, to anyone, regardless of that person's qualification. If a person is giving charity, he can select anyone to take it.

Without the mercy of Caitanya Mahāprabhu, understanding Kṛṣṇa is very, very difficult. *Manuṣyāṇāṁ sahasreṣu kaścid yatati siddhaye* (*Bhagavad-gītā* 7.3): out of many millions of people, hardly one tries to make his life spiritually successful. People simply work like animals, not knowing how to make a success of human life. One's human life is successful when one understands Kṛṣṇa; otherwise one remains an animal. Anyone who is not Kṛṣṇa conscious, who does not know who Kṛṣṇa is, is no better than an animal. But Caitanya Mahāprabhu gave this concession to the fallen souls of this age: "Simply chant the Hare Kṛṣṇa *mahā-mantra* and you will be delivered." This is Caitanya Mahāprabhu's special concession (*kīrtanād eva kṛṣṇasya mukta-saṅgaḥ paraṁ vrajet, Bhāgavatam* 12.3.51).

Now, Kuntī was not an ordinary devotee. She had become one of the relatives of Kṛṣṇa, and therefore Kṛṣṇa had come to offer her respects. But still she said, "Kṛṣṇa, I have become attached to two families, my father's family and my husband's family. Kindly help me become detached from these families." Thus she illustrated that one must become detached from society, friendship, and love, all of which will otherwise entangle us.

As long as I think, "I belong to this family," "I belong to this nation," "I belong to this religion," "I belong to this color," and so on, there is no possibility of becoming Kṛṣṇa conscious. As long as one thinks that one is American, Indian, or African, that one belongs to this family or that family, or that one is the father, mother, husband, or wife of this or that person, one is attached to material designations. I am spirit soul, and all these attachments belong to the body, but I am not this body. This is the essence of understanding. If I am not this body, then whose father or whose mother am I? The supreme father and mother is Kṛṣṇa. We are simply playing the parts of father, mother, sister, or brother, as if on stage. *Māyā,* the material nature, is causing us to dance, telling us, "You are a member of this family and a member of this nation." Thus we are dancing like monkeys.

In the *Bhagavad-gītā* (3.27) it is said:

prakṛteḥ kriyamāṇāni
guṇaiḥ karmāṇi sarvaśaḥ
ahaṅkāra-vimūḍhātmā
kartāham iti manyate

This verse indicates that because the living entity has associated with a certain quality of nature, nature is making him dance according to that quality, and thus one is thinking, "I am this" or "I am that." This information provided in *Bhagavad-gītā* is the basic principle of understanding, and it will give one freedom.

The most essential education is that which enables one to become free from the bodily concept of life, but unfortunately scientists, philosophers, politicians, and other so-called leaders are misleading people so that they become more attached to the body. It is the human life that offers the opportunity to become Kṛṣṇa conscious, but these rascals are stopping that opportunity by alluring people to bodily designations, and therefore they are the greatest enemies of human civilization.

One attains a human body after evolving through 8,400,000 life-forms, from aquatics to plants, and then to trees, insects, birds, beasts, and so on. Now, people do not know what is the next step in evolution, but that is explained in *Bhagavad-gītā* (9.25). *Yānti deva-vratā devān.* As the next step in evolution, one may, if one desires, go to a higher planetary system. Although every night people see so many planets and stars, they do not know what these higher planetary systems are. But from the *śāstra,* the Vedic literature, we can understand that on these higher planetary systems, material comforts are available that are many, many times greater than those on this planet. On this planet we may live for at most one hundred years, but on the higher planetary systems one can live for a lifetime we cannot even calculate. For example, the lifetime of Brahmā, who lives on the highest planet, is stated in *Bhagavad-gītā* (8.17): *sahasra-yuga-paryantam ahar yad brahmaṇo viduḥ.* We cannot calculate even twelve hours of Brahmā with our mathematical figures, but even Brahmā has to die. Even though one may have a long duration of life, no one can live permanently in this material world. Nonetheless, if one prepares oneself one may go to the higher planetary systems, or similarly one may go to the Pitṛlokas. There one may meet one's forefathers, if they have been eligible to go there. Similarly, if one desires, one may also remain here on earth. Or *yānti mad-yājino 'pi mām:* if one becomes a devotee of Kṛṣṇa, one can go to Him.

One may go to hell, one may go to heaven, or one may go back home, back to Godhead, as one likes. Therefore an intelligent person should think, "If I have to prepare for my next life, why not prepare to go back home, back to Godhead?" One's present body will be finished, and then one will have to accept another body. What kind of body one will accept is stated in *Bhagavad-gītā* (14.18). *Ūrdhvaṁ gacchanti sattva-sthāḥ:* those who are in the mode of goodness, avoiding the four principles of sinful life, will live their next life on a higher planetary system. Even if one does not become a pure devotee of the Lord, if one follows the regulative principles for avoiding sinful life one will remain in goodness and get this opportunity. Human life is meant for this purpose. But if we waste our life just living like cats and dogs, eating, sleeping, mating, and defending, then we shall lose this opportunity.

Rascals, however, do not know this. They do not believe that there is a next life. In Russia a professor, Professor Kotovsky, told me, "Swamiji, after this body is finished, everything is finished." He is a big professor, yet still he said that. Such men may pose as scientists and philosophers, but actually they have no knowledge, and they simply mislead others. This is our greatest source of grief, and therefore I have requested the members of the Kṛṣṇa consciousness movement to challenge and defeat these rascals, who are misleading the entire human society. People should not think that the devotees of Kṛṣṇa are mere sentimentalists. On the contrary, the devotees are the greatest philosophers and the greatest scientists.

Kṛṣṇa has two engagements: *paritrāṇāya sādhūnāṁ vināśāya ca duṣkṛtām* – giving protection to the *sādhus,* the devotees, and killing the demons. Kṛṣṇa gave protection to the Pāṇḍavas and Vṛṣṇis because they were devotees, and He also killed demons like Kaṁsa, Aghāsura, and Bakāsura. Of the two engagements, His killing of the demons was His major occupation. If we examine how much time He devoted to killing and how much time He devoted to protecting, we shall find that He devoted more time to killing. Similarly, those who are Kṛṣṇa conscious should also kill – not by weapons but by logic, by reasoning, and by education. If one is a demon, we can use logic and arguments to kill his demoniac propensities and turn him into a devotee, a saintly person. Especially in this present age, Kali-yuga, people are already poverty-stricken, and physical killing is too much for them. They should be killed by argument, reasoning, and scientific spiritual understanding.

Kuntī addresses Kṛṣṇa as *viśveśa,* the Lord of the universe (*viśva* means "universe," and *īśa* means "lord" or "controller"). The universal affairs are going on so nicely, with the sun rising just on time, the seasons changing, and the seasonal fruits and flowers making their appearance. Thus there is no mismanagement. But how are these things going on so nicely if there is no controller? If we see any establishment going on very well, we immediately understand that the manager, director, or controller of the institution is expert. Similarly, if we see the universal affairs going on nicely, we must know that behind them is a good controller. And who is that controller? That controller is Kṛṣṇa, as stated in *Bhagavad-gītā* (*mayādhyakṣeṇa prakṛtiḥ sūyate sa-carācaram*). Therefore Kuntī addresses Him as *viśveśa,* the controller of the universe. People are interested only in pictures of Kṛṣṇa embracing Rādhārāṇī that depict the dealings of Rādhā and Kṛṣṇa to be like those of ordinary boys and girls. They don't understand Kṛṣṇa. Such obnoxious pictures should be avoided. Kṛṣṇa is the supreme controller. Let there be a picture showing how Kṛṣṇa is controlling the whole universe. That kind of picture is wanted, not these cheap pictures.

Unless the living force is present within the body, the body cannot move or work nicely, and similarly within the universe, the cosmic manifestation, Kṛṣṇa is present as the living force – Kṣīrodaka-śāyī Viṣṇu, or Paramātmā. Therefore Kuntī addresses Kṛṣṇa as *viśvātmā,* the soul of the universe. Rascals do not know how this world is moving and how this universe is acting, and therefore they should learn from *Śrīmad-Bhāgavatam.*

Kuntīdevī also addresses Kṛṣṇa as *viśva-mūrti,* the personality of the form of the universe. When Arjuna wanted to see Kṛṣṇa's universal form, Kṛṣṇa immediately manifested it. This is another of Kṛṣṇa's opulences (*vibhūti*). The original form of the Lord, however, is Kṛṣṇa with two hands, playing on the flute. Because Arjuna was a devotee and wanted to see the universal form, Kṛṣṇa showed it to him, but that was not His actual form. A person may dress himself as a king, but his real, natural appearance is shown at home. Similarly, Kṛṣṇa's real form is seen at home in Vṛndāvana, and all other forms are expansions of His plenary portions. As stated in the *Brahma-saṁhitā, advaitam acyutam anādim ananta-rūpam:* He can expand Himself in millions and millions of forms (*ananta-rūpam*), but He is one (*advaita*), and He is infallible (*acyuta*). His real form, however, is the *dvi-bhuja muralī-dhara* – the form with two hands holding a flute. Therefore Kuntīdevī says, "You have Your universal form, but the form in which You are standing before me is Your real form."

Kuntīdevī prays, "Please sever my tie of affection for my kinsmen." We are thinking, "This is my own, that is my own," but this is *moha*, illusion (*janasya moho 'yam ahaṁ mameti*). How does this illusion come into existence? It begins with the natural attraction between man and woman. A male seeks a female, and a female seeks a male. This is true not only in human society, but also in bird society, beast society, and so on. This is the beginning of material attachment. When a man finds a woman and they unite, this attachment becomes even more firmly established (*tayor mitho hṛdaya-granthim āhuḥ*). Now, after the attachment increases to some degree, the man and woman look for an apartment in which to live together, and then, of course, the man needs to earn money. When they are well settled, they must have children and also some friends to come and praise them: "Oh, you have such a nice apartment and such nice children." In this way one's attachment increases.

A student's education, therefore, should begin with *brahmacarya*, which means freedom from sexual attachment. If he can, he should try to avoid all this nonsense. If not, he can marry and then after some time enter *vānaprastha*, retired life. At that time one thinks, "Now that I have enjoyed this attachment so much, let me leave home." Then the man travels all over to various places of pilgrimage to become detached, and the wife goes with him as an assistant. After two or three months he again comes home to see that his children are doing nicely and then again goes away. This is the beginning of detachment. When the detachment is complete, the man tells his wife, "Now go live with your children, and I shall take *sannyāsa*, the renounced order of life." This is final detachment. The whole Vedic way of life is meant for detachment, and therefore Kuntī prays, "Kindly help detach me from this family attraction." This is Kuntīdevī's instruction.

25

Unalloyed Devotion

tvayi me 'nanya-viṣayā
matir madhu-pate 'sakṛt
ratim udvahatād addhā
gaṅgevaugham udanvati

O Lord of Madhu, as the Ganges forever flows to the sea without hindrance, let my attraction be constantly drawn unto You, without being diverted to anyone else.

Śrīmad-Bhāgavatam 1.8.42

Perfection of pure devotional service is attained when all attention is diverted toward the transcendental loving service of the Lord. To cut off the tie of all other affections does not mean complete negation of the finer elements, like affection for someone else. This is not possible. A living being, whoever he may be, must have this feeling of affection for others because this is a symptom of life. The symptoms of life, such as desire, anger, hankerings, and feelings of attraction, cannot be annihilated. Only the objective has to be changed. Desire cannot be negated, but in devotional service the desire is changed only for the service of the Lord in place of desire for sense gratification. The so-called affection for family, society, country, etc., consists of different phases of sense gratification. When this desire is changed for the satisfaction of the Lord, it is called devotional service.

In the *Bhagavad-gītā* we can see that Arjuna desired not to fight with his brothers and relations just to satisfy his own personal desires. But when he heard the message of the Lord, *Śrīmad Bhagavad-gītā,* he changed his decision and served the Lord. And for his doing so, he became a famous devotee of the Lord, for it is declared in all the scriptures that Arjuna attained spiritual perfection by devotional service to the Lord in friendship. The fighting was there, the friendship was there, Arjuna was there, and Kṛṣṇa was there, but Arjuna became a different person by devotional service. Therefore, the prayers of Kuntī also indicate the same categorical changes in activities. Śrīmatī Kuntī wanted to serve the Lord without diversion, and that was her prayer. This unalloyed devotion is the ultimate goal of life. Our attention is usually diverted to the service of something which is nongodly or not in the program of the Lord. When the program is changed into the service of the Lord, that is to say when the senses are purified in relation with the service of the Lord, it is called pure, unalloyed devotional service. Śrīmatī Kuntīdevī wanted that perfection and prayed for it from the Lord.

Her affection for the Pāṇḍavas and the Vṛṣṇis is not out of the range of devotional service, because the service of the Lord and the service of the devotees are identical. Sometimes service to the devotee is more valuable than service to the Lord. But here the affection of Kuntīdevī for the Pāṇḍavas and the Vṛṣṇis was due to family relation. This tie of affection in terms of material relation is the relation of *māyā,* because the relations of the body or the mind are due to the influence of the external energy. Relations of the soul, established in relation with the Supreme Soul, are factual relations. When Kuntīdevī wanted to cut off the family relation, she meant to cut off the relation of the skin. The skin relation is the cause of material bondage, but the relation of the soul is the cause of freedom. This relation of the soul to the soul can be established by the via medium of the relation with the Supersoul. Seeing in the darkness is not seeing. But seeing by the light of the sun means seeing the sun and everything else which was unseen in the darkness. That is the way of devotional service.

In the previous verse of *Śrīmad-Bhāgavatam* Queen Kuntī prayed that the Lord kindly cut off her attraction for her kinsmen, the Pāṇḍava and Vṛṣṇi families. However, giving up one's attraction for material things is not sufficient. The Māyāvādī philosophers say, *brahma satyaṁ jagan mithyā:* "This world is false, and Brahman [spirit] is truth." We admit this, but qualify it. As living entities, we want enjoyment. Enjoyment means variety. It is not possible to enjoy anything without variety. Why has God created so many colors and so many forms? In order to create enjoyment out of variety, for variety is the mother of enjoyment.

Māyāvādī philosophers, impersonalists, want to negate this variety, but what is the result? Because they do not engage in devotional service, they simply undertake the hard labor of austerities and penances without achieving any permanent result. This is explained by a prayer in *Śrīmad-Bhāgavatam* (10.2.32):

> *ye 'nye 'ravindākṣa vimukta-māninas*
> *tvayy asta-bhāvād aviśuddha-buddhayaḥ*
> *āruhya kṛcchreṇa paraṁ padaṁ tataḥ*
> *patanty adho 'nādṛta-yuṣmad-aṅghrayaḥ*

"O lotus-eyed Lord, those who think they are liberated in this life but do not render devotional service to You must be of impure intelligence. Although they accept severe austerities and penances and rise to the spiritual position, to impersonal Brahman realization, they fall down again because they neglect to worship Your lotus feet."

The human form of life is meant for reestablishing our relationship with God and acting according to that relationship. Even in ordinary dealings, one businessman who intends to do business with another must first establish some relationship with him, and then transactions can take place. Similarly, a husband and wife establish a relationship by marriage, and then they live together. In a similar way, human life is meant for reestablishing our relationship with God. The material world means forgetfulness of this relationship. There is no Kṛṣṇa consciousness in this material world, for as soon as there is Kṛṣṇa consciousness, as soon as there is action on the basis of Kṛṣṇa, it is no longer the material world but the spiritual world.

As a woman, Kuntīdevī had a relationship with two families. That was her attachment. Therefore she prayed to Kṛṣṇa to cut off these relationships and free her. But after becoming free, what should she do? That is the question. One may be employed in some business and, feeling inconvenience, resign. That resignation may be all right, but if by resigning one becomes unemployed and has no engagement, then what is the value of resigning?

Those who are frustrated and confused want to negate this material world. They know what they don't want, but they do not know what they do want. People are always saying, "I don't want this." But what *do* they want? That they do not know.

What one should actually want is explained by Kuntīdevī. She says, "Let my family relationships cease, but let my relationship with You be confirmed." In other words, she does not want to be attracted to anything but Kṛṣṇa. This is perfection, and this is actually wanted.

The word *ananya-viṣayā* means *ananya-bhakti,* undeviating devotional service. We must simply be attached to Kṛṣṇa twenty-four hours a day without deviation. In this way our renunciation can be perfect. If we think we can be attached to Kṛṣṇa and material things at the same time, we are mistaken. We cannot ignite a fire and at the same time pour water on it. If we do, the fire will not act.

The Māyāvādī *sannyāsīs* renounce this world (*brahma satyaṁ jagan mithyā*). It is very good to preach renunciation of the world, but side by side we must have attraction for something, otherwise our renunciation will not remain. We see many Māyāvādī *sannyāsīs* who say *brahma satyaṁ jagan mithyā,* but after they take *sannyāsa* they return to the material world to open hospitals and do philanthropic work. Why? If they have left this world, considering it *mithyā,* false, why do they return to take up politics, philanthropy, and sociology? Actually this is bound to happen, for we are living entities and are active. If out of frustration we try to become inactive, we shall fail in our attempt. We must engage in activities.

The supreme activity, the Brahman (spiritual) activity, is devotional service. Unfortunately the Māyāvādīs do not know this. They think that the spiritual world is void. However, the spiritual world is exactly like the material world in that it has varieties. In the spiritual world there are also houses, trees, roads, chariots – everything is there, but without the material inebrieties. As described in *Brahma-saṁhitā* (5.29):

cintāmaṇi-prakara-sadmasu kalpa-vṛkṣa-
lakṣāvṛteṣu surabhīr abhipālayantam
lakṣmī-sahasra-śata-sambhrama-sevyamānaṁ
govindam ādi-puruṣaṁ tam ahaṁ bhajāmi

"I worship Govinda, the primeval Lord, the first progenitor, who is tending the cows, yielding all desires, in abodes built with spiritual gems, surrounded by millions of purpose trees, and always served with great reverence and affection by hundreds of thousands of goddesses of fortune, or *gopīs.*"

In the spiritual world there are *kalpa-vṛkṣa* trees, which yield whatever type of fruit we desire. In the material world a mango tree cannot supply grapes, nor can a grapevine supply mangoes. In the spiritual world, however, if we take a mango from a tree and at the same time desire grapes, the tree will supply them. This is called a "desire tree." These are some of the actualities of the spiritual world.

In this material world we require sunlight and moonlight, but in the spiritual world there is no need of sunlight and moonlight because everything and everyone is effulgent. In *kṛṣṇa-līlā,* Kṛṣṇa stole butter, and the neighborhood friends of mother Yaśodā complained. Actually they were not complaining, but were just enjoying the bodily features and the fun of Kṛṣṇa. They told mother Yaśodā, "Your son comes to our house and steals butter. We try to conceal it in the dark so that He cannot see it, but somehow He still finds it out. You had better take away all His ornaments because we think that the light of His jewels helps Him find the butterpot." Mother Yaśodā replied, "Yes, I will take off all His ornaments." But the neighbors would reply, "No, no. It is useless. Somehow this boy has an effulgence that comes out of Himself. He can find the butter even without the ornaments." Thus the transcendental body is effulgent.

It is because of the effulgence of Kṛṣṇa's transcendental body that there is light. Whatever light we see is simply borrowed light from Kṛṣṇa's effulgence. As stated in the *Brahma-saṁhitā* (5.40):

yasya prabhā prabhavato jagad-aṇḍa-koṭi-
koṭiṣv aśeṣa-vasudhādi vibhūti-bhinnam
tad brahma niṣkalam anantam aśeṣa-bhūtaṁ
govindam ādi-puruṣaṁ tam ahaṁ bhajāmi

"In the millions and millions of universes there are innumerable planets, and each of them is different from the others by its cosmic constitution. All of these planets are situated within the spiritual effulgence called the *brahma-jyotir*. This *brahma-jyotir* is the bodily effulgence of the Supreme Personality of Godhead, whom I worship."

The bodily effulgence of Kṛṣṇa generates millions of universes. In this solar system the sun produces many planets, and because of sunshine the planets are warm and the seasons change. Because of the sun there are trees, green foliage, fruits, and flowers. Similarly, whatever we see in creation is all due to Kṛṣṇa's bodily effulgence.

The Māyāvādīs simply see the effulgence, which is impersonal. They cannot see anything more. We may see an airplane rise in the sky, but after a while it passes out of our sight due to the dazzling sunshine. The airplane is there, but we cannot see it. Similarly, if we simply try to see the effulgent *brahma-jyotir,* we are unable to see within it. One of the *mantras* in the *Īśopaniṣad* therefore petitions the Lord to wind up His effulgence so that He can be seen properly.

The Māyāvādī philosophers cannot see the personal activities of Kṛṣṇa nor the planet where Kṛṣṇa is personally active. The *Bhāgavatam* says, *āruhya kṛcchreṇa paraṁ padaṁ tataḥ patanty adho 'nādṛta-yuṣmad-aṅghrayaḥ:* because they do not see the lotus feet of Kṛṣṇa, they have to return to this material world, despite all their serious penances and austerities. Thus renunciation in itself will not help us. We may artificially renounce, but again we shall become so-called enjoyers. Such renunciation and enjoyment is like a pendulum that goes this way and that. On one side we become false renunciants, and on the other we become false enjoyers. The remedy, however, is here. If we really want to become detached from this material world, we must increase our attachment for Kṛṣṇa consciousness. Renunciation alone will not help us. Therefore Kuntīdevī prays, *tvayi me 'nanya-viṣayā.* She prays that her attraction be constantly drawn unto Kṛṣṇa without being diverted to anything else. This is *bhakti,* pure devotional service, for as mentioned by Rūpa Gosvāmī, devotional service should be unalloyed (*anyābhilāṣitā-śūnyaṁ jñāna-karmādy-anāvṛtam*).

In this material world there are *jñānīs* and *karmīs.* The *karmīs* are fools who unnecessarily work very hard, and the *jñānīs* are those who, when a little elevated, think, "Why work so hard? So many things are not required. Why accumulate so much money and food and so much false prestige?" The *jñānī* thinks in this way. The *bhakta,* however, is beyond the *karmī* and the *jñānī.* The *karmī* has many desires, and the *jñānī* tries to get rid of all desires, but desirelessness can be possible only when we desire to serve Kṛṣṇa. Otherwise it is not possible to get rid of desires. *Jñāna-karmādy-anāvṛtam.* As *bhaktas,* we should have no desires for *jñāna* and *karma.* We should be without attachment for material things, but we must have attachment for Kṛṣṇa. In this way our detachment will be fixed.

We must cultivate Kṛṣṇa consciousness favorably (*ānukūlyena kṛṣṇānuśīlanam*). This means thinking of how Kṛṣṇa will be satisfied. We must always think of Kṛṣṇa, just like the *gopīs.* The Kṛṣṇa consciousness of the *gopīs* was perfect because they had no desire other than to try to please Kṛṣṇa. That is perfection. Therefore Caitanya Mahāprabhu recommends, *ramyā kācid upāsanā vraja-vadhū-vargeṇa yā kalpitā:* there is no better process by which to worship the Supreme Personality of Godhead than that method adopted by the *gopīs.*

The *gopīs* had no desire other than to satisfy Kṛṣṇa. All the *gopīs* tried to satisfy Him, including the elder *gopīs,* Yaśodā and her friends, and so also did the elderly *gopas* like Nanda Mahārāja and his friends.

The boys and girls of Vṛndāvana who were of the same age as Kṛṣṇa also tried to satisfy Him. Everyone tried to satisfy Kṛṣṇa – even the cows, the flowers, the fruits, and the water of Vṛndāvana. This is because everything in Vṛndāvana is spiritual; nothing is material.

We should understand the difference between spiritual and material. That which is material has no living symptoms, and that which is spiritual has all living symptoms. Both the trees in the spiritual world and those in the material world are living entities, but in trees here the living symptoms are absent. A human being is a living entity, and the devotees in the spiritual world are also living entities, but in the human beings who are not Kṛṣṇa conscious the real symptoms of life are absent.

Actually there is no other consciousness but Kṛṣṇa consciousness. And that consciousness is spiritual. Thus even while in this material world, if we simply increase our Kṛṣṇa consciousness we shall live in the spiritual world. If we live in the temple, we live in the spiritual world because in the temple there is no business other than Kṛṣṇa consciousness. There are so many engagements carried out for Kṛṣṇa. Those who strictly follow the regulations of Kṛṣṇa consciousness actually live in the spiritual world, not the material world. We may think we are living in New York, Los Angeles, or elsewhere, but we are actually living in Vaikuṇṭha.

It is a question of consciousness. A bug may sit on the same seat with the spiritual master, but because the spiritual master has developed consciousness and the bug does not, they are different. They may be sitting in the same place, but the bug remains a bug, and the spiritual master remains the spiritual master. The position in space may remain the same, just as we remain in the material world or the spiritual world, but if our Kṛṣṇa consciousness is strong, we are not in the material world.

Thus renunciation by itself, the simple giving up of worldly things, is not sufficient. Renunciation may be a helpful process, but it will not help absolutely. When we increase our attachment for Kṛṣṇa, our renunciation will be perfect. As we increase attachment for Kṛṣṇa, attachment for this material world will automatically diminish. Attachment for Kṛṣṇa and the material world cannot go hand in hand. If a woman is attached to two men – her husband and her paramour – she cannot maintain her attachment for both. Her attachment will increase for her paramour.

Although she may work at her husband's home very nicely, her mind will be attached to her paramour, and she will think, "When shall I meet him tonight?" In the same way, if we increase our attachment for Kṛṣṇa, detachment or renunciation of this material world will automatically come (*bhaktiḥ pareśānubhavo viraktir anyatra ca, Bhāgavatam* 11.2.42).

Thus Kuntīdevī prays to Kṛṣṇa that He may grant her His mercy by which she can become attached to Him. We cannot increase our attachment for Kṛṣṇa without Kṛṣṇa's mercy. We cannot become devotees without Kṛṣṇa's mercy; therefore we simply have to serve Kṛṣṇa, for by service Kṛṣṇa is satisfied.

Kṛṣṇa does not require anyone's service, for He is perfect in Himself. However, if we give Him service wholeheartedly and sincerely, then, by His mercy, we shall make advancement. *Sevonmukhe hi jihvādau svayam eva sphurat adaḥ.* God will reveal Himself to us. We cannot see God with our blunt eyes. How then can we see Him? *Premāñjana-cchurita-bhakti-vilocanena, santaḥ sadaiva hṛdayeṣu vilokayanti* (*Brahma-saṁhitā* 5.38). We have to smear our eyes with the ointment of love; then Kṛṣṇa will reveal Himself. Kṛṣṇa will actually come in front of us.

When Dhruva Mahārāja was undergoing penance and meditating upon the form of Viṣṇu within his heart, the Viṣṇu form suddenly disappeared, and his meditation broke. Upon opening his eyes, Dhruva Mahārāja immediately saw Viṣṇu before him. Like Dhruva Mahārāja, we should always think of Kṛṣṇa, and when we attain perfection we shall see Kṛṣṇa before us. This is the process. We should not be too hasty. We should wait for the mature time. Of course, it is good to be eager to see Kṛṣṇa, but we should not become discouraged if we do not see Him immediately. If a woman gets married and wants a child immediately, she will be disappointed. It is not possible to have a child immediately. She must wait. Similarly, we cannot expect that just because we engage ourselves in Kṛṣṇa consciousness we can see Kṛṣṇa immediately. But we must have faith that we will see Him. We must have firm faith that because we are engaged in Kṛṣṇa consciousness we shall be able to see Kṛṣṇa face to face. We should not be disappointed. We should simply go on with our Kṛṣṇa conscious activities, and the time will come when we will see Kṛṣṇa, just as Kuntīdevī sees Him face to face. There is no doubt about this.

In the *Bhagavad-gītā* it is stated that even if one is sometimes found to be somewhat misbehaved, he is to be considered saintly if he engages steadily in the service of Kṛṣṇa. Sometimes American or European devotees may be criticized because they make mistakes and fall short of the system for worshiping the Deity as practiced in India, but still, according to *Bhagavad-gītā,* they must be considered saintly. We must fix our minds upon serving Kṛṣṇa sincerely and seriously, and then, even if there is some mistake, Kṛṣṇa will excuse it. Rūpa Gosvāmī says, *tasmāt kenāpy upāyena manaḥ kṛṣṇe niveśayet:* we should first fix our minds upon Kṛṣṇa, and then the ability to follow the other rules and regulations will automatically follow. In the beginning we should try our best to fix our minds upon the lotus feet of Kṛṣṇa, and then everything else will automatically become correct.

Kuntīdevī addresses Kṛṣṇa as Madhupati. Kṛṣṇa has thousands of names, and the name Madhupati indicates that He killed the demon Madhu. Kṛṣṇa consciousness is likened to a river, but not an ordinary river. It is like the River Ganges, which is very pure and directly connected to Kṛṣṇa. Kuntīdevī prays that just as the River Ganges flows toward the sea, her attraction will flow incessantly toward Kṛṣṇa's lotus feet. This is called *ananya-bhakti,* unalloyed devotion. Thus Kuntīdevī prays that her attraction for Kṛṣṇa will flow without hindrance.

26

Enchantment by Kṛṣṇa's Glories

śrī-kṛṣṇa kṛṣṇa-sakha vṛṣṇy-ṛṣabhāvani-dhrug-
rājanya-vaṁśa-dahanānapavarga-vīrya
govinda go-dvija-surārti-harāvatāra
yogeśvarākhila-guro bhagavan namas te

O Kṛṣṇa, O friend of Arjuna, O chief among the descendants of Vṛṣṇi, You are the destroyer of those political parties which are disturbing elements on this earth. Your prowess never deteriorates. You are the proprietor of the transcendental abode, and You descend to relieve the distresses of the cows, the brāhmaṇas, and the devotees, You possess all mystic powers, and You are the preceptor of the entire universe. You are the almighty God, and I offer You my respectful obeisances.

Śrīmad-Bhāgavatam 1.8.43

A summary of the Supreme Lord, Śrī Kṛṣṇa, is made herein by Śrīmatī Kuntīdevī. The almighty Lord has His eternal, transcendental abode, where He is engaged in keeping *surabhi* cows. He is served by hundreds and thousands of goddesses of fortune. He descends on the material world to reclaim His devotees and to annihilate the disturbing elements in groups of political parties and kings who are supposed to be in charge of administration work. He creates, maintains, and annihilates by His unlimited energies, and still He is always full with prowess and does not deteriorate in potency. The cows, the *brāhmaṇas,* and the devotees of the Lord are all objects of His special attention because they are very important factors for the general welfare of living beings.

Kuntī addresses Lord Kṛṣṇa as *kṛṣṇa-sakha* because she knows that although Arjuna, who is also known as Kṛṣṇa, is her son and therefore subordinate to her, Lord Kṛṣṇa is more intimately related with Arjuna than with her. Kṛṣṇā is also a name of Draupadī, and so the word *kṛṣṇa-sakha* also indicates Lord Kṛṣṇa's relationship with Draupadī, whom He saved from being insulted when Duryodhana and Karṇa attempted to strip her naked. Kuntī also addresses Lord Kṛṣṇa as *vṛṣṇi-ṛṣabha,* the child of the dynasty of Vṛṣṇi. It was because Kṛṣṇa appeared in the Vṛṣṇi dynasty that this dynasty became famous, just as Malaysia and the Malaya Hills became famous because of the sandalwood that grows there.

Kuntīdevī also addresses Lord Kṛṣṇa as the destroyer of the political parties or royal dynasties that disturb the earth. In every monarchy, the king is honored very gorgeously. Why? Since he is a human being and the other citizens are also human beings, why is the king so honored? The answer is that the king, like the spiritual master, is meant to be the representative of God. In the Vedic literature it is said, *ācāryaṁ māṁ vijānīyān nāvamanyeta karhicit* (*Bhāgavatam* 11.17.27): the spiritual master should not be regarded as an ordinary human being. Similarly, a king or president is also not treated like an ordinary human being.

In the Sanskrit language the king is also called *naradeva,* which means "God in human form." His duty is like that of Kṛṣṇa. As God is the supreme living being in the universe and is the maintainer of all other living beings, the king is the supreme citizen in the state and is responsible for the welfare of all others.

Just as we are all living beings, Kṛṣṇa, God, is also a living being. Kṛṣṇa is not impersonal. Because we are all individual persons but our knowledge and opulence are limited, the impersonalists cannot adjust to the idea that the Supreme, the original, unlimited cause of everything, can also be a person. Because we are limited and God is unlimited, the Māyāvādīs, or impersonalists, with their poor fund of knowledge, think that God must be impersonal. Making a material comparison, they say that just as the sky, which we think of as unlimited, is impersonal, if God is unlimited He must also be impersonal.

But that is not the Vedic instruction. The *Vedas* instruct that God is a person. Kṛṣṇa is a person, and we are also persons, but the difference is that He is to be worshiped whereas we are to be worshipers. The king or president is a person, and the citizens are also persons, but the difference is that the president or king is an exalted person who should be offered all respect.

Now, why should so many persons worship one person? Because that one person provides for the others. *Eko bahūnāṁ yo vidadhāti kāmān.* God is one, and we are many, but He is worshiped because He provides for everyone. It is God who provides food and all the other necessities of life. We need water, and God has nicely arranged for oceans of water, with salt mixed in to preserve it all nicely. Then, because we need drinking water, by God's arrangement the sunshine evaporates the water from the ocean, takes it high in the sky, and then distributes clear, distilled water. Just see how God is providing everything that everyone needs.

Even in ordinary life the state has a heating department, lighting department, plumbing department, and so on. Why? Because these are amenities we require. But these arrangements are subordinate; the first arrangement is that of God. It is God who originally supplies heat, light, and water. It is God who supplies the rainwater that fills our wells and reservoirs. Therefore the original supplier is God.

God is an intelligent person who knows that we need heat, light, water, and so on. Without water we cannot produce food. Even those who eat animals cannot do so without God's arrangement, for the animal also must be provided with grass before one can take it to the slaughterhouse. Thus it is God who is supplying food, but still we are creating rebellion against Him. The word *dhruk* means "rebellious." Those rascals who are going against the law of God are rebellious.

The king's duty is to act as the representative of Kṛṣṇa, or God. Otherwise what right does he have to take so much honor from the citizens? Monarchy was formerly present in every country, but because the kings rebelled against God and violated His laws, because they tried to usurp the power of God and did not act as His representatives, the monarchies of the world have nearly all disappeared. The kings thought that their kingdoms were their personal property. "I have so much property, such a big kingdom," they thought. "I am God. I am the lord of all I survey." But that is not actually the fact. That fact is that everything belongs to God (*īśāvāsyam idaṁ sarvam*). Therefore the representative of God must be very obedient to God, and then his position will be legitimate.

Greedy, self-interested kings are like false spiritual masters who proclaim that they themselves are God. Because such false masters are rebellious, they have no position. A spiritual master is supposed to act not as God but as the most confidential servant of God by spreading God consciousness, Kṛṣṇa consciousness. Viśvanātha Cakravartī Ṭhākura says, *sākṣād-dharitvena samasta-śāstrair uktaḥ:* all the *śāstras,* the Vedic literatures, state that the spiritual master is to be honored as the Supreme Personality of Godhead. Thus the idea that the spiritual master is as good as God is not bogus. It is stated in the *śāstras,* and therefore those who are advanced in spiritual life accept this spiritual injunction (*uktas tathā bhāvyata eva sadbhiḥ*). Then is the spiritual master as good as God? *Kintu prabhor yaḥ priya eva tasya:* the spiritual master is not God, but is the confidential representative of God. The distinction is that between *sevya-bhagavān* (he who is worshiped) and *sevaka-bhagavān* (he who is the worshiper). The spiritual master is God, and Kṛṣṇa is God, but Kṛṣṇa is the worshipable God whereas the spiritual master is the worshiper God.

The Māyāvādīs cannot understand this. They think, "Because the spiritual master has to be accepted as God and because I have become a spiritual master, I have become God." This is rebellious. Those who are given a position by God but who want to usurp His power, which they actually cannot do, are rebellious fools and rascals who require punishment. Therefore Kuntīdevī says, *avani-dhrug-rājanya-vaṁśa-dahana:* "You descend to kill all these rascals who rebelliously claim Your position." When various kings or landholders are subordinate to an emperor, they sometimes rebel and refuse to pay taxes. Similarly, there are rebellious persons who deny the supremacy of God and declare themselves God, and Kṛṣṇa's business is to kill them.

The word *anapavarga* indicates that Kṛṣṇa's prowess is without deterioration. This word is the opposite of the word *pavarga,* which refers to the path of material tribulation. According to Sanskrit linguistics, the word *pa-varga* also refers to the Sanskrit letters *pa, pha, ba, bha,* and *ma*. Thus when the word *pavarga* is used to refer to the path of material tribulation, its meaning is understood through words beginning with these five letters.

The letter *pa* is for *pariśrama,* which means "labor." In this material world, one must work very hard to maintain oneself. In *Bhagavad-gītā* (3.8) it is said, *śarīra-yātrāpi ca te na prasiddhyed akarmaṇaḥ:* "One cannot even maintain one's own body without work." Kṛṣṇa never advised Arjuna, "I am your friend, and I shall do everything. You just sit down and smoke *gañjā.*" Kṛṣṇa was doing everything, but still He told Arjuna, "You must fight." Nor did Arjuna say to Kṛṣṇa, "You are my great friend. Better for You to fight and let me sit down and smoke *gañjā.*" No, that is not Kṛṣṇa consciousness. A God conscious person does not say, "God, You please do everything for me and let me smoke *gañjā.*" Rather, a God conscious person must work for God. But even if one does not work for the sake of God, one must work, for without work one cannot even maintain one's body. This material world, therefore, is meant for *pariśrama,* hard labor.

Even a lion, although king of the beasts, must still look for its own prey in the jungle. It is said, *na hi suptasya siṁhasya praviśanti mukhe mṛgāḥ*. A lion cannot think, "Since I am king of the forest, let me sleep, and all the animals will come into my mouth." That is not possible. "No, sir. Although you are a lion, you must go search for your food." Thus even the lion, although so powerful, must endeavor with great difficulty to find another animal to eat, and similarly everyone in this material world must work with great difficulty to continue his life.

Thus *pa* indicates *pariśrama,* labor, and *pha* is for *phena,* which means "foam." While working very hard a horse foams at the mouth, and similarly human beings must also work hard in this way. Such hard labor, however, is *vyartha,* futile, and this is what is indicated by the letter *ba.* And *bha* indicates *bhaya,* fear. Despite working so hard, one is always somewhat fearful that things will not be done as he desires. The nature of the body is that it involves eating, sleeping, mating, and fearing (*āhāra-nidrā-bhaya-maithunaṁ ca*). Although one may eat very nicely, one must consider whether one is overeating, so that he will not fall sick. Thus even eating involves fear. A bird, while eating, looks this way and that way, fearful that some enemy may be coming. And for all living entities, everything finally ends in death, *mṛtyu,* and this is what is indicated by the letter *ma.*

Thus *pavarga* and its component letters *pa, pha, ba, bha,* and *ma* indicate hard labor (*pariśrama*), foam at the mouth (*phena*), frustration (*vyartha*), fear (*bhaya*), and death (*mṛtyu*). This is called *pavarga,* the path of material tribulation. *Apavarga,* however, indicates just the opposite – the spiritual world, where there is no labor, no foam, no frustration, no fear, and no death. Thus Kṛṣṇa is known as *anapavarga-vīrya,* for He shows the path to the spiritual world.

Why should one suffer from these five kinds of tribulation? Because one has a material body. As soon as one accepts a material body – whether it is that of a president or a common man, a demigod or a human being, an insect or a Brahmā – one must go through these tribulations. This is called material existence. Kṛṣṇa comes, therefore, to show one the path to *apavarga,* freedom from these tribulations, and when Kṛṣṇa shows this path, we should accept it. Kṛṣṇa says very clearly, "Surrender unto Me. I shall give you *apavarga.*" *Ahaṁ tvāṁ sarva-pāpebhyo mokṣayiṣyāmi:* "I shall give you protection." And Kṛṣṇa has the power with which to fulfill this guarantee.

Kuntīdevī addresses Kṛṣṇa as Govinda because He is the giver of pleasure both to the cows and to the senses. *Govindam ādi-puruṣaṁ tam ahaṁ bhajāmi.* Govinda, Kṛṣṇa, is the *ādi-puruṣa,* the original person. *Aham ādir hi devānām* (*Bhagavad-gītā* 10.2): He is the origin even of demigods like Brahmā, Viṣṇu, and Śiva. People should not think that Brahmā, Viṣṇu, and Śiva are the origin of everything. No. Kṛṣṇa says, *aham ādir hi devānām:* "I am the origin even of these demigods." Therefore we repeatedly emphasize that we worship no one but the original person (*govindam ādi-puruṣaṁ tam ahaṁ bhajāmi*).

When Kuntī prays, *go-dvija-surārti-harāvatāra,* she indicates that Govinda, Kṛṣṇa, descends to this world especially to protect the cows, the *brāhmaṇas,* and the devotees. The demoniac in this world are the greatest enemies of the cows, for they maintain hundreds and thousands of slaughterhouses. Although the innocent cows give milk, the most important food, and although even after death the cows give their skin for shoes, people are such rascals that they kill the cows, but still they want to be happy in this world. How sinful they are.

Why is cow protection so much advocated? Because the cow is the most important animal. There is no injunction that one should not eat the flesh of tigers or other such animals. In the Vedic culture those who are meat-eaters are recommended to eat the flesh of goats, dogs, hogs, or other lower animals, but never the flesh of cows, the most important animals. While living, the cows give important service by giving milk, and even after death they give service by making available their skin, hooves, and horns, which may be used in many ways. Nonetheless, the present human society is so ungrateful that they needlessly kill these innocent cows. Therefore Kṛṣṇa comes to punish them.

Kṛṣṇa is worshiped with this prayer:

namo brahmaṇya-devāya
go-brāhmaṇa-hitāya ca
jagad-dhitāya kṛṣṇāya
govindāya namo namaḥ

"My Lord, You are the well-wisher of the cows and the *brāhmaṇas,* and You are the well-wisher of the entire human society and world." For perfect human society there must be protection of *go-dvija* – the cows and the *brāhmaṇas.* The word *dvija* refers to the *brāhmaṇa,* or one who knows Brahman (God). When the demoniac give too much trouble to the *brāhmaṇas* and the cows, Kṛṣṇa descends to reestablish religious principles. As the Lord says in *Bhagavad-gītā* (4.7):

yadā yadā hi dharmasya
glānir bhavati bhārata
abhyutthānam adharmasya
tadātmānaṁ sṛjāmy aham

"Whenever and wherever there is a decline in religious practice, O descendant of Bharata, and a predominant rise of irreligion – at that time I descend Myself." In the present age, Kali-yuga, people are very much sinful and are consequently suffering greatly. Therefore Kṛṣṇa has incarnated in the form of His name, as found in the *mahā-mantra:* Hare Kṛṣṇa, Hare Kṛṣṇa, Kṛṣṇa Kṛṣṇa, Hare Hare/ Hare Rāma, Hare Rāma, Rāma Rāma, Hare Hare.

Queen Kuntī prayed to the Lord just to enunciate a fragment of His glories. The Lord, upon hearing her prayers, which were composed in choice words for His glorification, responded by smiling, and His smile was as enchanting as His mystic power. The conditioned souls, who are engaged in trying to lord it over the material world, are also enchanted by the Lord's mystic powers, but His devotees are enchanted in a different way by the glories of the Lord. Thus all the devotees worship the Lord by chosen words. No amount of chosen words are sufficient to enumerate the Lord's glory, yet He is satisfied by such prayers, just as a father is satisfied even by the broken linguistic attempts of a growing child. Thus the Lord smiled and accepted the prayers of Queen Kuntī.

Appendixes

The Author

His Divine Grace A.C. Bhaktivedanta Swami Prabhupāda appeared in this world in 1896 in Calcutta, India. He first met his spiritual master, Śrīla Bhaktisiddhānta Sarasvatī Gosvāmī, in Calcutta in 1922. Bhaktisiddhānta Sarasvatī, a prominent religious scholar and the founder of sixty-four Gauḍīya Maṭhas (Vedic institutes), liked this educated young man and convinced him to dedicate his life to teaching Vedic knowledge. Śrīla Prabhupāda became his student and, in 1933, his formally initiated disciple.

At their first meeting, in 1922, Śrīla Bhaktisiddhānta Sarasvatī requested Śrīla Prabhupāda to broadcast Vedic knowledge in English. In the years that followed, Śrīla Prabhupāda wrote a commentary on the *Bhagavad-gītā,* assisted the Gauḍīya Maṭha in its work and, in 1944, started *Back to Godhead,* an English fortnightly magazine. Singlehandedly, Śrīla Prabhupāda edited it, typed the manuscripts, checked the galley proofs, and even distributed the individual copies. The magazine is now being continued by his disciples.

In 1950 Śrīla Prabhupāda retired from married life, adopting the *vānaprastha* (retired) order to devote more time to his studies and writing. He traveled to the holy city of Vṛndāvana, where he lived in humble circumstances in the historic temple of Rādhā-Dāmodara. There he engaged for several years in deep study and writing. He accepted the renounced order of life (*sannyāsa*) in 1959. At Rādhā-Dāmodara, Śrīla Prabhupāda began work on his life's masterpiece: a multi-volume commentated translation of the eighteen-thousand-verse *Śrīmad-Bhāgavatam* (*Bhāgavata Purāṇa*). He also wrote *Easy Journey to Other Planets.*

After publishing three volumes of the *Bhāgavatam*, Śrīla Prabhupāda came to the United States, in September 1965, to fulfill the mission of his spiritual master. Subsequently, His Divine Grace wrote more than fifty volumes of authoritative commentated translations and summary studies of the philosophical and religious classics of India.

When he first arrived by freighter in New York City, Śrīla Prabhupāda was practically penniless. Only after almost a year of great difficulty did he establish the International Society for Krishna Consciousness, in July of 1966. Before he passed away on November 14, 1977, he had guided the Society and seen it grow to a worldwide confederation of more than one hundred *āśramas*, schools, temples, institutes, and farm communities.

In 1972 His Divine Grace introduced the Vedic system of primary and secondary education in the West by founding the *gurukula* school in Dallas, Texas. Since then his disciples have established similar schools throughout the United States and the rest of the world.

Śrīla Prabhupāda also inspired the construction of several large international cultural centers in India. At Śrīdhāma Māyāpur, in West Bengal, devotees are building a spiritual city centered on a magnificent temple – an ambitious project for which construction will extend over many years to come. In Vṛndāvana are the Kṛṣṇa-Balarāma Temple and International Guesthouse, *gurukula* school, and Śrīla Prabhupāda Memorial and Museum. There are also major temples and cultural centers in Mumbai, New Delhi, Ahmedabad, Siliguri, and Ujjain. Other centers are planned in many important locations on the Indian subcontinent.

Śrīla Prabhupāda's most significant contribution, however, is his books. Highly respected by scholars for their authority, depth, and clarity, they are used as textbooks in numerous college courses. His writings have been translated into over fifty languages. The Bhaktivedanta Book Trust, established in 1972 to publish the works of His Divine Grace, has thus become the world's largest publisher of books in the field of Indian religion and philosophy.

In just twelve years, despite his advanced age, Śrīla Prabhupāda circled the globe fourteen times on lecture tours that took him to six continents. In spite of such a vigorous schedule, Śrīla Prabhupāda continued to write prolifically. His writings constitute a veritable library of Vedic philosophy, religion, literature, and culture.

References

The text of *Teachings of Queen Kunti* is confirmed by standard Vedic authorities. The following authentic scriptures are specifically cited in this volume:

Bhagavad-gītā

Brahma-saṁhitā

Caitanya-caritāmṛta

Hari-bhakti-sudhodaya

Īśopaniṣad

Kaṭha Upaniṣad

Muṇḍaka Upaniṣad

Śikṣāṣṭaka

Śrīmad-Bhāgavatam

Śvetāśvatara Upaniṣad

Vedānta-sūtra

Viṣṇu Purāṇa

Glossary

Ācārya – a spiritual master who teaches by example.

Arcā-vigraha – the Deity incarnation of the Supreme Lord, manifest within material substances such as wood or stone.

Aṣṭāṅga-yoga – the mystic *yoga* system propounded by Patañjali in his *Yoga-sūtras.*

Asuras – atheistic demons.

Ātmā – the eternal spirit soul who is living within the temporary, material body.

Avatāra – an incarnation, or "descent," of the Supreme Lord.

Bhagavad-gītā – the discourse between the Supreme Lord, Kṛṣṇa, and His devotee Arjuna expounding devotional service as both the principal means and the ultimate end of spiritual perfection.

Bhakta – a devotee of God.

Bhakti – devotional service to Lord Kṛṣṇa.

Brahmacarya – celibate student life; the first order of Vedic spiritual life.

Brahma-jyotir – the brilliant effulgence emanating from the Supreme Lord's personal form, which is experienced by impersonalists as formless, limitless light, and thus mistaken by them to be the ultimate realization of the Absolute.

Brahman – the Absolute Truth; especially the impersonal aspect of the Absolute.

Brāhmaṇa – one wise in the *Vedas* who can guide society; the first Vedic social order.

Brahmāstra – in Vedic military science, an advanced nuclear weapon powered by the chanting of certain *mantras.*

Dharma – occupational duty; religious principles.

Gañjā – marijuana.
Goloka (Kṛṣṇaloka) – the highest spiritual planet, containing Kṛṣṇa's personal abodes, Dvārakā, Mathurā, and Vṛndāvana.
Gopas – cowherd men (or boys).
Gopīs – Krsna's cowherd girlfriends, His most confidential servitors.
Guru – a spiritual master.
Hare Kṛṣṇa mantra – *See: Mahā-mantra*
Jñānī – one who cultivates knowledge by empirical speculation.
Kali-yuga (Age of Kali) – the present age, characterized by quarrel; it is last in the cycle of four and began five thousand years ago.
Karma – fruitive action, for which there is always reaction, good or bad.
Karmī – a person satisfied with working hard for flickering sense gratification.
Kṛṣṇaloka – *See:* Goloka
Kṣatriya – a warrior or administrator; the second Vedic social order.
Līlā – the pastimes of the Supreme Lord, which He performs simply for His own pleasure and that of His devotees.
Mahābhārata – the history of the Kurukṣetra war, compiled by Vyāsadeva.
Mahā-mantra – the great chanting for deliverance: Hare Kṛṣṇa, Hare Kṛṣṇa, Kṛṣṇa Kṛṣṇa, Hare Hare/ Hare Rāma, Hare Rāma, Rāma Rāma, Hare Hare.
Mahātmā – a great soul.
Mantra – a sound vibration that can deliver the mind from illusion.
Māyā – illusion; forgetfulness of one's relationship with Kṛṣṇa.
Māyāvādīs – impersonal philosophers who say that the Lord cannot have a transcendental body.
Munis – thoughtful sages.
Paramahaṁsa – "topmost swan," a person who knows perfectly how to separate spirit from matter.
Paramātmā – the Supersoul, Lord Viṣṇu sitting within the heart of each and every living being.
Pātāla-loka – the lower planetary system, where the demons live.
Prakṛti – material nature, who controls all phenomena in this world, as well as all conditioned living beings, but is herself directly controlled by the Supreme Lord.

Prasāda – food spiritualized by being offered to the Lord.

Purāṇas – supplements to the original *Vedas* which recount the history of the universe from its very creation and describe the Supreme Lord's various incarnations.

Ṛṣis – sages.

Sannyāsa – renounced life; the fourth order of Vedic spiritual life.

Sārī – the standard woman's garment in Vedic culture.

Śāstras – revealed scriptures.

Śrīmad-Bhāgavatam – the "spotless *Purāna,*" which explains pure devotional service to the Supreme Lord.

Śruti – the original four *Vedas* together with the *Upaniṣads.*

Śūdra – a laborer; the fourth of the Vedic social orders.

Surabhis – the transcendental cows of the spiritual world, who can be milked to get the fulfillment of any possible desire.

Svayaṁvara – the ceremony in which a king's daughter is allowed to choose her own husband.

Tilaka – auspicious clay marks that sanctify a devotee's body as a temple of the Lord.

Tulasī – a sacred plant worshiped by devotees of Viṣṇu.

Upaniṣads – philosophical sections of the *Vedas,* designed to bring the student closer to the Absolute Truth.

Vaikuṇṭha – the spiritual world.

Vaiṣṇava – a devotee of Lord Viṣṇu, Kṛṣṇa.

Vānaprastha – one who has retired from family life; the third order of Vedic spiritual life.

Vedānta-sūtra – the summary of Vedic knowledge compiled by Srī Vyāsadeva in short codes.

Vedas – the original literature, comprising all branches of philosophy, science, art, and spiritual knowledge, which was first spoken by Lord Viṣṇu Himself to the creator Brahmā.

Vṛndāvana – Krsna's personal abode, where He fully manifests His quality of sweetness.

Yogī – a transcendentalist who, in one way or another, is striving for union with the Supreme.

Zamīndār – a landlord.

Guide to Sanskrit Pronunciation

The system of transliteration used in this book conforms to a system that scholars have accepted to indicate the pronunciation of each sound in the Sanskrit language.

The short vowel **a** is pronounced like the **u** in b**u**t, long **ā** like the **a** in f**a**r. Short **i** is pronounced as **i** in p**i**n, long **ī** as in p**i**que, short **u** as in p**u**ll, and long **ū** as in r**u**le. The vowel **ṛ** is pronounced like **ri** in **ri**m, **e** like the **ey** in th**ey**, **o** like the **o** in g**o**, **ai** like the **ai** in **ai**sle, and **au** like the **ow** in h**ow**. The *anusvara* (**ṁ**) is pronounced like the **n** in the French word *bo***n**, and *visarga* (**ḥ**) is pronounced as a final **h** sound. At the end of a couplet, **aḥ** is pronounced **aha**, and **iḥ** is pronounced **ihi**.

The guttural consonants – **k, kh, g, gh,** and **ṅ** – are pronounced from the throat in much the same manner as in English. **K** is pronounced as in **k**ite, **kh** as in Ec**kh**art, **g** as in **g**ive, **gh** as in di**g-h**ard and **ṅ** as in si**ng**.

The palatal consonants – **c, ch, j, jh,** and **ñ** – are pronounced with the tongue touching the firm ridge behind the teeth. **C** is pronounced as in **ch**air, **ch** as in staun**ch-h**eart, **j** as in **j**oy, **jh** as in he**dgeh**og, and **ñ** as in ca**ny**on.

The cerebral consonants – **ṭ, ṭh, ḍ, ḍh,** and **ṇ** – are pronounced with the tip of the tongue turned up and drawn back against the dome of the palate. **Ṭ** is pronounced as in **t**ub, **ṭh** as in ligh**t-h**eart, **ḍ** as in **d**ove, **ḍh** as in re**d-h**ot, and **ṇ** as in **n**ut.

The dental consonants – **t, th, d, dh,** and **n** – are pronounced in the same manner as the cerebrals, but with the forepart of the tongue against the teeth.

The labial consonants – **p, ph, b, bh,** and **m** – are pronounced with the lips. **P** is pronounced as in **p**ine, **ph** as in u**ph**ill, **b** as in **b**ird, **bh** as in ru**b-h**ard, and **m** as in **m**other.

The semivowels – **y, r, l,** and **v** – are pronounced as in **y**es, **r**un, **l**ight, and **v**ine respectively. The sibilants – **ś, ṣ,** and **s** – are pronounced, respectively, as in the German word *sprechen* and the English words **sh**ine and **s**un. The letter **h** is pronounced as in **h**ome.

Centers of the International Society for Krishna Consciousness

Founder-*Ācārya:* His Divine Grace A. C. Bhaktivedanta Swami Prabhupāda

For further information on classes, programs, festivals, residential courses, and local meetings, please contact the center nearest you.

✦ *Temples with restaurants or dining.*

UNITED KINGDOM AND IRELAND

Belfast, Northern Ireland — 140 Upper Dunmurray Lane, Belfast BT17 OHE; Tel. +44-28-90620530; belfast@iskcon.org.uk; www.iskcon.org.uk/belfast

Birmingham, England — 84 Stanmore Road, Edgebaston, Birmingham B16 9TB; Tel. +44-121-4204999; birmingham@iskcon.org.uk; www.iskconbirmingham.org

Cardiff, Wales — The Soul Centre, 116 Cowbridge Road East, Canton, Cardiff, CF11 9DX; Tel. +44-2920-390391; the.soul.centre@pamho.net; www.thesoulcentre.net

✦ **Dublin, Ireland** — 83 Middle Abbey Street, Dublin 1; Tel. +353-1-8729775; dublin@krishna.ie; www.krishna.ie; restaurant: www.govindas.ie

Lanarkshire, Scotland — Karuna Bhavan, Bankhouse Road, Lesmahagow, Lanarkshire, ML11 0ES; Tel. +44-1555-894790; Fax +44-1555-894526; karunabhavan@aol.com; www.iskcon.org.uk/scotland

Leicester, England — 21 Thoresby Street, North Evington, Leicester LE5 4GU; Tel. +44-116-2762587; leicester@iskcon.org.uk; www.iskconleicester.org

✦ **London, England** (city) — 10 Soho Street, London W1D 3DL; Tel. +44-20-74373662; shop: 72870269; Govinda's restaurant: 74374928; Fax +44-20-74391127; london@pamho.net; www.iskcon-london.org

✦ **London, England** (country) — Bhaktivedanta Manor, Dharam Marg, Hilfield Lane, Aldenham, near Watford, Herts WD25 8EZ; Tel. +44-1923-857244; Fax +44-1923-852896; bhaktivedanta.manor@pamho.net; for accommodations: accommodations.requests@pamho.net; www.krishnatemple.com

London, England (south) — 42 Enmore Road, South Norwood, London SE25 5NG; Tel. +44-20-86564296; www.iskcon.org.uk/snorwood

Manchester, England — 20 Mayfield Road, Whalley Range, Manchester M16 8FT; Tel. +44-161-2264416; manchester@iskcon.org.uk; www.iskcon.org.uk/manchester

Newcastle, England — 304 Westgate Road, Newcastle-upon-Tyne, Tyne & Wear NE4 6AR; Tel. +44-191-2721911; newcastle@iskcon.org.uk; www.iskcon.org.uk/newcastle

✦ **Swansea, Wales** — 8 Craddock Street, Swansea SA1 3EN; Tel. +44-1792-468469; iskcon.swansea@pamho.net; restaurant: govindas.swansea@pamho.net; www.iskconwales.org

RURAL COMMUNITIES

London, England — (contact Bhaktivedanta Manor)

Upper Lough Erne, Northern Ireland (Govindadwipa) — Inisrath Island, Derrylin, Co. Fermanagh BT92 9GN; Tel. +44-28-67721512; bbt@krishnaisland.com; www.krishnaisland.com

ADDITIONAL RESTAURANTS

Dublin, Ireland — Govinda's, 4 Aungier Street, Dublin 2; Tel. +353-1-4750309; info@govindas.ie; www.govindas.ie

Dublin, Ireland — Govinda's, 18 Merrion Row, Dublin 2; Tel. +353-1-6615095; info@govindas.ie; www.govindas.ie

Hare Krishna meetings are held regularly in more than 40 centers in the UK and Ireland. For more information, contact the temple nearest you or go to www.iskcon.org.uk.